THE COMPLETE BOOK OF
THE
WATERGARDEN

THE COMPLETE BOOK OF
THE
WATER GARDEN

PHILIP SWINDELLS
and
DAVID MASON

Edited by Alan Toogood

The Overlook Press
Woodstock, New York

First published in 1990 by
The Overlook Press
Lewis Hollow Road
Woodstock, New York 12498
Second hard cover printing 1990

Fourth printing 1995

Library of Congress Cataloging-in-Publication Data
Swindells, Philip.
    The complete book of the water garden/by Philip Swindells and David Mason.
    p.   cm.
    Originally published: Ward Lock Publishers, Ltd. (London) 1989.
    1. Water gardens   I. Mason, David. 1946-   II. Title.
SB423.S92   1990   635.9'674--dc20

ISBN 0-87951-385-3

Printed in Italy

CONTENTS

Preface

Water is one of the most attractive features in a garden. Not only does it provide the gardener with the opportunity to grow a wide range of interesting aquatics, but it also adds a unique reflective quality to the garden. This can be used to great advantage, especially on the smaller plot where the mirror-like surface of the water will enhance the scale of its surroundings.

There are also tremendous opportunities for the use of moving water, either the splashing and spraying of a fountain or the gentle murmer of a waterfall. These add a further unique dimension to the garden and are so easily contrived with modern technology. The modern submersible pump has presented endless opportunities for the adventurous gardener.

Then there are the plants. Few garden features can offer conditions for such a diversity of subjects. What is lovelier than the broad verdant pads of the water lilies with their brightly coloured and beautifully sculptured blossoms? Or the sweetly scented water hawthorn? There are strange floating aquatics that do not require planting, fern-like submerged plants that gently sway beneath the surface and a myriad of marginal aquatics that throng the poolside with colour. Fish add the final touch to a living canvas, a picture in the garden of unparalleled beauty. Within these pages some of the wonderful world of water is explored; we hope that you will come to know and love it, just as we have.

P.S. & D.M.

Acknowledgements

The publishers are grateful to the following for granting permission to reproduce the colour photographs: David Mason (pp. *ix*, *xvii* (upper) and *xxxii*); Photos Horticultural Picture Library (pp. *i*, *iii*, *viii*, *xiii*, *xxi*, *xxvi*, *xxvii*, *xxix* and *xxx*); Harry Smith Horticultural Photographic Collection (pp. *ii*, *iv*, *vi*, *vii*, *xvii* (lower), *xix*, *xx*, *xxii* (upper), *xxv*, *xxviii* and *xxxi*); Hugh Palmer (pp. *xiv* and *xv*); Pat Brindley (pp. *xxii* (lower), *xxiii* and *xxiv*); Andrew Lawson (pp. *xvi*); Michael Boys (pp. *v*). The photographs on pp. *x*, *xi* and *xii* were taken by Bob Challinor.

All the line drawings were drawn by Peter Bull Art.

Publisher's Note

Readers are requested to note that in order to make the text intelligible in both hemispheres, plant flowering times, etc. are described in terms of seasons, not months.

The following table provides an approximate 'translation' of seasons into months for the two hemispheres.

NORTHERN HEMISPHERE				SOUTHERN HEMISPHERE
Mid-winter	=	January	=	Mid-summer
Late winter	=	February	=	Late summer
Early spring	=	March	=	Early autumn
Mid-spring	=	April	=	Mid-autumn
Late spring	=	May	=	Late autumn
Early summer	=	June	=	Early winter
Mid-summer	=	July	=	Mid-winter
Late summer	=	August	=	Late winter
Early autumn	=	September	=	Early spring
Mid-autumn	=	October	=	Mid-spring
Late autumn	=	November	=	Late spring
Early winter	=	December	=	Early summer

PART 1

THE HISTORY OF
WATER IN THE GARDEN

SITING WATER FEATURES

DESIGN

CONSTRUCTION

CHAPTER 1
The History of Water in the Garden

Egypt and Mesopotamia

Water has been a persistent theme in gardens from the beginning. Its use, whether practical, symbolic or aesthetic in nature, may be traced back to the early civilizations of man as they began to flourish in Egypt and Mesopotamia. In these desert environments population centres were located near great rivers: in the valley of the Nile in Egypt and between the Tigris and Euphrates in Mesopotamia. Water from these rivers had to be controlled, saved and channelled and therefore a sound system of hydraulic engineering was developed.

The first Egyptian gardens served as areas of food production and were necessarily irrigated. As time passed the irrigation channels and storage ponds evolved into decorative canals and pools, the latter containing lotus, papyrus and fish. Initially a practical necessity, water became a beautifying element and gardens began to afford pleasure as well as food. Those built by kings or associated with religious temples became quite elaborate and frequently contained large pools and, in some cases, lakes. Gardens came to be thought of as earthly manifestations of the real paradise, an oasis where water flowed freely to nourish trees, fruits, flowers and the spirits of men.

In Mesopotamia water management included the construction of lakes, reservoirs and canals. It is believed that the fabled hanging gardens of Babylon, possibly built by Nebuchadnezzar II (604–562 BC), were supplied with water by an intricate combination of machinery and conduits which drew from the Euphrates.

Islam

In ancient Persia (Iran) where environmental conditions were similar to those of Egypt, the theme of the garden as an oasis was repeated. Reflecting man's desire to shelter himself from the inhospitable desert, the traditional Persian garden, *chahar bagh* or 'fourfold' garden, was a level enclosed square divided into four by two canals crossing at the centre. A pool, fountain or pavilion was located in the central position. The canals radiating from the point of intersection represented the four rivers of paradise. An abundance of shade and fruit trees and flowers grew in the quadrants which were filled with networks of irrigation and ornamental canals.

The precise origins of these paradise gardens are lost in history. Their design is revealed in old carpets and paintings. The basic plan seemed to incorporate themes from the royal hunting parks, *pairidaeza*, and the protective oasis.

The historical importance of the Persian garden is that its basic layout served as the prototype of the Islamic garden. When the Muslim Arabs conquered Persia in the seventh century they assimilated elements from her culture. The design of the Persian garden was eagerly embraced as it coincided with the descriptions of the garden of paradise found in the Koran. The paradise garden followed the spread of Islam to Syria, Egypt, North Africa, Spain, Turkey and India.

The treatment of water

Wherever Islamic gardens were found water remained the essential element, its irrigating conduits forming the framework of their distinctive style.

At most locations a scarce supply dictated thriftiness in use. Islamic architects were highly skilled in the ability to make less appear more. Their artistic treatment of a basically practical system of storage and irrigation converted pools and canals into design forms which explored and took full advantage of the qualities inherent in water. Canals were not hidden or covered but exposed so the passage of water could be seen. Fountains were often a single frail column providing a musical sound and a cooling splash. Large reflecting pools mirrored beautiful surroundings and suggested a large quantity of water though they were often very shallow.

Spain

When climate and other conditions allowed, the style of the Islamic garden became less restrained and water was often used with exuberance. In southern Spain the Alhambra and Generalife palaces represent the peak of Moorish artistic achievement. Begun by kings of the Nasrid dynasty in the thirteenth century, they contain the finest examples of the paradise garden remaining today. These palaces, perched majestically in the foothills of the Sierra Nevada overlooking Granada, the last Moorish stronghold in Spain, enjoyed an uninterrupted supply of water delivered from the mountains by a series of aqueducts. In the Alhambra, the winter palace, each patio and courtyard displays water in a manner representative of a theme in the philosophy of Islam. In the gardens of the nearby Generalife, the summer palace, there are many pools and fountains, even a watered stairway. Here cooling water is used joyously and generously.

India

Yet another manifestation of Islamic garden design can be found in India. At about the time building began on the Alhambra and Generalife in Granada the Monguls were beginning the conquest of lands formerly belonging to Persia. Their descendants, the Moguls, pushed into India, carrying their love of the Persian garden with them.

These Mogul emperors were passionate gardeners and during the sixteenth and seventeenth centuries they built fabulous water gardens such as Shalamar and Achabel in the valley of Kashmir and later the exquisite Taj Mahal at Agra. Again we see water used more freely and with more imagination as the original oasis scheme is adapted and expanded to take advantage of a more kindly environment.

One expression of an ample water supply was the use of water chutes known as *chadars*, a word meaning shawl, whose carved, uneven surfaces enhanced the texture of the flowing water, increasing its visual impact. *Chadars* appeared again in the gardens of Renaissance Italy and are found today in modern designs.

China

Profoundly influenced by the philosophy of Taoism, the ancient Chinese revered nature. Their gardens, inspired by landscape painting and poems and often designed by artists, poets or monks, were artistic representations of the natural environment in which water and mountains played the major roles.

In lavish imperial gardens and in the smaller private gardens of scholars and painters water appeared in every conceivable natural form: stream, river, waterfall, pond and lake. However, in the garden, as in the scroll painting of the landscape artist, the natural world was often suggested rather than copied exactly; a few rocks placed in a small pond might indicate islands in a lake or ocean.

The garden was created as a place of beauty and tranquillity where man could contemplate and observe nature, discover its harmony and his place in the natural order. A calm, reflecting surface of water expanded his sense of peace, creating an atmosphere conducive to thought.

In addition to creating a mood, water was used as a means of guiding the visitor through a garden by linking together its various parts. Like the natural world the garden held mysteries which were unravelled slowly as one followed the path of a winding stream bed or irregular shoreline, the view ahead temporarily concealed by a curve in a river or a mound of rock.

Water, rocks, earth and plants were carefully composed into an exquisite living painting which illustrated the essence of nature. During the eighteenth century in England garden architects also found inspiration in landscape paintings. During this period written descriptions of Chinese gardens began to appear.

Although the flowing, natural forms of Chinese landscapes contrast sharply with the rigid symmetry of the Islamic garden, water is the common denominator of both styles, illustrating its high adaptability to different design requirements.

Japan

With the spread of Buddhism, Chinese art forms reached Japan during the sixth and seventh centuries. The Chinese influence in garden design gradually waned and by the seventeenth century a more clearly defined Japanese style had evolved. This style, though retaining the original theme of man's relationship with nature, was more precise, formal and symbolic than the Chinese. It emanated from the philosophy of the Zen Buddhist monks who were the designers for many gardens. The use of symbolism is especially evident in the 'dry' garden where water was unavailable; a pool denoted by a bed of raked sand, a stream bed by the placement of rocks or pieces of wood.

The idea of the garden as a symbolic representation of nature persists in Japanese designs today and water, real or suggested, is crucial to this theme.

Greece and Italy

Water was an integral part of the gardens of the Greeks and Romans, not surprising to anyone who has experienced the heat of a Mediterranean summer.

In Greece and Italy the earliest gardens not associated with food production were located near natural springs which were believed to be gifts from the gods and therefore sacred. Often a temple, honouring a god or goddess, was constructed near the source of the spring. Groves of trees and gardens were added to the site. Water from the spring was piped into decorative basins. As time passed these basins were adorned with statuary which was sometimes used to propel water in jets or streams. From these beginnings evolved more elaborate models and fountains could be found throughout Greece and Italy. Originally their function was threefold; religious, utilitarian and aesthetic.

During the Hellenistic period in Greece, which began with Alexander the Great, sophisticated aqueducts and water systems were widespread. Illustrated writings from this time describe machinery for operating the joke fountains, water organs, etc. found in the gardens of Renaissance Italy. Often thought to be the creations of sixteenth century architects, they were, in fact, copies of early Greek inventions.

Public and private pleasure gardens began appearing, reflecting ideas which Alexander brought with him on his return from victories in Persia and India. These were gardens to enrich the spirit of man, not to please the gods or provide food.

The Romans incorporated the best elements of the Greek pleasure gardens in designs for splendid villa gardens. The villas and adjoining gardens were summer retreats from the heat and crowds of Rome. Pools, canals, fountains, cascades and baths refreshed the air and body and gave pleasure to the eye. The remains of the Emperor Hadrian's villa at Tivoli, completed about 136 AD, illustrate the grand scale of water use in these classical gardens.

A superb aqueduct system allowed lavish use of water not only in gardens but also in the fountains and baths of Rome itself. Still known as the city of fountains, today's Rome can only suggest her former glory during the Empire when there were more than one thousand fountains and nearly as many baths. The fountains were grand affairs, decorated with statues of gods and nymphs—a theme which, like so many others, reappeared during the Renaissance.

Because the Romans were highly skilled as well as prolific builders, the ideas they borrowed from the Greeks and from other cultures within their vast empire have endured long after the fall of Rome. The durability of their structures provided a legacy of classical designs which was drawn upon by the artists and architects of the Renaissance.

The Middle Ages

Most mediaeval gardens in Europe and England were found within the protective confines of monastery and castle walls. The use of water was limited mainly to wells, fish ponds, tanks and moats. Occasionally decorative fountains or wells were used as a central feature at the intersection of pathways; an idea possibly carried home from the east by the crusaders.

Renaissance Italy

Ancient Greece and Rome provided the backbone for the enlightened thinking of the Renaissance. Humanism had been rediscovered; from the early fifteenth century the individuality and spirit of man were expressed through his creative genius. Having jumped clear of the hide-bound thinking of the Middle Ages into an era of freedom and discovery, the artists presented ideas borrowed from classical times in fresh, imaginative, harmonious designs which integrated the house, garden and surrounding countryside.

Gardens developed during this period were visual extravaganzas. Water was the heart and soul of many. It was used in copious amounts and often with a sense of amusement. Water jets were secreted, designed to deliver bursts to unsuspecting visitors. Almost anything that could emit water was made to do so. Dragons, serpents, dolphins and other creatures were popular, as well as the human form which spouted water from extraordinary places! Balustraded terraces were decorated with elaborate, gushing fountains and linked by glistening cascades.

The Villa d'Este

One of the finest examples of a water garden built during the Renaissance, or perhaps during any period, is the Villa d'Este at Tivoli, some 32 km (20 miles) from Rome. This magnificent spectacle, designed by Pirro Ligorio, was begun about 1550, taking 30 years to complete. The nearby ruins of Hadrian's Villa inspired the imaginative Ligorio.

Italy is predominantly hilly and this garden, like many others, was created on a slope, providing ample site for falling water. Used in a multitude of ways to set various moods, water is the connecting link in the many-terraced garden. The Villa d'Este revelled in the scope and variety of its water features which still enthral visitors today.

The Fountains of the Organ, the Owl and the Dragon are clever designs in which water is used to make various sounds imitating music, bird song and gunfire. One terrace contains the Pathway of One Hundred Fountains where water escapes in a series of jets, sprays and streams to cool the atmosphere on a hot summer day. Pools are surrounded by fountains which create an effect of perpetual rainfall, filling the air with rainbows on a sunny day. Symbolizing fertility, water spurts from each nipple of a multi-breasted statue of the goddess Diana. Rills and cascades provide additional feelings of motion and joy. In some areas water rests quietly in pools and tanks, appearing reflective and calming.

The imaginative, diverse and complex employment of water in this garden illustrated the Renaissance idea that man's intellect was boundless.

The Villa Lante

The design of the Villa Lante near Viterbo represented another Renaissance theme: man's triumph over nature. Simplicity, rather than complexity, is the hallmark of this garden by Vignola. It was constructed in the second half of the sixteenth century. The water begins its route through the garden from a rustic hillside grotto as a naturalistic rill which forms a pool. From the pool it descends to a lower terrace where it rises from an elegant fountain. Dropping again through a sculptured cascade, the water reaches another terrace. Here it passes through a stone dining table, set between two fountains, where it serves to cool wine, finally ending its journey at the lowest point of the garden in a formal water parterre with a central fountain. At each stage along the way the water increases in volume and stature; at its wooded source a simple offering of nature, at its climax an element in a sophisticated architectural design.

The recently restored Villa Lante is the best existing example of the gardens of the period.

13

The French tradition

Although it was not until the seventeenth century that the classic French style reached its zenith, its roots were to be found in the moats and fish ponds of the Middle Ages. As the fifteenth and sixteenth centuries unfolded, the functional mediaeval gardens were transformed into gardens for enjoyment and artistic displays. Ancient ponds and moats were enlarged to become water allées. There was a great influx of ideas from Italy and Italian designers were imported. Gardens were filled with classical statuary, fountains and grottos as well as parterres. One of the most significant characteristics of the Italian style to reach and take hold in France was the complementary relationship between house and garden. No longer was the garden treated as a separate entity. Architecture began to overshadow horticulture as the garden's *raison d'etre*.

By the early seventeenth century a nearly pure French style had evolved. Gardens were being created for the aristocracy and were used as vehicles for the display of wealth and power in an age which glorified both.

André Le Nôtre

The remarkable André Le Nôtre developed the design of the classic French garden with such strength and clarity that it became the framework for gardens the world over. In France the grandiose, formal and controlled Le Nôtre style represented man's intellectual freedom and his triumph over nature as well as the power of the crown and the aristocracy. Though ostentatious and politically motivated, the gardens exhibited a lasting strength of character founded on impeccable taste and a love of the arts.

Le Nôtre took advantage of the huge flat landscape of the countryside, so different from that of Italy. He converted moated castles, such as the Château de Chantilly near Paris, into huge waterscapes filled with geometric canals, pools and fountains. A large formal expanse of water was a trademark of the French tradition. His ambitious designs were no doubt made easier to accomplish by the generally high water table and, most importantly, the undisputed

fundamental requirement for any development — wealthy clients.

Versailles

Nowhere was this wealth more evident than at Versailles Palace, belonging to King Louis XIV. Here in the early 1660s Le Nôtre began the layout of a spectacle hailed by many as the most magnificent water gardens ever built. One of the motivations behind this extravaganza was the prior design by Le Nôtre of the garden, Vaux le Vicomte, for one of the King's ministers, Nicolas Fouquet. Vaux, designed and executed over a period of five years, is the purest example of Le Nôtre's genius. King Louis viewed Fouquet's superb garden as a threat to his royal status and his own Versailles had to be bigger and better than anything built previously or likely to be in the foreseeable future. Expense was no concern.

The focal point and heart of the garden was a mile-long canal dissected by another almost as long. Fountains were found everywhere in a variety of shapes and sizes. The largest single fountain, known as The Sheaf, had 140 jets of its own. Approximately 14 000 jets were used in all. Water was provided for the garden by pumping from the River Seine via an aqueduct, but even with all 14 waterwheels in operation it was impossible to produce sufficient pressure for everything to work simultaneously. The fountains of Versailles could play only in sequential groups; flowing in synchronism with the progression of King Louis and his party on their tour through the gardens.

The influence of Versailles was felt in most civilized countries throughout the world and copies can be seen from the Soviet Union to the United States.

English Renaissance gardens

As internal peace came to Tudor England with the conclusion of the Wars of the Roses in 1485, the enclosed mediaeval garden began to be replaced by the Renaissance pleasure garden. The inspiration for the new gardens came from France. Henry VIII built one of the first royal gardens in the Renaissance style at Hampton Court.

The only important water feature was a fountain located at the centre of the square plan.

French influence continued to dominate during Elizabethan times. The idea of the pleasure garden spread to the country estates of the nobility.

Water assumed greater importance in gardens during the reign of James I. As people were able to travel more freely, more information reached England from the continent. Italian styles became popular. The Frenchman, Salomon de Caus, came to England after studying garden design in Italy. He was a skilled engineer as well and brought with him a sound knowledge of hydraulics and the Italian theme of integrating house and garden. Gardens were built or redesigned to include grottos, fountains and various automata. One can only eulogize the endless and novel ways that were invented for displaying water.

The formal garden in England

In England, as on the continent, the model for the formal garden came from the French. When Charles II was restored to the throne in 1660 he returned from France with his mind full of pictures of the fabulous gardens being created there by Le Nôtre. French gardeners were brought to England and English gardeners studied in France.

Chatsworth House, Derbyshire

The popularity of the French style prompted the First Duke of Devonshire to employ Grillet, a pupil of Le Nôtre. Although long canals were the usual water feature of the day, at Chatsworth Grillet created the famous water cascade or staircase in 1694, which was enlarged a few years later. During this period the Willow Tree Fountain was designed; made of hollow copper tubing, each branch produced a thin jet of water at the touch of a switch. Like the Italian joke fountains, it was often used to surprise visitors. Today's Willow Tree Fountain is a replacement of the original. Succeeding dukes added grottos, lakes, fountains and cascades, making Chatsworth one of the best water landscapes to be seen today.

Royal parks

It was a French gardener, André Mollet, who first laid out St. James Park for Charles II. He designed a *patte d'oie*, or goosefoot, with the middle toe taking the shape of a large canal some 852 m (2800 ft) long and 30 m (100 ft) wide, transformed into the lake we see today during the reign of King George IV.

At Hampton Court Charles had Mollet's goosefoot plan repeated and again the middle toe forms the Long Canal. It was during the reign of William and Mary, 1689–1702, that the gardens of Hampton Court came into their full glory when the Great Fountain Garden was designed by another Frenchman, Daniel Marot. He combined the Dutch canal garden with garden ornamentation in the style of Louis XIV, resulting in a Franco-Dutch hybrid. The Fountain Garden, located between the palace and a semi-circular canal, contained 13 flowing fountains. The Dutch influence, with its emphasis on longer, narrower canals, was fundamentally an echo of the French style, a style which was beginning to lose favour in England.

The English landscape garden

Towards the end of the seventeenth century the popularity of the formal French style began to wane. By the beginning of the eighteenth century a new style was evolving. Although indigenous to England the 'landscape garden' contained veins of influence from other times and places. Naturalism was the watchword of this movement which received impetus from different sectors of society.

Writers such as Pope, Addison and Steele extolled nature and the natural landscape while criticizing the rigid formality of French designs. Accounts of the Chinese tradition of naturalistic landscapes began to appear.

The landscape paintings of seventeenth century artists were very popular, especially those of Claude Lorraine, who depicted scenes of the Roman countryside embellished with classical buildings. Like China centuries before, paintings became the inspiration for many new gardens.

Huge country estates began to be formed as Acts of Parliament allowed the aristocracy to enclose large areas of common land. The wealthy landowners travelled abroad, especially to Italy, returning to England with an enthusiasm for Palladian architecture. They were determined to build new homes or remodel old ones in the style of Palladio within a Claudian setting.

Water — a central theme

Water was plentiful in every great landscape garden and as fundamental to the success of the design as it was at Versailles, though used in a different guise.

Vast expanses of quiet water were the hallmark of the designs of the new gardens. Fountains disappeared and water was no longer constrained in canals or formal pools. Streams were dammed to form lakes with natural contours or slowly moving rivers. Rushing streams and waterfalls were shunned by the purists. Cascades essential to water-management schemes were hidden. Water was used to connect the sections of a garden. More importantly, a placid lake contributed a mood of serenity and a feeling of space, expanding the visitor's outlook as it disappeared behind a curving shoreline or into a woodland. The reflective surface of still water was used to capture nature's rhythms; passing birds, scudding clouds, daily variations of light and seasonal tints. It also mirrored the perfect proportions of classical structures.

Major personalities

The shift away from the formal to the natural in garden design was a gradual one with many individuals contributing to the landscape movement; architects, gardeners, designers and private landowners. Although the majority of the plans were laid out and executed by professionals, amateurs were responsible, wholly or in part, for some outstanding gardens.

John Aislabie

A fine example of an early eighteenth century design is Studley Royal near Ripon in North Yorkshire. In 1722 John Aislabie, former Chancellor of the Exchequer, began to fashion his own water garden in a style which illustrates the transition from the age of formal gardens to that of the natural landscape. Though most of the water features are formal in shape, they are set in a natural wooded valley with grass allowed to grow down to the water's edge.

William Kent

William Kent (1685–1748), an architect with a painter's eye, was a pioneer among the professionals and the first to make a real impact on the countryside. As an artist he had travelled and studied in Italy and was obviously influenced by the landscape paintings of the Italian countryside. His ideal landscapes were three dimensional representations of the paintings he admired. He designed temples and bridges as the focal points for his water features. The beautiful garden of Stowe in Buckinghamshire is a showcase for his work. Kent's ideas carried great weight and were incorporated into the plans of many professionals and amateurs, notably Hoare at Stourhead.

Henry Hoare II

Although several descendents of Henry Hoare were involved in the creation of Stourhead in Wiltshire, he was the major contributor, beginning the gardens in the 1740s. Many feel Stourhead is a perfectly composed landscape. A large, irregular lake forms the heart of the garden and reflects the plantings of trees and rhododendrons as well as the many classical buildings dotted around it. This artificial lake was one of many to be created during the course of the century. Other water features include a grotto in which a sleeping nymph lies over a cascade formed from natural springs and a river god's cave where water pours from an urn.

Caves and grottos were very fashionable during the eighteenth century and often had water dripping through them. No doubt their popularity has diminished in England due to climatic considerations.

'Capability' Brown

Lancelot 'Capability' Brown (1716–1783)

was the most influential and well-known personality of the naturalistic school. The landscape movement reached its apex during his career. Fully committed to the use of natural shapes, he swept away any remnants of the formal style. Brown's strength was his ability to develop a particular site to its full potential. With great skill and, one must remember, adequate manpower as there were no bulldozers, he designed or contributed to many gardens known and admired today. Water was a dominant theme in his work and he was a master at creating great lakes by damming small rills and streams.

Perhaps the ultimate expression of his genius may be seen in the lake he created for Blenheim Palace in Oxfordshire. His lake provided a perfect setting for a bridge designed earlier by the respected architect, Van Brugh. Before Brown's lake was constructed the bridge had lacked a setting of adequate dimensions.

Humphry Repton
Humphry Repton (1752–1818) was the last of the great landscapers. For the most part he followed Brown's design principles. However, being of a more flexible nature than his predecessor, Repton allowed terraces, balustrades and flower beds near the house while favouring a Brownian approach for more distant areas of the garden. His use of water included the reintroduction of the fountain; the symbol of artificiality which had been outlawed by Brown and others.

The nineteenth century
By the turn of the century the original concepts underlying the landscape park were becoming diluted. Nevertheless, garden design throughout most of Europe had come under its influence. The theme of the English landscape garden continues today in gardens and parks in Europe and North America.

With the decline of the landscape movement there was a return to a more formal style. Classical designs were brought back but lacked innovations to breathe new life

into them. In some eclectic gardens the attempt to harmonize features from various traditions usually failed. With the regurgitation of old schemes and ideas there was little to differentiate the use of water in the 1800s from the preceding centuries.

Exotic plants
Perhaps the most exciting development to occur and one which would affect the employment of water, was the great flood of new plants into England and western Europe from the New World and the Orient. Among these were types suitable for growing in the water or at its edge.

Attempts were made to create environments suited to the new plants by providing settings similar to their natural habitats. Waterfalls became popular features of rock gardens. Mountain settings were built, occasionally designed to depict a specific mountain such as the Matterhorn, by incorporating recognizable characteristics. Cascades led to pools or appeared at the back of cave-like structures.

Water lilies
The only hardy water lily grown during the first part of the nineteenth century was the white *Nymphaea alba* which grew in places like the River Cherwell in Oxford. About midway through the century a Frenchman, Joseph Borg Latour-Marliac, began his work in the cross breeding of *N. alba* with coloured species. His first success came in 1879 and he was able to produce over 70 new hardy cultivars before his death in 1911. The descendants of his cultivars live on in the water gardens of today but the secret of his success died with him and remains to be rediscovered.

The conservatory
Many of the new plants originated in warmer climates and required protected growing conditions. Huge temple-like glass buildings were constructed to provide the necessary shelter. Often these conservatories contained pools. In such a pool in 1849 Sir Joseph Paxton became the first man in England to flower the giant water lily, *Victoria amazonica*.

Oriental gardens

The appearance of new plants from the Orient stimulated interest in reproducing oriental-style gardens, especially Japanese. These reproductions were superficial in nature and often required the presence of a stone lantern or other ornament to substantiate the Japanese connection. However, water was a consistent element in these gardens and provided the correct setting for Japanese primulas and various iris species.

William Robinson and Gertrude Jekyll

Towards the end of the nineteenth century appeared two personalities whose attitudes and ideas regarding the use of plant material are still valid today. William Robinson (1838–1935) and Gertrude Jekyll (1843–1932) shared a respect for the colour, foliage and shape of plants. They believed these virtues are shown to best advantage when plants are grown in a natural, informal way within an appropriate setting. These ideas led to the development of the wild or informal garden. The most successful gardens of this type evolved around a pre-existing natural feature such as a pond, stream or woodland. In her book *Wall and Water Gardens* Miss Jekyll discusses the development of natural water features and describes the excitement and pleasures inherent in water gardening. With Robinson and Jekyll we see the beginning of a style of water gardening which enjoys such popularity today.

The United States

America's first settlers were Dutch and English. Their gardens reflected the styles of their native lands but adapted to a new environment. As time passed immigrants poured in from all corners of the globe, bringing influences from various cultures. Today gardens can be seen which are representative of nearly every garden tradition: Moorish, Chinese, Japanese, Italian, French and English. Generally the water features in American gardens followed the dictates of these imported traditions.

Plantation gardens

The earliest American gardens on a grand scale were built by planters along the east coast. The plantations sat on high ground above tidal rivers and were joined to the water by a series of descending terraces called 'falls'. Unique to America, the falls were plain architectural features which framed the great houses when viewed from the river, or led the eye to the river when viewed from the house. Water, though not integrated with the gardens, was the focal point of their vistas.

The country place era

At the beginning of the nineteenth century the English ideas of natural landscape design began to filter into the United States. However, it was during the period from the 1880s to the 1920s, when many American financiers amassed great wealth, that the finest landscape gardens were built with strong European overtones. These years were known as the 'country place era'. Italian villa gardens were the most popular models of the day. The Vizcaya Garden

Water use today

Faced with the practical realities of today's world, few communities or individuals can duplicate the lavish waterscapes of the past and must discover simpler and more economical ways of using water without sacrificing artistic quality.

The development of synthetic materials for waterproofing has greatly expanded the possibilities for the use of water features from a geographical as well as a monetary point of view; for example; roof gardens with pools and fountains, reservoirs, ornamental lakes constructed around buildings, and pools and lakes in desert environments.

Water is a major element in civic and private design the world over. Imaginative layouts and structures for the display of water are being created; or should we say the qualities inherent in water are stimulating a new era of creativity? For whether it is moving or still, musical or silent, water inspires today's generation as it did those of the past. Certainly it adds life and interest to any garden of any style in any place.

near Miami, Florida is an outstanding example of a sixteenth century Italian garden. Vizcaya was built between 1912 and 1916. Water assumes an importance here equal to that at the Villa Lante. Perhaps the most famous Italian gardens in America are at Hearst Castle in San Simeon, California. Begun by William Randolph Hearst in 1922, the gardens boast an exquisite water feature in the form of the classical Neptune Pool complete with a Graeco-Roman temple.

The French formal garden style was also evident in gardens built at this time. Longwood Gardens in Pennsylvania, though echoing several traditions, contains the Fountain Garden which is on a par with the one at Versailles. The nearby Nemours Foundation at Wilmington, Delaware is a classic French Renaissance garden with pools and fountains in a magnificent setting. Both gardens belong to the DuPont family and are reflections of their ancestral homeland.

With the advent of the income tax and the crash of 1929 the 'country place era' came to an end.

Contemporary gardens

Contemporary gardens in the United States have a flavour more truly American than their grand predecessors. Today's garden is a functional extension of the house. When well designed it is also a work of art which satisfies the needs of people and the requirements of the site. Water commonly enters the picture in the form of a swimming pool which is the focal point of the garden. Concrete is often used in the construction of pools, allowing designers to create an infinite variety of beautiful and interesting shapes. The importance of such water shapes to the overall success of many contemporary designs is illustrated at El Novillero, a garden created by Thomas Church (1902–1978) in Sonoma, California and considered to be one of the most outstanding gardens of this century.

CHAPTER 2
Siting Water Features

Whether you have many acres or just a few square feet, it is vitally important to consider the impact of any water feature from every possible angle before deciding on its final position. Most new schemes in a garden, particularly flower beds, can be moved with relative ease, if you happen to position them wrongly. The inclusion of a water feature, whatever the size or scale, requires a good deal more thought if you are to avoid the very substantial consequences should your original positioning be wrong.

Water in a garden usually provides the focal point, or is a strong influence in creating an atmosphere. The amount of time you spend considering the various aspects involved should not be underestimated nor underrated. Before deciding on a site for a water feature it is as well to think of possible alternative ideas for that particular position. Would a rose border, or possibly a croquet lawn, look better there? Having looked at these options and concluded that water will be the right choice, further plans can be made.

Maybe your particular interest embraces water lilies or fish. Possibly you like the idea of the tranquillity provided by calm stretches of water, or the sound it can make tumbling from a fountain or waterfall. Whatever your area of interest, each one of these features, or a combination of them, has specific needs if it is to function well and be seen to best advantage.

It will be too late if, after you have perfectly constructed a beautifully designed pond you find yourself thinking, 'It would have been so much better from my sitting-room window if the fountain were just a few yards to the right!' or, 'If only I had noticed the amount of shade that tree casts, I would have moved the pool to another position!' Whatever your aspirations and no matter how well designed and con-structed, a water feature in the wrong place will rarely be satisfactory.

A formal pool

This is defined here as a design of geometric shape, most probably set into a hard land-scape, surrounded by stone or brick paving (Fig. 1). It may be of any size and could include a fountain in the overall design. You may be wanting to take advantage of the reflective qualities of water in addition to growing water lilies. A pool of this kind provides the opportunity to have fish. It is a peaceful kind of design, just right for relaxing in a chair armed with a gin and tonic after a hard day's work, or a refreshing cup of tea on a hot summer afternoon!

Viewpoint

Wherever you have considered positioning the formal pool, make sure you look at the site from the places you will see it, both indoors and out. You may want the pool to be seen when first entering the garden, or possibly not noticed until a certain point is reached. Look at these angles and make a mental note of the outside scene, then go indoors and sit in your favourite armchair. What will be the view from there? Take a look through the kitchen window, probably the most looked-out-of window in the whole house, especially if the sink is in front of it! It is of little value to have the best view from behind the lawnmower if you are trying to concentrate on making a straight line!

Ensure you have the best angle of view from a frequently used path or position in the garden. If not, you will gain little from your efforts. Of course, there can and should be many viewpoints, each revealing something different. This is particularly important in relation to the background which can make a substantial contribution to the end product.

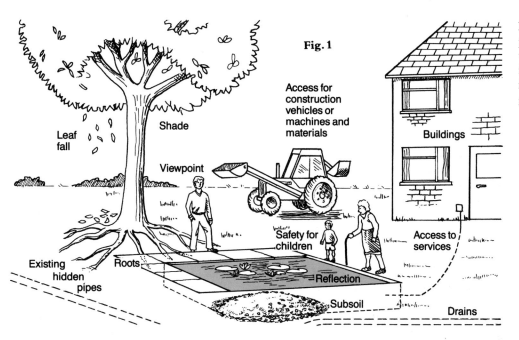

Fig. 1

Access for
construction
vehicles or
machines and
materials

Shade

Leaf
fall

Viewpoint

Buildings

Safety for
children

Access to
services

Existing
hidden
pipes

Roots

Reflection

Subsoil

Drains

Fig. 1 Important points to consider when siting a formal pool – that is, a pool of geometric shape.

Reflection

The reflection is a dimension unavailable in any other form of gardening and is a special characteristic of water. The position of a pool can produce a good or bad image depending on the surrounding buildings, landscape or whatever is adjacent to your garden and the angle you view it from. To judge this without the presence of water is difficult, but try to imagine a mirror and visualize the image you see from the various points of view. The image on water will not be so clear but the principle is the same and a little time spent could prevent your neighbour's washing line being repeated in your pool! A good tree is certainly worth taking into account as would a garden ornament or statuary. From your chosen viewpoint look from the ground to the skyline: all of what you see can be duplicated in a pool, upside down.

Trees

Because of the great variety of trees and the effects they can produce it is realistic to be aware that while some gardens are blessed with trees others are cursed by them. Every tree, no matter what its size, has good and bad characteristics. These should be recog-

nized and their qualities used to influence the development of your garden. Rarely will mature trees coincide with your requirements and while there is often little you can do to change the tree, how you deal with its effects can lead to success or disaster. It is a question of balancing one advantage or preference against those factors that are undesirable.

In most northerly latitudes it is unlikely that any form of shade will be beneficial to this sort of pool, particularly if you intend to grow water lilies. These plants do well only in good light; they will produce weak growth with few flowers beneath the overhanging canopy of a tree. Also the water will remain cool through lack of sunlight, a further discouragement to growth. If you happen to be planning your water garden in the winter when the trees have no leaves, remember that conditions will change dramatically by early summer and the pool could be in dense shade at the most critical time for plant growth.

Many leaves, particularly laburnum and holly, will create toxic gases if allowed to build up in the water. It is advisable to keep clear of all deciduous and evergreen trees that are likely to cast their leaves into the water. Netting can be used to prevent this but it needs positioning before any leaf fall and that is not always convenient with some aquatic plants still in growth. Holly, it should be remembered, tends to have a leaf cast during late spring just as growth is at its peak.

Many large vigorous trees such as aspen and ash send out their penetrating roots great distances in search of water and anchorage. These roots can be extremely damaging to pond structures. In some instances they have been known to fracture concrete pools, uplift paving and even raise preformed fibreglass structures out of the ground!

Trees for shape
Not all trees are detrimental near pools and some have excellent qualitites which should be used. Most of these are coniferous. *Taxus baccata* (English yew) in its fastigiate form known as the Irish yew can be handsome and is reminiscent of the columnar cypress so typical of Italian gardens. Upright junipers are acceptable as are the various species of pine. Alternatively you may have evergreen shrubs such as *Prunus lusitanica* (Portugal laurel). This responds well to pruning and can be trimmed to shape (even an old specimen) to fit in with the envisaged formality of the pool. The list could go on, but it is important to remember other factors with each one considered and whether they will enhance the setting without introducing too many of the undesirable effects already discussed.

Buildings
Whether the structure is a garden shed or your home, it is important to consider how a building may affect the success of your pool.

In comparison to a tree, the shade cast by a building can have a different effect. All buildings will cast solid shade, depending on the sun's position, whereas shade from a tree is variable, dependent on the time of year and kind of tree. Shade from a building or wall is usually to be avoided and a poorly lit alcove will severely limit your success with plants. Because the dark or cold side of a building rarely sees sunshine, the damp conditions are ideal for encouraging unwanted liverworts and mosses. This will cause path surfaces to become slippery and dangerous, as well as being unsightly.

From the safety angle, especially where small children or elderly people are concerned, care should be taken to allow sufficient space for a pathway between pool and building. Tricycles and people with walking sticks need a remarkable amount of space and the path should be sufficient for them to pass easily and without fear.

Allow for essential services to the house: window cleaners, painters or any structural-maintenance people all need sufficient space to work, especially when using ladders.

A building as a background can either enhance or detract from the beauty of a pool. Depending on the style and colour of the building, you may or may not want to see it, or be distracted by it. This is a matter of personal choice and will be discussed in Chapter 3. Sufficient to say at this stage that buildings can be altered in appearance with careful use of climbing plants and shrubs.

Access to services
The services you need will depend on the complexity of your pool design. Starting with water supply, it is inevitable that during the summer there will be a need for occasional topping up, a difficult operation if using a bucket and the tap is some distance from the pool. A hosepipe is the obvious answer, but that may not be easy if it involves passing the hose through delicate bedding plants. It would be wise, therefore, to ensure an underground water supply is fed as close as possible to the poolside. Provision for this should be made from the first stage to avoid later upheaval. Further advice on water supply appears in Chapter 4.

Good access to drains facilitates emptying the pool for periodic cleaning and can prevent embarrassing flooding of the neighbour's garden. Again this can be dealt with at the construction stage but should be considered right from the start.

If a fountain or lighting is included in

your design you will need to provide an electricity supply. The position to choose should have good access to a safe socket which you will most likely want to control from indoors. At this stage you need to look at the route such a supply would take and the feasibility of digging a trench which, if direct from the mains, will need to be 60 cm (2 ft) beneath the ground. A reduced supply from a transformer can be in a shallower trench.

Whenever any excavation is considered, particularly if it is near a house or building of some age, there is the possibility of hidden dangers beneath the ground. You are likely to be digging down below any previous trenches that have been made and, with electricity and water supplies especially, it is important to know of their whereabouts. Drainpipes, too, are significant and if you happen to be on a septic tank system, remember the overflow pipes which are usually laid in a V formation from the main tank.

Access for construction

It does not matter how large or small a pool you are intending to build, in each instance you must take into account the feasibility of getting the various building materials to the proposed site. There should be at least space to manoeuvre a wheelbarrow. If you intend to use a preformed fibreglass pool do not forget to take into account the structure's overall dimensions to avoid later embarrassment. With some modern houses it is surprising how little space there is between one house and another and it may not always be possible to wheel concrete slabs or bring a cement mixer through the living room! For large-scale work you may be considering hiring a mechanical digger. It is wise to actually discuss access with the operator on site. The driver is far better equipped to decide how much space he needs to work than you are. Give him as much information as you can, particularly if you suspect hidden cables or pipes. These are not only dangerous, but can cause a

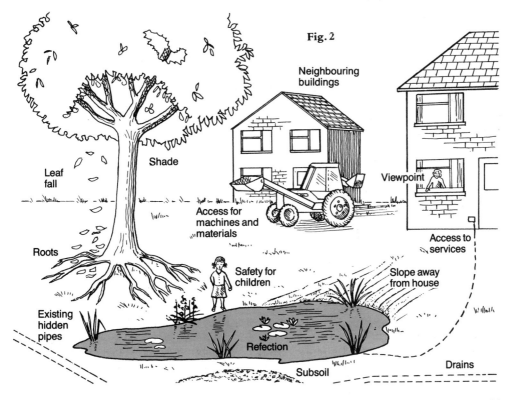

Fig. 2

Neighbouring buildings

Shade

Leaf fall

Roots

Access for machines and materials

Safety for children

Existing hidden pipes

Refection

Subsoil

Slope away from house

Viewpoint

Access to services

Drains

Fig. 2 Major points to bear in mind when siting an informal pool — that is, one which is designed to appear as a natural part of the garden.

23

great deal of inconvenience to many people if damaged and you will not be popular if your street loses its power or water supply! Make sure the driver is covered with adequate insurance should an accident occur.

An informal pool

This heading is intended to deal with a man-made pool which is designed to appear as a natural part of the garden (Fig. 2). It is asymmetrical in shape, unlikely to have a fountain, but may include a waterfall and may have a bog garden attached. We would expect to find an irregularly shaped pool with occasional water lilies. The margins would be planted with shallow-water plants next to plantings of moisture-loving perennials. A rock garden may feature as part of the overall design.

Viewpoint

Usually a natural pond is found at the lower end of a hill or slope. Therefore a pool in the garden, if it is to appear natural, should be looked down upon. If your garden slopes away from the house the situation is ideal and it should be easy to select the most logical place. Should you have a flat site the position will have to be judged in relation to other garden features and will be a question of balance (see Chapter 3). An uphill site is going to present problems from the construction point of view and unless you include a waterfall it will not be satisfactory.

It is not always a good idea to take advantage of a 'wet spot' in a garden. This may seem contradictory, but it is important to first ascertain why it is wet and if it can be controlled. Flooding may occur during the winter and with it may come high concentrations of fertilizers from surrounding farmland. If this were to run into your pool it would be damaging to fish and plants alike. It is also feasible that a rigid pool could be lifted by water beneath it and that could mean rebuilding.

Trees and buildings

Generally speaking, trees provide the ideal setting to any natural pool, but some are better than others and careful positioning is necessary. The points already discussed for a formal pool apply and should be observed. Smaller pools are at greater risk than larger ones, as the concentration of toxicity from rotting leaves is multiplied and builds up more quickly, leaving little margin for error. Unlike a formal pool, some shade may be desirable if you have a bog garden adjoining, but this should be from trees like oak and birch that have a thin canopy with filtered light passing through (see bog-garden siting).

It is probable that neighbouring buildings will be in conflict with a proposed site rather than your own home or garage. This is because an informal pool is usually positioned some distance from your own house (refer to the earlier section on formal pools for further points).

Fountains

Here we are looking at fountains in their own right, not as part of a pool design (Fig. 3). Positioning a fountain is rather like locating the best place for speakers of a hi-fi set. By placing the fountain where you can hear its splash or plip-plop sound you enhance the atmosphere of the garden by adding an extra dimension.

Fountains are available in a wide variety of shapes and forms and each one requires its own particular setting. A choice can be made between great gushing affairs and those producing only a single frail jet. Usually, deciding on a fountain style to suit a garden is difficult, as the exact effect cannot be imagined easily. There are various points to consider. Those that follow are of a general nature. Further details appear in Chapter 3.

Viewpoint

Generally speaking a fountain should be isolated and uncluttered by surrounding objects or encroaching plants. Trees and large shrubs should be kept clear and not allowed to overhang. Not only will they detract from the shape and visual effect of the fountain, but mosses and lichen will develop in the receptacle or on the surrounding pathway causing it to be slippery and dangerous.

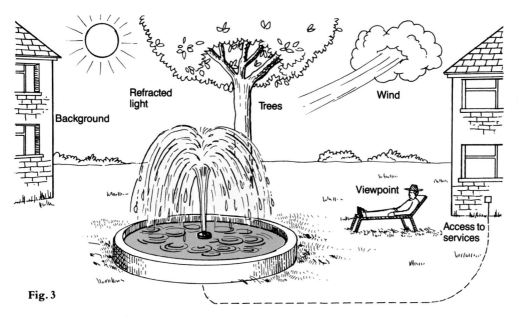

Fig. 3

Whatever shape you have it will be a focal point in the garden. The background is of utmost importance. Remember, a fountain is partially transparent and your view extends beyond the initial eyecatching spray of water. Anything that lies through, beyond and around it is just as important. Large fountains in a landscape setting will help to take the eye up and on to the surrounding scenery. In a smaller town or country garden you will not want to see neighbouring houses or buildings and you should try to focus attention lower down on a particular plant grouping.

On a smaller scale still, in a city garden or tiny town yard, a bubble fountain is the ideal thing. Here it is a good idea to have the fountain set in coloured stones. This will provide interest around and through the fountain and help focus attention on that area. Patios make ideal places for bubble fountains. They can be set in a sunken tank or even housed in a tub or barrel. Their low profile allows use in a windy location, or they can be included in a conservatory or garden room. Not only does a fountain of this kind provide movement but it also increases humidity when used indoors, benefiting plants. Good light is essential and the best position to provide

this should be sought. If there is likely to be a danger of winter frosts, provision should be made for the fountain to be drained of water during the coldest months.

Refraction
Particularly with a multi-jetted fountain there is the added potential of the effects of light passing through water, providing glistening sprays; at times a rainbow will be seen. By placing the fountain where it will receive many hours of direct sunlight you will be able to enjoy the magical qualities of light meeting water for most of the day and from various viewpoints.

Wind
Possibly the biggest enemy of the fountain is wind, so a draughty position should be avoided. Choose, if you can, a site sheltered from the prevailing wind. In some areas dominant winter and summer winds will vary in direction. Because it is likely that your fountain will be drained down for frost protection in the winter, it should be the prevailing summer winds that are considered. Not only does wind blow water around but it carries with it particles of dust and dirt. Over a period of time these will accumulate, making the water appear

Fig. 4 Siting a waterfall. This feature can be formal or informal.

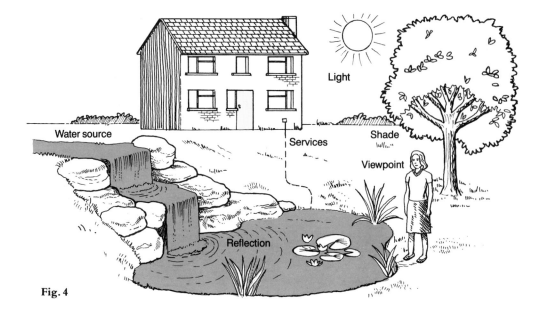

Fig. 4

dirty and ultimately causing jets and filters to become blocked.

Access to services

As with a pool, you will need to ensure that adequate drainage is available for emptying and cleaning. Also that you have an accessible electricity supply for a circulating pump. If your fountain is integrated in the pool design this may already be taken care of, otherwise you will need to consider the feasibility of bringing the supply from a transformer. If you are using mains supply for a more powerful circulating pump this will mean burying a cable as described later: a thought worth considering if your chosen position for the fountain lies directly across your prize lawn!

Fig. 5 A house situated on a sloping site may be thought of as ideal for a waterfall set in a stream, feeding into a pool. The importance of correctly positioning the waterfall is shown here.

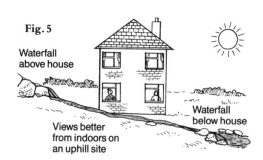

A waterfall

A waterfall or spout can be formal or informal (Fig. 4). It can be a very shallow, barely noticeable change in water level or, by contrast, a high thunderous affair involving many gallons of water. It can be artificially contrived in a pool or can appear part way down a natural water course. In common with a fountain, a waterfall may be a very distinct focal point and its position is important.

Viewpoint

Unless dealing merely with a subtle change in water level, a waterfall will be creating a strong eyecatching feature and should therefore occupy a prominent position. As it will be integrated into a stream or pool the criteria for siting to obtain maximum visual benefit have already been discussed and similar principles apply.

A house situated on a sloping site may be thought of as ideal for a waterfall set in a stream, feeding into a pool. In Fig. 5 the importance of positioning is illustrated.

Because of climate sitting outdoors may be limited to rare summer evenings, so the most frequent vantage point would be from indoors. This should be considered when planning any garden feature.

Reflection and light

Reflection will be diminished once you introduce moving water of any kind. The movement created by a waterfall will depend on the size of the pool in relation to the size of the fall. The ripples from moving water travel some distance and a small pool will loose its reflective qualities if fed by a large busy waterfall.

While not seriously affecting the function of a waterfall, heavy shade diminishes the beauty of the dancing highlights that can be created by sun moving on water.

Practicalities

Water source is particularly important if you wish to create a natural waterfall. Water should emerge from an appropriate place and not look contrived. Shrubs or rocks can mask the head of a small spring or rill. Maybe the source could be secreted beneath a summerhouse with access through a trap door. There are endless possibilities and some will be discussed in the design section. Before the design emerges practical thought should be given to the potential sites and the practicalities of bringing water to them.

Large rocks may need to be brought in and the feasibility of doing so should be studied. Make sure there is room to store them at delivery time. Lorry drivers do not usually have time to wait until you clear a space.

As water will nearly always need circulating, electricity will be needed and a supply assured. The feasibility of providing the supply to the pool is just as important as the suitability of the site itself. If in doubt, advice from a qualified electrician should be sought.

Stream or rill

A water course of this type may be anything from a trickle of water as an individual feature, to an element of a larger design leading to a waterfall, or connecting separate pools. The requirements differ little from those already discussed under pools and waterfalls and in choosing a site keep them in mind. From a practical point of view it is obviously necessary to have a slope and sensible beginning and end. The beginning could be from a gargoyle or overflowing trough leading down to a pool where it is recirculated. If you plan a stream with banks that you intend to plant, note should be made of the species you are aspiring to grow. This is important, especially if trees are present and are likly to cast shade.

Water wheel

A water wheel can add interest and extra sound to a stream and makes an unusual feature. With a little ingenuity it should be possible to generate your own electricity to power the water-circulating pump. It may be necessary to place the water wheel at the foot of a waterfall or a narrow part of the stream to increase the flow sufficiently to make this effective.

Circulating pumps

Most pumps suitable for the average garden are submersible and sit in the pond. If a more powerful one is needed it may be necessary to consider an above-ground model. It is as well to remember the noise a pump makes. Although relatively silent, an endless drone on a Sunday afternoon spoils the peaceful sound of water playing on the pool. The pump should be positioned so that it is out of earshot but easily accessible for maintenance and draining down to prevent damage during the winter.

Ponds above ground

Any container that holds water, or can be used to hold water, is a potential pond. Ideally it should be ornamental, probably a half whisky barrel or a decorative fibreglass tank similar to those made for plants in office buildings. They can be used almost anywhere. Placed to brighten up a corner or on a patio, they make ideal alternatives to pots of annuals or conifers. The most important factor is that of light, particularly if you anticipate growing water lilies. Several tubs together can be effective when a variety of plants is used. They can be set among containers of other plants or grouped independently. Apart from an occasional top up with water they need little attention.

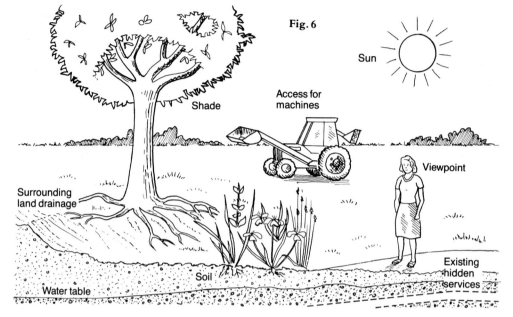

Fig. 6

Sun

Shade

Access for machines

Viewpoint

Surrounding land drainage

Soil

Existing hidden services

Water table

A bog garden

Strictly speaking, the term bog garden (Fig. 6) is applied to a place for growing plants that thrive in wet or constantly moist soil. To appear 'right' in its position the most natural place is at the lowest part of the garden, or adjacent to, or linked with, an informal pool. You may be in the fortunate position of having a wet garden and so before dealing with the position for an artificially created bog garden, let us look at how to identify the suitability of a naturally occurring bog.

A natural bog

Before going ahead with planting plans at least a full year's knowledge of the garden is necessary. It is important to notice any variations in moisture that may occur on the proposed site. Many plants enjoy constant moisture but they will not tolerate flooded conditions for several weeks of the year during the winter. Similarly when rain is inconsistent during the growing season, particularly spring and early summer, a fall in the water table will result in plants drying out at a time when they need water most. An ideal site, then, is one that is constantly moist during the summer while not flooding for long periods during the winter.

Controlled bog

If you have a fluctuating water table it must be controlled to be successful. This can be done and will be dealt with in Chapter 4. It is also important to take into account the possibility of a change in the water source. Farming techniques are constantly under review but land is still being drained in some areas. Also, a new housing development or major road can dramatically change the subterranean water levels for some distance around.

It is apparent now that the initial instinctive choice, a naturally correct one, of the lowest part of the garden, may be less suitable than at first supposed. The site should be drainable in extreme conditions or be where winter flooding is unlikely to occur.

Viewpoint

Unlike a fountain, a bog garden will not necessarily attract immediate attention, unless a significant plant is displaying well. In fact, because of its naturalistic style, it is easy to hide the bog behind other plantings, or in a shady nook or corner. Many bog plants look well and thrive in such a location. This principle of concealment provides any garden with a little mystery and is especially effective in a small garden where it affords an illusion of space as well as the element of surprise. There is, however, no reason why a bog cannot be made adjacent to your house provided other conditions are met.

Trees and light

The quality of shade cast by trees is an important condition for a successful bog garden. It is particularly applicable since most bog plants are perennial and rely entirely on one season's vegetative growth for their beauty and interest. Many of these plants produce large tender leaves during spring and early summer; a time when frosts may still be experienced, followed by warm sunshine. Protection from these extremes is essential to avoid a season of scorched disfigured plants.

The dappled shade from some species of trees will provide ideal protection. In many plant catalogues the term half shade is used to describe dappled light and should be understood as meaning the same. A recommended list of trees for inclusion in a design appears in Chapter 3.

Soil

Whatever form of terrestrial plant cultivation is in question, it is worth remembering that the plant we see above ground is reliant for healthy growth on that unseen part beneath the ground. Whether a bog is natural or aritificial, the soil structure is of utmost importance.

If you do have a choice of soils, and most of us don't, the type of subsoil is just as important as the topsoil in which the plant roots will attempt to grow. It is the ability of the subsoil to retain or discharge surplus water that will determine a site's suitability. Subsoil can vary over a small area and it is prudent to excavate a pilot hole in the chosen position before starting major excavations. Once down to the subsoil pour in some water. If it drains quickly then modification will be necessary. If the hole remains full of water for some time you may still have some amendments to make, but they will be of a different kind. Should you encounter solid bedrock you may have to think again and move to another position. If you come across roots from nearby trees it will also pay to move some distance away since their feeding roots will be in direct competition with your plants. See tree table on p. 50.

While giving consideration to things beneath the ground, remember, as mentioned in pool siting, any hidden cables, land drains or septic-tank outlets. It is sometimes easier to avoid them at this stage than go to the expense of re-routing them later. The feasibility of supplying water to a sub-irrigation system should be considered and a route contemplated for the proposed pipework.

If you intend to develop a wet area by damming an existing stream, beware of adjacent mature trees. If you change the established level of water to which they are accustomed you may be endangering their lives. Alteration of the water table in this way will kill many feeding roots which lie beneath the new water table. Over a period of years this loss will gradually show, especially if the tree's attempt to adjust by creating a new feeding zone has been unsuccessful. Subsequently the tree will die.

CHAPTER 3
Design

Garden design is an art form full of complexities. Unlike painting, where the image you create on canvas can remain for thousands of years, a garden is in a state of continual evolution and, if left unattended for as little as a few months, can be lost.

No matter how good the design concept is in terms of visual beauty, it must have the technical strength and soundness to survive the forces of nature and man. Thus it is necessary for the designer to have some basic knowledge of construction techniques and to be aware of the effects of a number of external forces, such as climate.

Comprehensive knowledge of a site is vital to the formation of a plan which will fully develop its potential. A good-looking workable design will be one that is in harmony with the site.

An understanding of plants, including their likes, dislikes and peculiarities, is as important as an awareness of their potential beauty. The treatment of their colours is naturally influenced by personal taste. However, colour associations in or around a water feature require the same sensitive handling as in other garden areas.

The first step in designing a new feature is to ask yourself a series of questions ranging from the suitability of the site for the feature you propose, to the extent of your ability, willingness and available time to maintain what you want to create. In addition, your use of and needs from the garden should be closely considered. Will what you have in mind fit into your existing way of life? Do you entertain a lot? If so, is the water feature you propose conducive to holding a barbecue or other outdoor social gathering? How does the family feel about its badminton lawn being dug up? Do you have to provide for the elderly or handicapped? And will small children be using the garden? If the answer is yes to these questions, will it be safe for them? All of these factors require thought and discussion if your new venture is to be successful.

A formal pool

One could simply say that a square, rectangle or circle is a formal pool. However if little thought is given to the shape of a pool in relation to its surroundings there will be a lack of unity and harmony. Looking back to the great formal gardens of yesteryear, in particular the French designs, there was always continuity between one area and another, irrespective of their grand scale. To appear right, a formal pool must be part of an overall design, not a lone object disconnected from other garden features but integrated into the general garden theme.

The strong and definite lines of a formal shape should be clearly visible and the pool edges uncluttered by irregular borders of plants. Some exceptions to this formula do exist and will be mentioned. An occasional potted specimen of an exotic greenhouse plant is appropriate as is a peripheral low hedge of a trimmed evergreen shrub echoing the geometric shape and separating whatever is beyond from the pool itself. Ideally the surrounding area should also be formal with geometrically shaped beds or neatly trimmed lawns, dissected by pathways converging on the pool at the heart of the design (Fig. 7).

Perspective and scale

Shapes positioned in a certain way appear to alter the true scale of a garden. The lines of a formal pool are a visual means of increasing or decreasing dimensions. Length can be suggested or emphasized by aligning a narrow canal-like pool with the long edge of a garden. A narrow space seems to become wider when a long pool is built across it. A central circular shape localizes the field of view, tending to diminish it (Fig. 8).

It is difficult to discuss how large or small a pool should be; there are no hard and fast rules. An extensive area of water, like a mirror, will enlarge the picture. However, if it is too big it will dominate the garden to the detriment of other features. The scale you use should be in proportion to the size of your house and garden and compatible with your requirements. It will be right if you feel comfortable and happy with it. For further points on scale see informal pools.

Using a suitable scale, draw your garden and house in position on a large sheet of graph paper. Include other salient features such as garage, shed or large trees and their overhang, not forgetting those next door which extend their limbs, producing shade or an invasive root run. Next draw a selection of pool shapes to the same scale on tracing paper or transparent acetate. Place this drawing over your garden plan and select the most suitable shape and location for your pool, remembering the points on siting. Do not be disappointed if the situation you choose fails to meet all of the suggested requirements. Normally one or several pre-existing conditions necessitate a few compromises.

It is a good idea to produce some sketches which give a more realistic view of the finished result. These are very useful if you are dealing with an undulating or sloping site, as they enable you to illustrate a dimension difficult to produce in plan form.

Shapes
The following is a selection of commonly found formal shapes and some suggestions as to how they can be used.

Square
A figure with four equal sides is very rigid and rarely used alone, unless absolute symmetry is needed to harmonize with other elements in the garden. However, squares used in a group formation are very effective.

In Fig. 9 small squares of different sizes

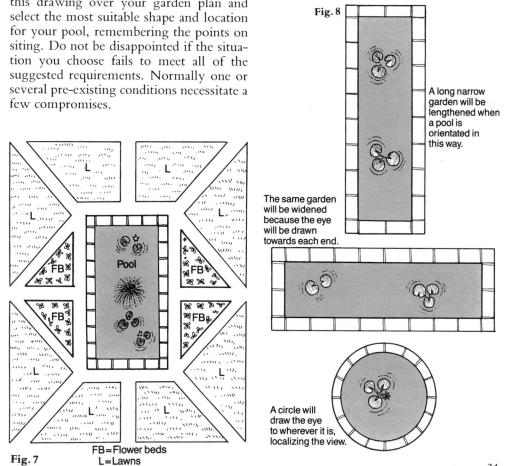

Fig. 8

A long narrow garden will be lengthened when a pool is orientated in this way.

The same garden will be widened because the eye will be drawn towards each end.

A circle will draw the eye to wherever it is, localizing the view.

FB = Flower beds
L = Lawns

Fig. 7

Fig. 7 A formal design with a pool at its centre.

Fig. 8 Pool shapes positioned in a certain way appear to alter the true scale of a garden.

Fig. 9 In garden design, squares used in a group formation are very effective. Some can be pools, others beds. They can be built above ground at varying heights.

Fig. 10 Here a circular fountain pool draws the eye on past the flower borders.

Fig. 11 A half circle. As illustrated with a circle, the eye will be drawn along the border to the fountains set against the dark background.

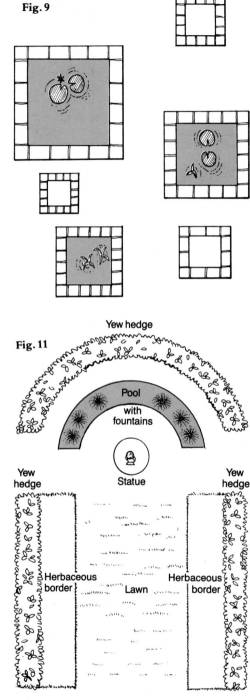

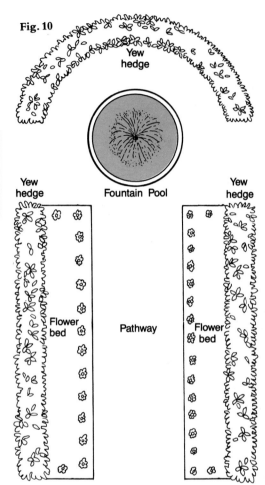

are placed at varying distances from one another. Each is filled with different species of plants and maintains its own identity.

The pathways between the squares can be constructed from shaped paving cobbles to soften the overall impact.

Circle

A circle is frequently used as a centre-piece to a garden, rather like a bull's eye to a dart board. It is a shape that lends itself well to a fountain and can also be used effectively as a focal point at the end of a path, where a formal evergreen hedge provides a good backdrop. (Fig. 10).

A half circle can be used in a similar way, with a seat or ornament at its heart (Fig. 11).

If a fountain is used, the light reflecting from it will be enhanced by the contrasting dark green of a yew hedge and, viewed

While aquatic and moisture-loving plants offer a great diversity of form and colour, do not overlook the opportunities presented by fuchsias and geraniums.

i

A well planted and colourful pool. The bearded iris in the foreground colonize the dry soil outside the pool.

This informal water feature rests easily in its setting. The alpine plants among the rocks and paving disguise the harsh pool edge.

A small and interesting water feature which is well integrated into its surroundings. The statuary provides a focal point.

from some distance, will produce an attractive focal point.

Oval

Like a circle or rectangle, an oval is frequently situated in the centre of a garden, or is at least related to another formal element. Although it is more difficult to construct than a rectangle, it provides a 'softer' look. It is more useful than a circle because it can create an illusion of greater length or breadth according to its orientation. (Fig. 12).

Rectangle

A rectangle can be used as the central point of a garden, or as the core of a separate area which is part of a large garden. For the sake of symmetry and continuity, plantings should be in a formal pattern and not spaced at random. The scheme in Fig. 13 reinforces the formality of the design by repeating the planting of *Scirpus tabernaemontani* 'Albescens' in each corner.

Depending upon the overall water area, water lilies placed at least 1.8 m (6 ft) apart line the centre. These require regular thinning to maintain their formality. The pool is surrounded by paving. The picture is completed by a neatly mown lawn, edged with a low-growing hedge or flower border. The rectangular water garden must be planted with simplicity and clarity. If your interest lies in a variety of plants this is not the design to choose.

Canal

A canal is really an extension of a rectangle and is used primarily to draw the eye to an object at its furthest point: a piece of sculpture, a fountain or a flower bed. The water rarely contains plants because of its narrowness but a canal may be edged with columnar conifers such as *Juniperus virginiana* 'Skyrocket'. At the gardens of the Generalife Palace in Granada, Spain, fountains line either side of a canal and play into it. At one end two tall cypresses accentuate the feeling of length and distance. (Fig. 14).

L-shape

This form can be used as a single unit or in

Fig. 12

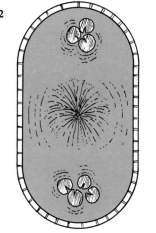

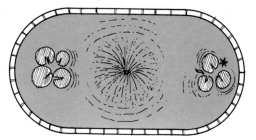

Fig. 12 An oval pool. Depending on its orientation, length or breadth can be accentuated. A central fountain would provide an opportunity to plant water lilies at either end, subject to the amount of water movement it created.

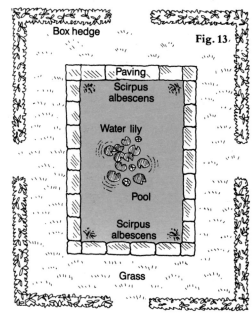

Box hedge   **Fig. 13**

Paving

Scirpus
albescens

Water lily

Pool

Scirpus
albescens

Grass

Fig. 13 In this rectangular pool, the planting reinforces the formality of the design.

Fig. 14 Canal planting. Water in the shape of a canal used to draw the eye to another object, yet it is part of the picture.

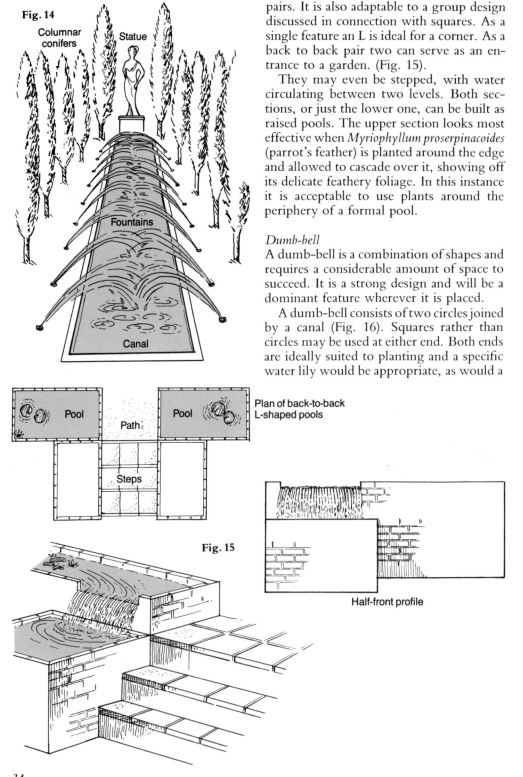

Fig. 14

Columnar conifers

Statue

Fountains

Canal

pairs. It is also adaptable to a group design discussed in connection with squares. As a single feature an L is ideal for a corner. As a back to back pair two can serve as an entrance to a garden. (Fig. 15).

They may even be stepped, with water circulating between two levels. Both sections, or just the lower one, can be built as raised pools. The upper section looks most effective when *Myriophyllum proserpinacoides* (parrot's feather) is planted around the edge and allowed to cascade over it, showing off its delicate feathery foliage. In this instance it is acceptable to use plants around the periphery of a formal pool.

Dumb-bell
A dumb-bell is a combination of shapes and requires a considerable amount of space to succeed. It is a strong design and will be a dominant feature wherever it is placed.

A dumb-bell consists of two circles joined by a canal (Fig. 16). Squares rather than circles may be used at either end. Both ends are ideally suited to planting and a specific water lily would be appropriate, as would a

Pool

Pool

Path

Steps

Plan of back-to-back L-shaped pools

Fig. 15

Half-front profile

Fig. 15 L-shaped pools can be used singly, in pairs or as part of a formal group design.

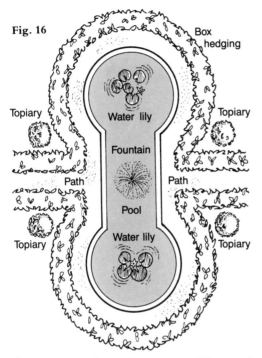

Fig. 16

Box hedging

Topiary

Water lily

Fountain

Topiary

Path

Path

Pool

Topiary

Water lily

Topiary

fountain or piece of statuary. The pool looks best set in an open space devoid of large trees. It should be surrounded by a path with pathways leading to and from it between sections of closely mown grass. Trimmed specimen bushes look attractive set in the corners of the lawn or arranged symmetrically. This is the perfect setting for the inclusion of topiary. The whole area can be enclosed by a clipped hedge or herbaceous border.

Triangle

Since the demise of the parterre in the seventeenth century, when it was just one of the many shapes found in a series of complex designs, the triangle has been little used. With a little imagination it can be integrated into a modern design where the angular shape creates an interesting effect. A modern home is the ideal setting for this out-of-the-ordinary feature. By using a circulating pump, several triangular pools of different dimensions and at different levels can be linked together with waterfalls. (Fig. 17). A swimming pool could be integrated into this design with tubs and planters providing colour during the summer.

Swimming pools

This book is primarily concerned with garden pools that are purely ornamental and/or provide an environment for growing water plants. However, an increasing number of swimming pools are being installed in the gardens of private homes and even water used for recreation should be pleasing to the eye. The same principles of design apply to both ornamental and swimming pools. All the factors discussed for healthy plant growth are necessary for the physical enjoyment of water. After all, you would not want to swim in a shady corner or in a draughty exposed position!

The one major difference, apart from those related to construction, is colour. Frequently the interiors of swimming pools are painted a pale turquoise. In a garden this colour is too glaring and detracts from the overall picture. Therefore it is better to use the dark navy blue paint now available which is more sympathetic to a garden setting. A pool for swimming must be chlorinated but adjoining pools need not share the same water supply and can be used for plants. In this way, the swimming pool blends into the garden as a whole. (Fig. 18).

Raised pools

Pools can be raised above ground and those in a formal style lend themselves to this treatment. The smaller pools may freeze in winter but provided fish are removed and the structure is sound, this does not matter. Raising a pool provides further design possibilities.

The placement of a pool on a sloping site should not present problems and can be accomplished in one of two ways, depending on preference and the degree of the slope.

Figure 19*a* requires a southerly aspect in order to catch the most light. The raised bed in Fig. 19*b* provides more versatility and, subject to light being available, will suit any aspect.

An informal pool

There is much in an informal garden that can be enhanced by the addition of water.

Fig. 17 With a little imagination, the triangle can be integrated into a modern design where the angular shape creates an interesting effect.

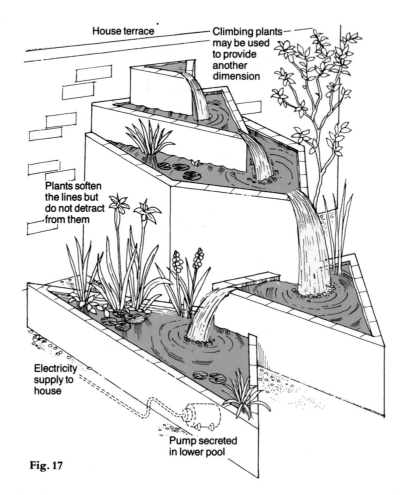

House terrace

Climbing plants may be used to provide another dimension

Plants soften the lines but do not detract from them

Electricity supply to house

Pump secreted in lower pool

Fig. 17

A rock garden is one example. Not only is water used in its own right to attract the eye but it also provides a habitat for a variety of plants and compliments many others growing in close proximity.

By using water of different depths one can demonstrate its versatility. Shallow water reveals a reflective quality when sunlight flickers across its surface. On the other hand, deep water offers an almost endless emptiness and plants stand out against a flattering background of contrasting darkness.

To most people quiet water by itself is a flat uninteresting medium. It is only when other elements are added or movement is introduced that its magical qualities are revealed. In his large-scale designs 'Capability' Brown did not rely on water alone. He found the interaction between water and countryside mutually enriching.

Scale

The overall harmony of a garden can be destroyed if the pool size is not in proportion to its surroundings. To produce a formula for scale is almost impossible and it is largely a question of relating features you propose adding to those already existing. For example, a 300 year old oak tree with a trunk diameter of 1.2 m (4 ft) is going to look like Gulliver in Lilliput with a 1.2 by 1.8 m (4 × 6 ft) pond adjacent to it, but the same tree will look splendid reflected in a large lake.

Deciding what will best suit your purpose can be daunting and whatever construction techniques you adopt, time spent

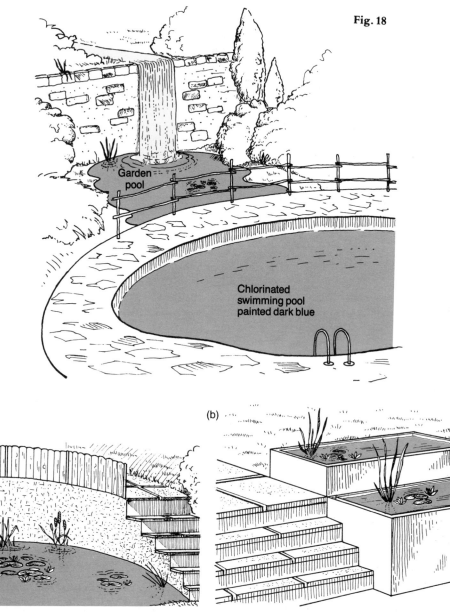

Fig. 18

Fig. 18 Swimming pool integrated into garden pool. The bridge is in fact a wall. It separates the two pools although they are designed as a whole unit.

Garden pool

Chlorinated swimming pool painted dark blue

(a)

(b)

Fig. 19

Fig. 19 A pool on a sloping site. (*a*) The pool recessed into a slope. (*b*) Pools raised above the slope.

looking at your garden from several angles, on separate days and even in different seasons will not be wasted.

Selecting any new feature for the garden is far more complicated than buying a piece of household furniture. Inside the house the scale is limited by walls and ceilings, whereas outside, even if you are surrounded by a solid boundary, the sky is infinite. In spite of the presence of this open space, most people underestimate how large the pool should be in relation to its surroundings. A scale drawing eliminates this problem and shows all related features in position, including the house when appropriate. If you are not inclined towards drawing, an alternative and effective method is to lay out a rope or hosepipe in the proposed shape and size at the location you have selected for your pool. Shape and size can be adjusted easily until they are suitable for the chosen site. If no amount of adjusting produces satisfactory results you need to consider a new location. Simply move your hosepipe or rope to a different spot and try again.

It is often difficult to judge the correct scale for any garden feature when you are starting from scratch on a piece of bare ground without any points of reference. It is useful to set out a familiar object you can relate to, such as a garden chair. It may not be advisable to leave it there once construction begins as it could well be too tempting!

Shape

You may create any shape you like for an informal pool. Deciding what will look right in your garden is largely a matter of personal choice but there are some basic guide lines to bear in mind from a visual

and practical point of view. Firstly, the overall shape should be simple: a smooth, flowing, uncomplicated line without sharp corners is best. Such a contour is naturalistic and easy on the eye.

Most aquatic plants are herbaceous and seasonal growth is visible for only half of the year. Therefore, the clear outline of the pond, stripped of its summer clothes, is important for its contribution to the garden in winter. It must harmonize with other aspects of the garden and cannot be judged purely on its ability to look attractive during the growing season.

Plants

When deciding on a shape for your pool consider the plants you intend to grow in it. Water lilies, in particular, need a broad body of water to be shown off to their best advantage and to have space to develop. It is important to provide access to plants deserving close inspection. Narrower sections of the pool are ideal for siting tall plantings. If located on the far side, away from the viewing area, they form a back-cloth.

On the main viewing side it is necessary to retain some open spaces so that the water and opposing plantings can be seen clearly. (Fig. 20). Individual groupings placed some distance from each other are desirable. Whenever plants are grown along the water's edge it is important to vary height and to avoid making a solid mass, producing a 'fringe'. This result is uninteresting and effectively cuts off any potential view of the pool from a distance.

Delightful contours can be produced by taking advantage of the great wealth of leaf shapes, from *Pontederia cordata* (pickerel weed) with its glossy heart-shaped leaves, to the tall slender grass-like foliage of *Scirpus tabernaemontani* 'Albescens'. Variation in texture, colour and seasonal interest is controlled by the planting you do and with careful planning it is possible to produce a rewarding picture from water level up to several feet from one spring to the next. If you are including a bog garden in your overall design, see p. 46 where associated planting details are discussed.

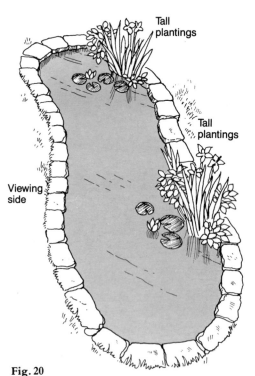

Fig. 20 When planting a pool, bear in mind that it is necessary to retain some open spaces on the viewing side so that the water and opposing plantings can be clearly seen.

Fig. 20

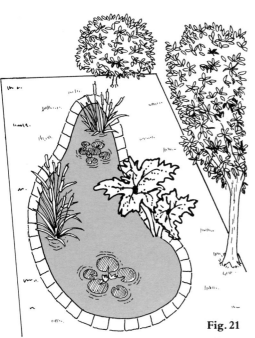

Fig. 21

Plants

The correct depth of water is vital to the success of aquatic plants. Some need deep water, others shallow. The deep-water plants are almost all water lilies and unless you are growing the miniature varieties such as *Nymphaea* × *pygmaea* 'Helvola', the pool depth should be at least 45 cm (18 in). Most water lilies are happiest between 60–75 cm (2–2½ ft) and unless you are building a large lake this is the optimum depth.

Shallow-water plants are usually accommodated around the pool edge on shelves or in specially constructed beds containing soil. The depth of water above the crowns of these plants can be as little as 5 cm (2 in) but the roots of many are vigorous. A container or pot at least 15 cm (6 in) deep is needed. The sort of plants suitable for these areas include scirpus, iris and pontederia.

Fish

Requirements for fish are similar to those for plants. They need a good depth of water, around 60–75 cm (2–2½ ft) to escape freezing conditions during winter, and they also enjoy shallow water for basking during the summer. Small shallow pools are particularly unsuitable, since they offer little protection from extremes of cold and heat.

Pumps and lights

Most modern submersible pumps and lights take up little space in a pool, but there must

Fig. 21 If the main shape for the garden is to be the sharply defined outline of a pool, then use marginal plants sparingly, choosing those that provide a strong outline.

Should you not be able or wish to grow bog plants, the sharply defined outline of the pool will be the main shape for the garden. An unplanted edge produces strong clear curves which break up the lines of a long narrow garden, creating a clean uncluttered feeling. Occasional statuesque plants can be used but only those that provide a strong outline (Fig. 21).

Design below water

For the effect above water to be successful the design of a pool below water must be sound and practical. While you may think only of the shape seen on the surface, it is just as important to consider the contours below. Underwater design must take into account plants, fish and ancillary equipment such as pumps and lights. If building your own pool, you have a free hand to manipulate the dimensions to satisfy the requirements of all the above categories.

Fig. 22

Mesh surrounding pump which can be removed and cleared occasionally

Section for pump can be separated from pool debris by a grill

Submerged pump

Fig. 22 Cut-away section of pool showing pump in deeper portion.

be sufficient space. The manufacturers' instructions will advise you regarding suitable placement but you must remember to include pumps and lights in your list of items to be placed in the pool and determine the amount of space they will occupy.

If a fountain is included a submersible pump will accommodate space at the deepest level. It should be possible to keep this clear of aquatic vegetation. A separate section or pocket, placed at the same depth or slightly deeper than the water lilies, is a good idea. A filter surrounding the pump will prevent the inevitable small organisms and debris blocking the works (Fig. 22).

Preformed pools

When choosing a preformed pool decide just what you want it to do and make sure these requirements are met. Most provide accommodation for deep- and shallow-water plants, but make sure the shelves are in the right places and, above all, that there is sufficient depth. Very few of these pools exceed 45 cm at their deepest point — just enough for the less-vigorous water lilies and barely enough to provide a good pocket of clear water beneath the ice for fish.

Streams and rills

Often a stream will lead into a pool. Sometimes one passes through a garden. A stream can be formal or informal. It can carry a large or small volume of water. Whatever its size or style it contributes to the interest of a garden in several ways.

Water moving in a stream or rill adds music and light to the atmosphere of any garden. Visual and auditory effects can be planned by design and many variations achieved. A stream bed littered with stones will produce more sound than one without. A high-powered circulating pump will move water more quickly than a low-powered one, thereby increasing the volume. A shallow stream in full sunlight, with many stones to interrupt the water's progress, has lovely reflective qualities. A deeper narrow stream flowing slowly through a wooded environment produces a feeling of peace or perhaps mystery.

A stream is able to connect one part of

the garden to another, visually as well as physically providing a sense of unity. The eye will naturally follow a strong positive movement. The garden is revealed as one follows the progression of the stream from one area to the next. In a large garden a foot-path following the stream's course carries the visitor through. Curves and bends encourage further investigation by concealing the next vista.

Planting

The banks of a stream make ideal habitats for many moisture-loving plants. The suitability of the water itself as an environment for plants depends on its speed and the construction of the stream. Swiftly moving

Fig. 23 The banks of a stream make ideal habitats for many moisture-loving plants.

Primula japonica 'Postford White'

Primula pulverulenta 'Bartley Strain'

Astilbe 'Fanal'

Primula bulleyana

Primula helodoxa

Hosta sieboldiana

Mimulus cardinalis

Fig. 23

water is not good for aquatic plants. They are not stable enough to resist the force of the flow and will be washed away. If the banks of the stream are composed of soil rather than concrete or plastic, moisture-loving primulas will be at home (see Chapter 4). Hostas, astilbes and mimulus will also do well and form a natural community (Fig. 23).

Waterfalls

Water can be made to spill over almost any solid object and a wide range of materials is used to create falls both in and out of doors. Waterfalls, which are so diverse in size and style, offer endless ways for displaying water. They can appear singly or in a series, tumbling one after the other. Wherever one is found in a garden it attracts attention. Therefore, the design and placement of a waterfall must be carefully thought out. Remember, as with a flat surface of calm water, shape can create illusions of height or breadth. A tall slender fall will draw the eye upward, lengthening and narrowing the picture; a broad shallow fall will shorten and widen it.

Natural waterfalls

Naturally occurring waterfalls appear in all sorts of shapes and sizes and for a variety of reasons. In warm climates they often appear only for brief periods of the year: during the rainy season, or in spring when fed by water from melting snow in the mountains. When the rain stops, or all the snow has gone, the falls dry up. In extreme conditions a sparse desert-like vegetation is left behind. In cooler climates there are falls that flow all the year round, often fed by underground springs that never dry up nor fluctuate with seasonal rainfall. The size, shape and vigour of the fall and the type of vegetation surrounding it depend entirely on the environment. In a man-made setting, such as a garden, it is possible to create the structures we want for a specific purpose, but it is to nature that we must turn for ideas about how they should look.

Scale
The scale of the waterfall must be compa-

tible with the garden as a whole. Although a waterfall is seen as a strong statement, in terms of an eyecatching feaure, it should not overpower other features. In the average urban plot it is a mistake to have a vigorous thundering waterfall that dominates the whole garden and drowns out other sounds. Such a waterfall is suitable only in spacious grounds. However, a high slender fall is acceptable in terms of scale and the sound and movement of a mere trickle of water can produce the desired effect. This version is often more appropriate in cooler climates and is less expensive to install.

Topography
If a waterfall is to look natural it must follow, or at least appear to follow, the lay of the land. Unless you are importing soil to create a high point, the slope of the land will govern the distance water can fall. For a design to appear 'right', it must 'fit in' with the topography and not look as if it has been put there just because there happened to be space! If you are building an artificial slope it is important to ensure that the rocks seem to be 'growing' out of the ground rather than placed on top of it. The rocky face of one of nature's waterfalls is part of a fault or weakness and in a garden it should be built to appear that way. Rocks vary in their constitution and erosion from water affects each type differently. A visit to a quarry or natural outcrop of the type of rock chosen is definitely a worthwhile excursion.

You will notice that the source of a fall is never from the highest point of the rock outcrop and in a garden setting this principle should be acknowledged and emulated. There is one deviation from copying nature that is acceptable. It concerns a common problem associated with a small volume of water: water clinging to the rock surface, leaving a barely visible sheen (Fig. 24*a*). This difficulty can be overcome by creating a lip or overhang from which the water will fall clear of the rocks beneath the overhang, and instead will splash directly into the pool below (Fig. 24*b*).

Very few gardens have the luxury of

Fig. 24 Small volume of water feeding a water fall. In (*a*) the water clings to the rock face resulting in an inconspicuous flow, whereas in (*b*), by creating an overhang, the flow of water into the lower pool is much move noticeable.

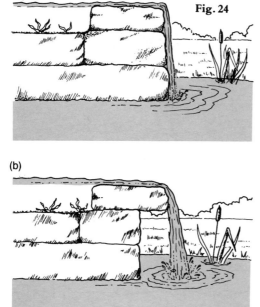

(a)

Fig. 24

(b)

natural water and therefore a circulating pump in a pool at the foot of the fall is necessary. It is important to conceal the supply at the head of the fall, as a hosepipe with water gushing from it can spoil the whole illusion. A rock can be positioned to hide the pipe or the pipe can also be disguised by feeding it into a pool secreted beneath a rock.

Planting

Because the overall effect is that of an alpine garden, care must be taken in selecting plants of an appropriate scale. Aspect will create positions for plants of different kinds, but rarely will planting be very close to the fall itself due to the constant splashing of water. Mosses are likely to develop on the rock surfaces; and in the crevices *Anagallis tenella* (bog pimpernel) can be established. Another corner will be suitable for *Pinguicula vulgaris* (butterwort) or ferns like *Blechnum spicant* (hard fern) and *Gymnocarpium dryopteris* (oak fern) which would enjoy the moist conditions. Away from the splashing, in beds to the side of the fall, but still benefiting from the moist conditions. primulas can be planted. Dependent on scale, some of the vast range of the candelabra group offer some possibilities. At the smaller end, *P.cockburniana* with orange flowers is quite lovely. The tall slender farina-covered stems of *P.pulverulenta*, especially the pale pink 'Bartley Strain', is also appropriate. In a pool leading away from splashing water *Iris laevigata* and *Acorus calamus* 'Variegatus' can be at home, planted in the shallow water near the edge. A continuation of this theme can be seen in Fig. 25.

Artificial waterfalls

New designs are appearing in many public

Fig. 25 Waterfall in a rock-garden setting, leading to a pool with a lower fall into a further pool.

Primula cockburniana

Thelypteris dryopteris

Pinguicula vulgaris

Anagalis tenella

Blechnum spicant

Iris laevigata

Acorus calamus 'Variegata'

Fig. 25

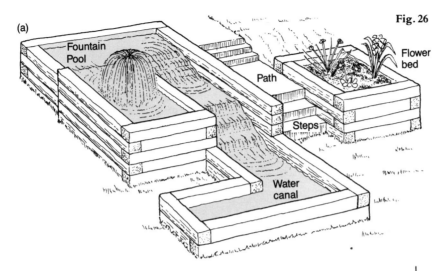

Fig. 26

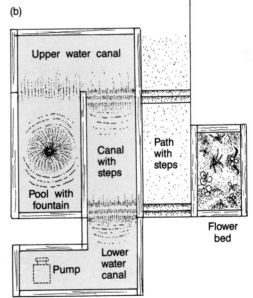

Fig. 26 Waterfall design items. (*a*) Shows a construction using railway sleepers throughout. Other hardwood timbers could be used but would be expensive. (*b*) Water is circulated from the lower canal up to a raised pool with a fountain. From there it flows back into the upper canal and down the staircase into the lower canal to be re-circulated again.

places, illustrating that the boundaries for artificial waterfalls are almost limitless. Hard angular structures are immediately softened and enlivened when water flows over or through them. Sadly some of the more adventurous designs that initially looked good on paper have proved too expensive to run and now sit like relics of a bygone era, waiting in vain for their life-giving water to return. To avoid creating a useless relic in your garden make sure your design is sound from an engineering as well as artistic point of view and that it can be maintained within a practical budget.

Raised tanks

Water falling between pools of different levels makes a very effective feature and can be created in or adjacent to a patio or other paved area. Each raised tank is the same shape but not necessarily the same size or depth. The tanks are linked by a channel, through which the water passes and falls from one to another. The water is recycled using a pump which is situated in the bottom pool. Because the tanks are of different depths waterfalls in a variety of heights can be achieved but remember, from a practical angle, the higher the fall the bigger the splash in the pool below. The size of each pool should increase towards the lowest point, not only for artistic balance, but also to prevent water from splashing areas you may prefer to keep dry.

Additional tanks can be linked to those flowing with water. These can accommodate plantings of infinite variety, from water lilies to bulrushes. Other containers can be planted with associated terrestrial plants. These appear the same outwardly but are not watertight and are filled with an appropriate planting compost.

Materials

The structures should be built with materials sympathetic to surrounding buildings. If your house is built of a particular kind of local brick, locate its source and use it. Unless you are aiming at a contrasting style, use stone similar to that of the area. Look-alike materials must be chosen carefully as they often appear incongruous. The area surrounding the water feature looks best paved in a pattern reflecting the tank shapes. Circular tanks are best surrounded by a pattern in swirls, whereas triangular ones can be set off with an angular zigzag pattern.

As an alternative, timber can be used throughout. It is much more versatile than brick or stone. Even decking, in the form of planked wood, can be recommended. The durability of some timbers in continual contact with water is well proven, particularly in the construction of water wheels. The use of hardwoods to create waterfalls is, therefore, not difficult to visualize and with a little thought an unusual feature can be produced with colour and texture very different from any other material (Fig. 26).

If you happen to live near the seashore and occasionally find nicely shaped pieces of driftwood, one might just form a chute through which water could flow. Hollowed-out bamboo, not the kind used to stake plants but the thicker sort that was once used for curtain rods, makes an interesting water pipe. When fitted between two half whiskey barrels you have the beginnings of a small Japanese-style garden. It is often such simple ideas that work most effectively. Waterfalls can be created from almost anything — even scrap metal. Use your imagination!

Fountains

Plants and fountains rarely combine successfully in the same pool. This is because fountains introduce movement to water and aquatic plants seldom thrive in turbulence. A vigorous multi-jetted fountain not only disturbs the water but also produces a constant bombardment of heavy droplets which damage leaves and flowers. Only when small fountains are used can plants share the same environment. Additionally a fountain is a beautiful object whose form should be distinct and separate from sur-

rounding features to be fully appreciated. Its existence is justified on its own merits without the introduction of other elements such as plants.

Not only do fountains appear as jets from concealed nozzles but also as sculpture. Familiar figures include cherubs and various forms of animal life. Finding the real thing in stone or lead can be an expensive proposition but reasonably priced reproductions are widely available. Sadly many of these fall far short of the originals and must be selected carefully to avoid disappointment.

Fountains are compatible with formal designs and can be shown off within a geometric pool. A very angular modern garden will benefit from the soft outlines provided by a fountain. Alternatively a single column of water in a similar setting produces a peaceful atmosphere.

Fountains should be looked at as embellishments to a design, providing flowing contours, sound, movement and light; a combination of qualities appealing to the eyes and ears.

Size and shape

A fountain, like any other water feature, must be in keeping with the rest of the garden: its size proportionally correct, its shape complimentary to existing forms.

As with a long canal or a high slender waterfall, a tall fountain will lift the eye and therefore can be used to draw attention to something beyond the highest point of the jet. A broad multi-jet fountain attracts light and concentrates the eye at a lower level.

At the smallest end of the scale are umbrella and bubble fountains which naturally pull the eye downward. There should be an additional interesting object nearby which will draw attention — a special ornament or an unusual plant. Umbrella and bubble fountains make ideal features for patios and can also be recommended for modern courtyards. A fountain in any form can be used as an initial attraction from which the viewer's eye is drawn to something else. This is the way most garden features work. You are lured by one thing which leads to another, and so on.

Sculpture

Included in this category are fountains consisting of free-standing figures and shapes. To make a definite statement they need to stand apart from other features and not be allowed to merge into a mass of vegetation. Although classical statuary has remained popular as an element in fountain design since the Renaissance, today's artists are producing original sculpture created specifically for fountains. These new imaginative shapes add a wonderful focus of interest to many gardens.

Any garden, whether or not it uses water, should have a strong design core. Sculpture can contribute to that strength, particularly in the winter when leaves have fallen and plants are resting. The position of a fountain is very important at this time when there is little to detract from it. The whole garden is seen more clearly and the need for balanced proportions becomes more apparent. It is significant to remember just how long the winter prevails, as during this time the success of your design will be judged more critically than in spring and summer when other attractions will help to conceal an otherwise unsatisfactory overall pattern or skeleton of the garden.

Wall fountains or gargoyles

Some of these gothic masks which eject water through their mouths are gruesome in appearance. Really it is rather like Beauty and the Beast. Flowering plants seem to look so much nicer near something as grotesque as a gargoyle. If only for that reason and the amusement they provide, they are worth having. Obviously you need a wall and a suitable tank for recirculating water. A wall-mounted fountain makes a good focal point at the T junction of a path. Paths need to have a start and finish. The start is usually obvious but often there is no conclusion, no reason for you to walk that path. A gargoyle provides the reason to proceed further.

Fountains and lighting

After dark, particularly during warm summer evenings, interesting effects can be created by using coloured lights to illuminate water playing from a fountain. Some of the grand public fountains in city centres make spectacular night-time displays. As the fountains change from one pattern to another, so the colour of light changes. It may be blue, red, green, then yellow, and so on.

All this sounds very technical and out of reach of the ordinary gardener, but it need not be so. Modestly priced kits can be bought to provide changing colours. They operate by having a coloured lens over the light. One design has four colours in segments on a transparent circular disc. The spray jet revolves the disc, showing each colour in turn. Other single lamps have interchangeable lenses. Not only are coloured lights available, but you can also find fountains with sequential changes in shape which automatically work through different patterns over a set period of time.

Miniature indoor fountains

Living rooms and conservatories usually provide an atmosphere more suitable for human habitation than plant life. Generally speaking, that is what they are designed to do but our need for humidity in the atmosphere is much less than that of a plant. Small indoor fountains are available which provide the ideal answer. The jets play in a small area and reach only a few centimetres high. Humidity is increased by them and the sound of moving water satisfies the human occupants, providing a useful and ornamental addition to the room. They function best placed in good light and near radiators where the dry warm air is most concentrated.

Water features that are safe for children

Shallow tanks, just deep enough to hide a submersible pump, can make ideal safe fountain containers. When stones or large pebbles are used to fill the tank there is no visible water surface or any depth of water to create a hazard. A variety of fountain styles can be used and their vigour is dictated by the size of container used. Because this type of fountain is usually small, it is appropriate in scale for children's gardens and the size should be judged in relation to them for it to appear right. This is important for the children also, as they can relate much better to smaller objects.

This is one of the few fountain types which is compatible with plants. Plant size must be kept in proportion to the size of the fountain. Pots are effective submerged among the stones.

Particularly suitable for permanent planting would be *Acorus gramineus* 'Variegatus' which rarely exceeds 30 cm (1 ft) in height and is one of the few evergreen plants for use in water. In addition, for a warm garden, the tiny cousin of *Gunnera manicata*, *G. magellanica*, could be planted. It has attractive, crinkled, rounded leaves which will scramble among the stones. Because growth can be restricted in pots, invasive plants like *Houttuynia cordata* are suitable and particularly showy is the form with multicoloured leaves named *H.cordata* 'Chameleon'.

Temporary seasonal plantings to provide colour might be the tiny yellow *Mimulus primuloides* or one of the recent F1 hybrids, *M.* 'Malibu', a larger plant with vivid orange flowers lasting all summer.

If you have made a fountain in a conservatory your choice of plants can be extended and can even include examples of carnivorous plants, or the feathery growths of *Myriophyllum proserpinacoides* (parrot's feather) which, if kept trimmed, will provide a lovely carpet, looking particularly effective with droplets of water hanging among the foliage.

Whatever planting is done it is important to ensure the fountain is the main attraction and the plantings are not allowed to dominate the scene.

Bog gardens

This style of gardening has steadily increased and many large public gardens now include an area devoted to moisture-loving plants. Unlike all previously mentioned features, bog gardens exist primarily to grow plants. Their increasing popularity is due to the availability of a wide range of suitable plants and the potential they offer. Also, the advent of plastic and, in particular,

the butyl-rubber sheet, has made the development of this feature possible in almost any garden. In addition, a cool temperate climate is very suitable.

The level to which you develop this sort of garden will depend on two things. The first will be the scale and complexity of the development. The second will be the time and enthusiasm you have and are prepared to commit to the project; not just in its development but also in its upkeep. The two are inseparable and the design should encompass these important factors.

Scale

Because many bog plants are vigorous growers with large leaves they will need a good deal of space to develop to their full potential. Plants such as *Gunnera manicata* and *Lysichiton americanum* are suitable only for large bog gardens and they should certainly be included in such instances.

There are, however, many smaller plants suitable for the average urban garden and these should be planted in such a way that they either 'float' into one another or stand as individuals. The individual plants are the 'fountains' or 'waterfalls' in effect and provide the focal point in a bog garden. They are structural anchor points to the design, linking some plants, separating others. The size of these individuals will determine the scale for further plantings and should be the first plants established.

Depending on the size of your garden and the available space, some species may be used as individuals while on a different scale the same plant would appear in large groups. Hostas may be used to illustrate this idea. In large public gardens these leafy plants are often seen in groups of several dozen. They would be separated by clumps of ligularia or peltiphyllum, creating a variation in height. On a smaller scale, in the urban garden, a hosta is planted as an individual, replacing the ligularia of larger-scale plantings. Between would be swathes of primula, mimulus or trollius planted in winding drifts.

One can go a stage further down the scale and consider a tiny courtyard. Here the individual plants are those used in drifts before. Thus an individual primula would provide the anchor point while weaving through would be *Salix reticulata* (dwarf willow) or *Anagallis tenella* (bog pimpernel), which has starry pink flowers sitting on a tight creeping carpet of tiny green leaves. The form known as *A. tenella* 'Studland' has deeper pink flowers but is not as hardy.

The overall proportions of planting in a bog must, therefore, relate to the size and scale of its surroundings. Despite that generalization, some gardeners may prefer a single large specimen as an individual display piece and this can look superb. *Gunnera manicata* used as an individual in its own right, just as a fountain would be, gives a very distinctive, strong focal point to the setting. It may even be the only plant in the garden and could be surrounded by lawn or an interesting pattern of paving.

Seasonal design

A continual show of colour and interest throughout the year is the ideal objective. Actually achieving it can be difficult and even the best-laid plans can go astray. Some of the finest displays are produced by unusual weather and each year will vary according to the seasonal patterns.

Winter

During which season do you expect most from your garden? Do you start your gardening calendar in spring and finish when all the leaves are off the trees? For many people, the idea of gardening during the winter is out of the question, but the garden is still alive and is seen, albeit from indoors in many cases. Winter is when the naked shape of the garden is most noticeable. The outlines of the pool and surrounding beds will be seen without plants to soften their edges and the design will show through.

There are trees and shrubs that should be included for colour during this time but the trimmed-back hummocks of grasses and sedges can also provide shape and texture. Woody plants, in particular cornus (dogwood) and salix (willow) offer the best range of plants happy in wet soil. The bright scarlet stems of *Cornus alba* 'Sibirica'

(Westonbirt dogwood) are particularly handsome as are the various coloured stems of *Salix alba* which, although potentially a tree, is specifically noteworthy in the variety *S. alba* 'Chermesina' which has stems of brilliant orange. To encourage the production of the coloured one-year-old wood it is essential to prune regularly. Each year, just as the buds are beginning to burst in mid-spring, all the previous season's growth should be pruned down to two or three buds from the base. This is a form of pollarding and the resultant growth during the ensuing summer will be long and vigorous. When the leaves fall in autumn the summer's growth will be conspicuous. If your bog is adjacent to water you will have the added beauty of reflection. Apply the same pruning technique to the Westonbirt dogwood.

Spring

Willows are worth mentioning at this time, particularly for their catkins. There are many dwarf willows suitable for small gardens. Of individual merit is *Salix melanostachys*, a native of Japan. It bears almost black catkins with red anthers. In *S. lanata* (woolly willow) there are fluffy grey catkins with yellow anthers which precede the emergence of soft, grey, rounded leaves. This is a slow-growing species and rarely exceeds 1.2 m (4 ft) and is one of the best for small or large gardens.

The first primula to emerge is usually *P. rosea* which has brilliant deep rose-pink flowers appearing before the leaves. From then on there is a long succession of great variety right through to mid-summer when *P. florindae* (Himalayan cowslip) produces 60–90 cm (2–3 ft) stems with uncountable numbers of fragrant yellow or burnished-bronze flowers onlax pedicles. Throughout spring the many primulas in the candelabra group will produce their almost unending tiers of flowers, as will the infinite variety of others available.

For the larger garden *Lysichiton americanum* and its cousin *L. camtschatcense* should not be left out. Their startling display usually appears before most woody plants have burst their buds and will really be a

47

striking herald of further things to come. The flowers of peltiphyllum are also produced at this time before their giant umbrella leaves emerge and it is amazing to think that a plant of this size is related to the tiny mountain saxifrages. The various forms of *Iris laevigata* should be planted to provide a link with summer-flowering plants.

Summer
For this season when luxuriant leafy growth is at its peak, careful planning is required to escape the monotony caused by an excess of vegetation. At this time it is necessary to punctuate the large leaves of lysichiton, and indeed the cabbage-like primula foliage, with focal points of colour or leaves of a different shape. In other words, focus must now be shifted away from plants which were centre stage earlier in the year but which have now become less attractive.

One of the best genera for adding new interest is trollius, in particular *T. ledebourii* 'Golden Queen' or *T. ranunculoides*. They produce orange-yellow buttercup-like flowers on 60–90 cm (2–3 ft) stems. When set against the green foil of other plants or seen against a background of water they are irresistible and they are easy to grow.

The many colours and sizes of astilbe are capable of a continuous display for several months. They range in size from the tiny *A. chinensis* 'Pumila', usually less than 30 cm (1 ft) high, through to the lofty 1.5 m (5 ft) high spikes of *A. chinensis* 'Davidii'. It is worth while leaving these plants until spring before cutting down as their brown plumes are handsome and reduce the starkness of the winter landscape.

Mimulus are worth considering, especially the American species *M. cardinalis* which, as its name suggests, has bright scarlet flowers, and *M. lewisii*, a pink-flowered species. Both will flower right through until the frosts of autumn but can be cut down in mid-season if they become straggly, after which they may flower again.

During the last decade new cultivars of perennial lobelia have been introduced from Canada. These are certainly worth inclu-

sion for late summer, when their scarlet flowers on 90 cm (3 ft) stems will arrest any casual observer's eye. With names such as 'Will Scarlet', 'Cherry Ripe' and 'Brightness' one can hardly resist. Care must be taken in positioning such intense colours as balance can be easily disturbed by using too much in any one place or in too many sites. Their value is most appreciated when light is allowed to shine through from behind, particularly in the late afternoon. Alternatively, they look superb against a background of solid large leaves.

Autumn
Usually frosts determine how long the summer-flowering plants continue. One of the few plants to flower in this season is *Cimicifuga simplex*, one of the bugbanes, which has 1.2 m (4 ft) wand-like white flowers over attractive divided foliage. Red admiral butterflies seem particularly attracted to it.

With the wane of most plants before dormancy some of the previously unnoticed plants come into prominence. *Osmunda regalis* (royal fern) which throughout the summer has been a delicate background foil to more colourful plants, begins to turn the most lovely shades of yellow and brown. *Rodgersia podophylla* also stands out with its burnished-bronze leaves and the long awaited, waxy, yellow bells of *Kirengeshoma palmata* make their debut.

It may require a good deal of research and time to plant an all-seasons garden, but it can be done and should be attempted. The rewards are many and your garden will thrive as a result.

Planning a bog garden
A study of the needs of plants and an understanding of wet-soil management will provide the basis for a successful design. It is then a question of applying this knowledge and turning it into an art form. You will need to visualize the end result and bring into play all the points discussed earlier in the chapter on siting. A large sheet of graph paper is the starting point on which you can plot all the main features of your garden before starting on the design proper.

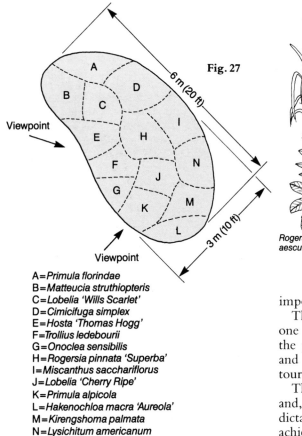

Fig. 27

Viewpoint

Viewpoint

A=*Primula florindae*
B=*Matteucia struthiopteris*
C=*Lobelia 'Wills Scarlet'*
D=*Cimicifuga simplex*
E=*Hosta 'Thomas Hogg'*
F=*Trollius ledebourii*
G=*Onoclea sensibilis*
H=*Rogersia pinnata 'Superba'*
I=*Miscanthus sacchariflorus*
J=*Lobelia 'Cherry Ripe'*
K=*Primula alpicola*
L=*Hakenochloa macra 'Aureola'*
M=*Kirengshoma palmata*
N=*Lysichitum americanum*

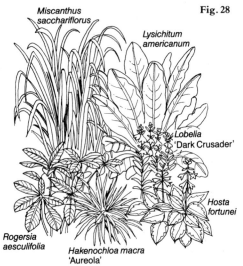

Fig. 28

Miscanthus sacchariflorus

Lysichitum americanum

Lobelia 'Dark Crusader'

Hosta fortunei

Rogersia aesculifolia

Hakenochloa macra 'Aureola'

Fig. 27 A bog-garden plan which will provide colour and interest over a long period and which features variation in height of plants.

Fig. 28 A selection of bog-garden plants showing a variety of shape, height and form.

On a second sheet of graph paper draw an enlarged shape of the proposed bog garden to a suitable scale. Now is the time to select the plants you want to include and it is a good idea to draw up a list of appropriate species. Against each one in a separate column note the season of flowering, habit, height/spread and the colour of flower or foliage.

Positioning the plants
Once you have a list of plants they can be considered for the plan. The first positions will be occupied by the boldest sorts — those which will stand tall or be focal points in the design. It will be wise to confirm this positioning by a quick look on site or through the window and imagine the new plants' mature size in relation to other surrounding features. Because these will create the framework of the design it is doubly

important to get it right.

The next development is a progressive one and involves the general balancing of the picture by relating colours to seasons and varying the overall height, using contours, dips and shapes (Fig. 27).

The size of each group of plants will vary and, to a large extent, personal taste will dictate what you do. Good balance can be achieved when small numbers of strong-coloured plants are intermingled with larger groups of more mellow shades. The resulting picture will catch the eye, but not totally dominate the garden. Shades of red and white are the most difficult colours to place and should be used positively but not overwhelmingly. Often the best place for these colours is against a background of plain green leaves.

A bog garden is rarely short of background plants and worthy of special mention, particularly if you have a cool shady corner, are ferns like *Matteuccia struthiopteris* (shuttlecock fern) and *Onoclea sensibilis* (sensitive fern). Many grass-like plants are also suitable as background material and provide an excellent foil. *Spartina pectinata* 'Aureomarginata' is an excellent candidate, but care must be taken not to detract from its natural shape and individual beauty by planting it too closely to plants of a similar height.

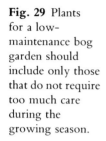

Fig. 29 Plants for a low-maintenance bog garden should include only those that do not require too much care during the growing season.

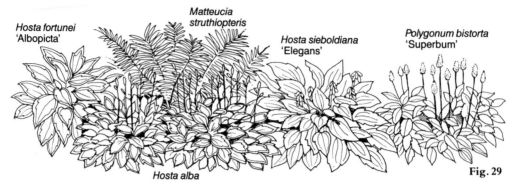

Hosta fortunei 'Albopicta'

Matteucia struthiopteris

Hosta sieboldiana 'Elegans'

Polygonum bistorta 'Superbum'

Hosta alba

Fig. 29

ORNAMENTAL TREES SUITABLE FOR PLANTING ADJACENT TO WATER

NAME	*BENEFICIAL CHARACTERISTICS*	*HEIGHT AFTER 10 YEARS*
Alnus species (alder)	Reliable on wet ground Medium to light canopy creating dappled shade Variability between species, with yellow dissected leaved forms among those available	3.6–4.5 m (12–15 ft)
Betula species (birch)	Tolerant of wet ground Light canopy, casting dappled shade Attractive bark and graceful habit Good autumn leaf colour Handsome catkins	5–6 m (16–20 ft)
Liquidambar styraciflua (sweet gum)	Tolerant of wet ground Excellent autumn foliage Upright habit casting little shade	5–6 m (16–20 ft)
Salix species (willow)	Versatility — can be a large tree or in certain forms can be pollarded to produce a compact shrub with coloured winter stems Early spring catkins are conspicuous in some species	6 m + (20 ft +) or 1.2–2m (4–6 ft) if pollarded
Taxodium distichum (swamp cypress)	Reliable in wet ground Narrow canopy casting little shade Attractive spring green and autumn bronze foliage Interesting roots when mature	5–6 m (16–20 ft)

A great variety of shapes should be well distributed over the area and while it is important to allow each species to show itself off as an individual or group, it should, wherever possible, complement adjacent plants, not detract from them. For example, grasses and narrow-leaved plants should stand above clumps of flowering plants with rounded leaves. They should be used to break the height between groups of similarly sized flowering plants or those grown for foliage effect such as hostas (Fig. 28).

Ease of upkeep
Because healthy bog gardens will produce a vigorous abundance of growth they are able to suppress most annual weeds. Planting density is important and, while large gaps should not be allowed, over-planting will look crowded and muddled, besides being expensive and wasteful. Perennial weeds are the real problem and it is essential to search thoroughly for the slightest vestige of their roots before beginning to plant. In particular couch grass and ground elder should be searched for and, if necessary, the ground should be left fallow for a season to ensure it is absolutely clean. It does not take long for any of these pernicious weeds to invade the roots of other plants, making it impossible to eradicate them. Having to begin all over again is hardly labour saving and is demoralizing.

Plants for a low-maintenance garden should include only those that do not require too much care once the growing season has started. Apart from occasional dead-heading, a fairly undemanding task, little work should be necessary. Avoid plants that need staking and those that require extra protection during the winter because they are not reliably hardy. Bog gardens offer a type of gardening that can be considered low maintenance, but they must have a sound design and thorough preparation (Fig. 29).

Relationship with other features
When a bog garden adjoins a pool or is associated with a stream bed it appears to be a natural adjunct. A bog garden on its own must look right in relation to other features and can be made to do so even if natural water does not occur in the immediate locality.

Level ground is the most unlikely place to find a bog garden and it may be necessary to create some artificial undulations in the surrounding ground to provide an appropriate setting (see Chapter 4). Contouring adds interest to the garden and forms a natural-looking hollow where moisture can collect. In gardening, producing the right effect often involves making something appear different to the way it really is.

CHAPTER 4
Construction

It is important with any form of construction to take accurate measurements and use sound techniques. It is doubly important where water constitutes part of that construction, or is the reason for it. Not only will water prove how accurate you are with a spirit level, but also it will test the ability of the best builders to form sound joints and make them watertight.

That is not to say that pool or waterfall construction is difficult, but success depends on thoroughness and commonsense. There are several ways to do most jobs and, if the way you mix cement or lay paving slabs works perfectly well, it would be silly to change to another method for the sake of it. You must choose a method that suits you and that you feel comfortable with.

Do not be over-ambitious or try something that may endanger you, your neighbours or surrounding property. A bag of cement is heavy and, like anything else, must be lifted sensibly and carefully. When hiring machinery make sure you follow the safety routine and do not force the machine to do more than it is intended to do. Guidelines for use are well based and thought out. If you injure yourself while misusing a hired machine compensation will be nil and so might your earnings for a month or two!

Selecting the construction material for pools

There are several ways of constructing a pool and basically there are four materials to choose from: preformed plastic or fibreglass, composite sheeting and concrete. Clay puddling, an ancient technique, is possible in some areas and will be discussed. Also, a relatively new technique using a composite material called Bentonite will be looked at.

Preformed pools

Initially these appear to offer the quickest and easiest way of making a garden pool. There are many styles available and you can choose elaborate curved shapes or straightforward squares and rectangles. Certainly with a little care they are easy to fit into the ground. Finishing and masking the edges is a little more difficult and the initial advantage gained can be easily lost.

The pools made of fibreglass are strong and will last virtually forever unless mistreated. The plastic kinds are cheaper but are made of tough material. They do not last as long as fibreglass. The edges become brittle with age, leading to easy damage and cracking.

The internal depth should be checked as some models are only 40 cm (16 in) deep which is not sufficient for the survival of fish during persistent frosts. A depth of 45 cm (18 in) is the minimum requirement, not only in cold areas but also in hot climates, where fish and plant roots need keeping cool. The internal colour is important, more from the aesthetic angle than any other. Also, recent tests have shown that paler colours deteriorate more rapidly in ultra-violet light than darker shades.

Flexible liners

Various materials are available and cost and quality will determine choice. The longevity of the material is the most important issue to consider and although the initial cost may be higher for a better-quality product, the idea of replacement, just when everything else in the garden is nicely established, can be a nightmare. With care, though, even 500 gauge black polythene can last several years.

The biggest enemy, as with rigid pools, is deterioration caused by ultra-violet light. After several years' exposure to any natural light the material becomes brittle and can then crack easily. These problems can be decreased by keeping the pool full at all times and ensuring the edges are well covered. You will want to do this anyway for the pool to look right.

P.V.C. liners
Single and double layers are available under a variety of manufacturers' brand names. The single layer will obviously not last as long as the double and those offered with plastic reinforcement should last longer still.

Butyl rubber
This material is much heavier to handle and is usually more costly than P.V.C., but it will certainly offer a longer lifespan and is less likely to be accidently damaged. It is normally only available in black, which is by far the best colour for the most natural-looking effect. If a hole does appear the damaged area can be patched. Some of the cheaper P.V.C. and plastic liners and difficult to mend.

Concrete
In the long term a well-constructed pool made of concrete is by far the best investment. Once built it is virtually indestructible and can be cleaned without fear of puncturing. Should any weakness develop it can be mended without disturbing surrounding features. It is also easy to mask the edges as stones can be cemented directly to it. On the minus side it is strenuous work and a great deal more complicated than either of the two previous methods.

Clay
If you happen to have a heavy clay subsoil and cost is a problem, then clay puddling can be a very effective method for making a pool. The clay must be very fine, smooth and of a plastic consistency. If well done, a pool made with clay can last almost indefinitely. Planting can be accomplished without fear of causing leaks.

Bentonite
This is a naturally occurring kind of clay and various uses have evolved for it. Its ability to absorb water is a desirable quality appropriate to pool construction. A technique has developed by which this material

is sandwiched between three layers of a tough polypropylene fabric. Thus, should a layer be punctured the expansion of the Bentonite between each layer quickly seals it off. It has been primarily developed for reservoir use, but should also be ideal for the private garden pool. It appears to be no more expensive than other liner materials.

Marking out
Having laid out the design on graph paper the next phase is that of transferring it onto the ground. If you have drawn the pool to scale in relation to the house or an adjacent wall it will be easy to plot. Measure from the building to the appropriate position and drive in a short stake to identify either the edge or centre of the pool. Further measurements are now made from this stake to create the pool shape.

Circular pools
A circular pool is the easiest of all and is made simply by attaching a piece of string, the length of the pool radius, to the centre stake. At the end of the string attach a cane to mark the circle. Walking round the stake with the string held taut, mark the ground as you go with the cane (Fig. 30).

A square
Here you will need to establish a base line which again can be done by measuring

Fig. 30

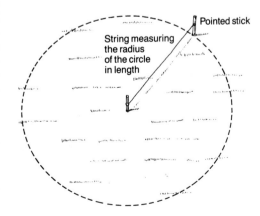

Pointed stick

String measuring the radius of the circle in length

Fig. 30 A circular pool is the easiest of all to mark out.

Fig. 31
Producing a right-angle. (*a*) Timber right-angle, useful for the marking out of squares, rectangles, etc. (*b*) 3−4−5 are the important numbers, whether working with metric or imperial measurements, e.g. 30−40−50 cm will also produce a right-angle.

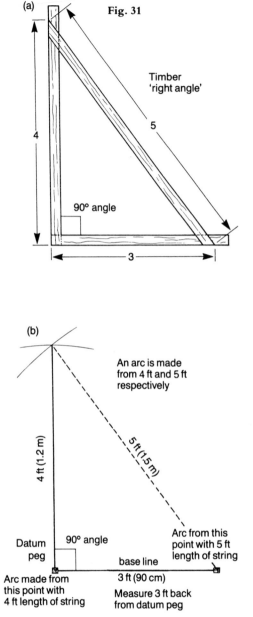

Fig. 31

Timber 'right angle'

5

4

90° angle

3

(b)

An arc is made from 4 ft and 5 ft respectively

4 ft (1.2 m)

5 ft (1.5 m)

Datum peg

90° angle

Arc from this point with 5 ft length of string

base line

Arc made from this point with 4 ft length of string

3 ft (90 cm)

Measure 3 ft back from datum peg

Fig. 32 Marking out an oval. (*a*) First stage in marking positions for pegs. (*b*) Plan of oval marking out principle. Procedure. 1. Mark the pool centre. 2. Mark each end of the pool. 3. In line with centre and end stakes mark a point either side of the centre, two-thirds of the distance from it and the peg at either end. 4. Cut a piece of string to twice the length of the distance between one end stake and the two-thirds stake furthest from it. 5. Join the ends together to make a loop. 6. Place the string around the two-thirds stakes.

from the building. Once this line is established you can either measure a right-angle using the 3−4−5 system, or a timber right-angle may be used. This can be simply made from good timber, preferably hardwood (Fig. 31*a*).

To measure with the 3−4−5 system, simply mark 90 cm (3 ft) back from the end peg of the base line. Then make an arc with string and stick approximately at right-angles 1.2 m (4 ft) away towards the next corner of the pool. From the 90 cm mark to where a 1.5 m (5 ft) length dissects the 1.2 m arc is a right angle to the base line. Proceed round the square or rectangle in the same way. As a check, measure diagonally across the corners. Both measurements should be exactly the same (Fig. 31*b*). Once you have a working knowledge of this simple geometry it is easy to apply to a rectangle, canal or L shape. A triangle can also be made.

An oval
A symmetrical oval is easy to produce. Two stout round stakes — broom handles are ideal — three bamboo canes and a piece of string are needed. From your plan plot the centre of the pool to its location and mark the spot with the first of your canes. Mark each end of the oval in a similar way using the other two canes. Next put in a stake in line with the centre and end canes at a point two-thirds of the distance from centre to end cane. Do this at both ends. Cut a piece of string to make a loop that will just fit round either peg to the cane farthest from it. This should fit both ends identically if your measurements are correct. Using the centre cane, take up the slack and keep the string taut while walking round the stakes and making a mark with the cane held against the string. When you have returned to the starting point, an oval will have been formed (Fig. 32).

For example, a pool 3 m (10 ft) long would have the stakes placed at 2 m (6½ ft) apart, each being 1 m (3¼ ft) from the centre: 1 m being two-thirds the distance from the centre of the pool to the edge. The string would be tied to form a circle, which would be double that of the distance from either peg to the end cane: in this case 2.5 m (8¼ ft).

A dumb-bell
This would simply be made by marking two parallel lines with a circle at either end (Fig. 33).

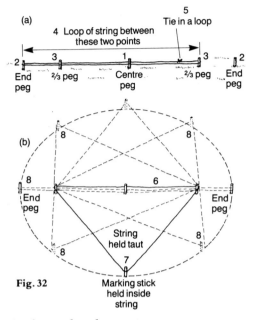

Fig. 32

(a)
5 Tie in a loop
4 Loop of string between these two points
2 End peg
3 ⅔ peg
1 Centre peg
3 ⅔ peg
2 End peg

(b)
8
8
8
End peg
6
End peg
8
String held taut
8
7
Marking stick held inside string

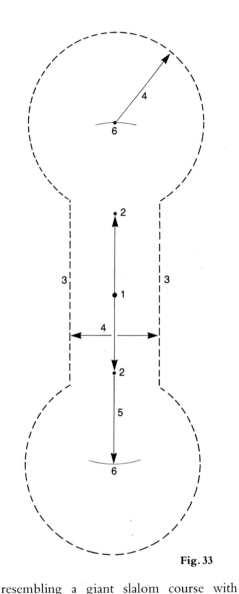

Fig. 33

Fig. 32 *contd.*
7. Pull the loop of string taut with a stick. 8. Keeping the loop taut, walk around, marking the ground with the stick until you return to the starting point.

Fig. 33 Marking out a dumb-bell. 1. Mark the centre of the design. 2. Measure and mark a straight line to the length of the straight part of the design. 3. Mark parallel lines either side of the centre to the width of the canal structure. 4. The width of the canal will form the radius of the circles at either end. 5. From the mark at either end at point 2 make an arc with stick and string equivalent to the width of the canal. Put in a stake. 6. From this point make a circle.

An irregular shape

Definitive exact measurement is not possible if there is no prescribed pattern. If you have made a drawing, points from it can be plotted on the ground and linked together with string or hosepipe. The latter is easier to see and can be adjusted to shape without difficulty. Once the final shape has been made, a shallow V-shaped trench should be made to provide a permanent edge — just in case you need the hosepipe elsewhere! Should you have bought a prefabricated pool, turn it upside down and mark around the shape with a spade.

Stream or rill

Measuring again from a permanent structure, plot the line of the proposed stream with bamboo canes. If you are linking this to a pool or other feature, plot the whole layout at the same time. This will ensure that the overall scale is correct and looks right. Adjustments are fairly painless at this stage. Later, they could be time consuming, frustrating and expensive.

Waterfalls

Again, using bamboo canes, mark out the position of each fall and, if possible, cut them to give an idea of the size of each one. By now you will have a garden somewhat resembling a giant slalom course with numerous gates (Fig. 34).

Access lines

If you intend to have a pump or lighting, the route for the electricity must also be plotted at this early stage, plus any overflow or supply pipes you have included in your plans. Nothing elaborate is necessary, but it is essential for the whole picture to be seen before construction work starts.

Fountains

To form the outline of the receptacle follow

Fig. 34 Marking out a waterfall. (a) Profile. (b) Plan.

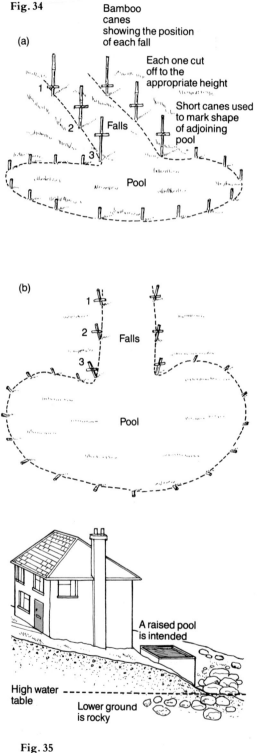

Fig. 34

(a)

Bamboo canes showing the position of each fall

Each one cut off to the appropriate height

Short canes used to mark shape of adjoining pool

1
2 Falls
3

Pool

(b)

1
2 Falls
3

Pool

Fig. 35 Starting point for levelling. House with garden sloping away from it.

A raised pool is intended

High water table

Lower ground is rocky

Fig. 35

the instructions already given which apply to the shape you have selected.

Levelling

A pool, half full at one end, yet brimming at the other, is unattractive and it offers little satisfaction to the constructor. Whatever its use, water provides an exacting challenge to any craftsman's ability and skill. Minor errors, resulting from a lack of sound preparation and attention to detail, are quickly exposed. Levelling the site for a pool requires patience and a good deal of care and as with most practical skills, success can be achieved by a series of easy, thoughtful and logical steps.

To begin, you will need a few simple tools: a spirit level — builders' metal ones are best; pointed wooden stakes — the number will depend on the size of the site; a club hammer; and a straight edge — usually a length of timber 2–3 m (6–10 ft) long, 10–15 cm (4–6 in) wide × 1–2 cm (⅜–¾ in) thick is appropriate. This must be absolutely straight from one end to the other. To check for irregularities look down its length. Alternatively, a very simple but accurate level can be made with a length of transparent hose pipe, two wooden pegs and some string.

Using a spirit level

If you have a reasonably level garden the first peg can be driven into the ground anywhere around the pool edge. This peg will be the starting point for all subsequent measurements and it must be soundly hammered into position. A dab of paint is useful for later identification should any measurements need reconfirming. If your garden is sloping, the positioning of this first peg is more important. Consider the following. The highest part of the area will be chosen if: your garden slopes steeply away from the house and you want the pool to be visible from it; the lower ground is very rocky and digging is almost impossible; you are building a raised pool; or you have a very wet garden and work is impossible at a lower level (Fig. 35).

The lowest point of the area will be chosen if: your garden slopes down to your house and you anticipate a rock garden or wall behind the pool; you intend building a natural water feature including a bog garden (Fig. 36a); or you want to avoid filling in the ground. It is much better to make a cutting through undisturbed ground than to rely on made-up earth which is likely to be unstable and sink (Fig. 36b).

In an undulating garden one should err toward the lower level as this will lead to a more 'comfortable' looking pool that will blend naturally into its surroundings.

From this single peg, which will now be referred to as the datum peg, all levels will be measured and it is important to avoid inadvertently knocking it or altering its height (Fig. 37). The next step is to insert pegs around the periphery of the pool at intervals of about 2 m (6½ ft). The object is to level all these with the datum peg. Starting with the peg nearest the datum, this should be tapped a little way into the ground. The distance between the two should then be spanned by the straight edge with the spirit level balancing on its narrow edge. The peg should be tapped down until the bubble in the spirit level can be centred. Repeat this process with each successive peg all the way around the proposed pool, eventually returning to the starting place. As a final check, compare the last peg to the datum to reveal any inaccuracies.

Levelling with a hosepipe

This is a simple but accurate alternative. Firstly, tie the translucent, water-filled hosepipe to the datum peg, leaving it a centimetre or so above the level. It is a good idea to cork the ends temporarily to avoid losing the water. Space the pegs at about 2 m (6½ ft) intervals around the proposed pool. Secure the hose to the first peg, remove the corks and adjust the peg according to the water in the hose. When the water is level with the datum and the new peg, move to the next one and repeat the process (Fig. 38). This system can be used when long distances are involved and is useful for quickly checking levels elsewhere.

Digging the hole

Whatever the pool shape, similar methods

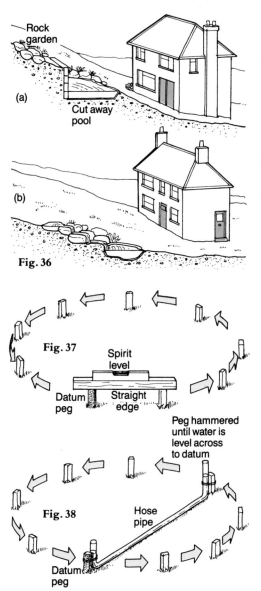

Fig. 36 House with garden sloping down to it, with rock garden or pool cut into the bank backed up by a wall. (a) Natural waterfall and bog garden. (b) Cutting undisturbed ground.

Fig. 37 Levelling with a spirit level. Level each peg in turn with the one before it.

Fig. 38 Levelling with a hosepipe. With a hose of sufficient length each peg can be levelled without detaching the datum end.

will be used to make the hole. The tools used will vary according to the size of the pool being constructed. Hand digging is the only possibility for most urban gardens due to limited access for a machine. Even where access is possible for a mechanical digger it may still be wise to do the job by hand unless the ground is very hard. A machine will cause considerable disturbance to existing areas of the garden. Repairing this damage can often take longer than if

Fig. 39 Digging hole for pool. (*i*) Dig out a single trench around the periphery. (*ii*) Dig across the pool at the same level. (*iii*) Put the soil onto the plastic sheet. (*iv*) Dig out around the inner edge. (*v*) Dig out across deep part of pool. (*vi*) Make a second heap for subsoil.

Fig. 39

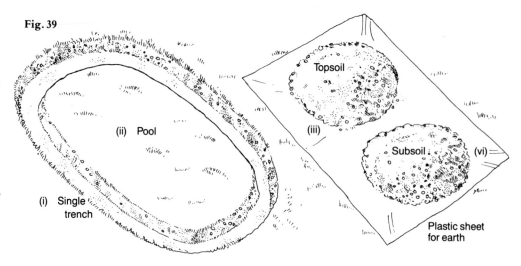

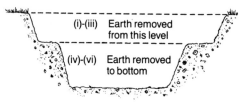

you had opted to dig the pool by hand in the first place. If you are starting a new garden it may be worth considering a machine, especially if contractors' vehicles have already ruined the soil structure by continual compression during their various activities.

Hand digging

A place to put the soil from the hole must be chosen before digging commences. You will be amazed how much space is needed and an area larger than the pool should be envisaged. Ideally, two areas should be used, keeping topsoil separate from the usually poorer subsoil. If you are putting the excavated material on grass it is a good idea to put a heavy-duty plastic sheet down first. It is much easier to clear up afterwards and is less damaging to the turf.

With a spade, dig a single trench all round the pool area, delineating the pool shape (Fig. 39). This will provide a good edge to work to. Next, remove all further

soil to the same depth across the whole area. You may want to use this soil to landscape around the pool. In most gardens this will be the extent of the topsoil.

Before further soil is removed you need to identify the locations of the shelves for shallow-water plants. It is important not to disturb this ground, as filling in later is rarely stable and sinking is likely to occur. The walls of the hole should incline only very slightly outwards to maintain stability. If the shope is very steep plants on the shelves will be too far away from the pool edge, looking isolated and unnatural. Only deep-water aquatics should have water all around them and plants like *Iris laevigata* should appear as part of the pool edge, not 'floating' separate from it. A well-constructed concrete pool is sufficiently sound to have near-vertical sides.

Most of the deeper part will be subsoil and not worth keeping, so it should be discarded. Using the same principle applied to the upper level, dig round the edge first, then remove the centre.

Mechanical digging

Hiring a machine and driver can either be a nightmare or a great saving in time and effort. The right person behind the wheel of a digger can make all the difference to subsequent work. Before committing yourself to an unknown contractor invite the actual driver to look at the job. The

Fig. 40

(i)

(iii)

Sand

Pool

(ii)

(iv)

Spirit level

Straight edge

Pool

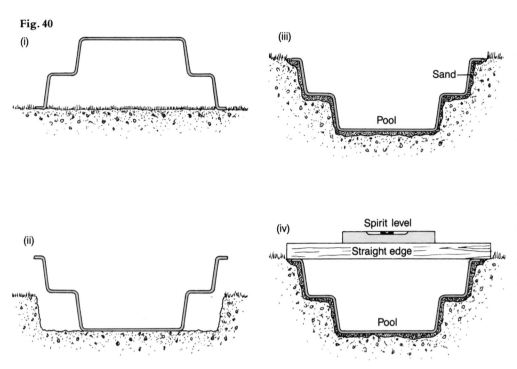

Fig. 40 Fitting a rigid pool. (*i*) Invert pool mould to mark shape. (*ii*) Mark deep portion with base of pool. (*iii*) Pool mould bedded onto sand. Check to prevent movement. (*iv*) Check to ensure pool is level using straight edge and spirit level spanned across the pool and its length. Fill in with soil or sand around the edges to make firm.

company director or representative will rarely offer any real indication of how adept his man is. Ask the driver if he has done this sort of work before and show him exactly what is needed.

Ideally you should be there to oversee the work as it is in progress. Try to be flexible about timing and avoid bringing any machinery into the garden after heavy rain. The most appropriate conditions for your garden occur during a cold spell when the ground is frozen hard, or a dry summer period. Neither of these conditions will present any problems to the diggers.

Fitting a rigid pool

Starting with level ground, the first stage is to determine the size and shape of the hole to be dug. To do this, simply invert the pool over the designated area and mark round it with a spade or turf edging iron (Fig. 40). If turf is to be removed it can be lifted carefully and laid to one side for use elsewhere, or it can be stacked to provide a future source of loam for potting soil.

Once the turf is disposed of the first depth of soil can be dug out as described under digging the hole. Then with the pool the right side up and lightly pressed in its final position, mark round the impression it leaves behind. This will be slightly smaller than the eventual size, due to the sloping sides, but it will provide a good guide to shape, particularly when many contours are present. The deeper part of the pool can now be excavated, leaving the shelves intact and undisturbed. Measure 2–3 cm (¾–1¼ in) deeper than the actual mould depth to allow for sand on which to bed the pool. Apply the same measuring principle to shelves and try the pool for size. It may require several attempts to find the exact fit.

It is important to make sure the pool neither rocks nor catches on a tight area which will lead to trouble later. Check with a straight edge right across the pool to make sure the height is correct. Then the sides can be gradually filled in with sand or loose soil. This should be tamped down at each stage of filling with a narrow stick to ensure no air pockets are left. Continue until the top is reached.

Fig. 41 Finishing the edges of rigid pool. Fit stones snugly and follow contours with complete stones. The remaining gaps can be filled with smaller pieces later or, if appropriate, planted with thyme or some similarly tolerant plant.

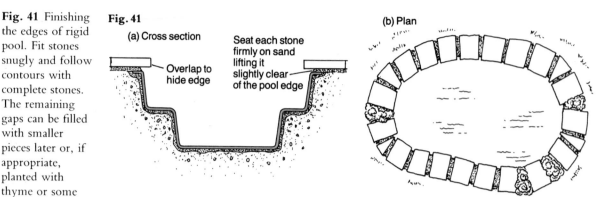

Fig. 41

(a) Cross section

Overlap to hide edge

Seat each stone firmly on sand lifting it slightly clear of the pool edge

(b) Plan

Finishing the edges

To achieve an acceptable finish to a rigid pool it is essential to provide a good overlap of some sort of stonework to hide the rim. Paving will have to fit snugly together to avoid gaps through which glimpses of the pool edge can be seen. Each stone must be seated firmly on the ground surrounding the pool using sand or cement (Fig. 41). It is best to avoid actual contact between pool and stone and care should be taken during this phase of construction to ensure the pool is not damaged.

Natural irregular rock is rarely satisfactory around a pool of this type because the stones seldom conform to a neat enough shape to both mask the pool edge sufficiently and to link properly with neighbouring stones.

Fitting a flexible pool liner

The first thing to be dealt with, having decided on the sort of liner that best suits your purpose and pocket, is the size required. To calculate the correct size for the liner use the following formula:

- To find the length required multiply the overall length of the pool by twice the depth.
- To find the width required multiply the overall width of the pool by twice the depth.

Therefore if you have a pool 5 m (16½ ft) long by 3 m (10 ft) wide with a depth of 75 cm (2½ ft), the calculation would be:

$$5 \times (2 \times 0.75) = 7.5 \text{ m long}$$
$$3 \times (2 \times 0.75) = 4.5 \text{ m wide}$$

Add to both length and breadth a further 30–45 cm (12–18 in) to provide enough material for overlap. If you are including a bog your sheet must be large enough for the combined areas of pool and bog. See bog construction, p. 85.

Installing the liner

Once the hole has been excavated to the chosen shape the shelves and flat parts should have a shallow blanket of sand spread over them to prevent any protruding sharp objects puncturing the material. Vertical faces or side walls should be covered also and newspaper or old carpet underlay provide the ideal answer. Any material that will stay in position long enough for the next phase to be completed and will not cause a lumpy finish is suitable (Fig. 42).

Lay out the liner over the hole and hold it in an even position with bricks, not allowing it to sag into the hole at this stage. Ensure the positioning is correct and that you have an even overlap at the widest and longest parts. With a hosepipe laid towards

Fig. 42 Preparation for a flexible pool liner.

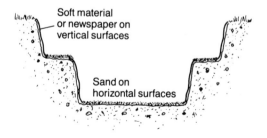

Fig. 42

Soft material or newspaper on vertical surfaces

Sand on horizontal surfaces

the centre of the sheet gradually start the water running. The sheet will begin stretching at first, then will start pulling the sides in. As the pool fills the water will pull the liner with even pressure all round until a shelf is reached. Then the liner will sink to the bottom, gradually filling all the contours (Fig. 43). As this is happening make sure the weights around the edge are sliding evenly. The results will be better and made easier if this is done in warm weather when the material is more pliable.

The overlap allowed around the edges will now need tucking neatly out of sight. If you are making a bog this will be dealt with later (p. 85). Otherwise, make a shallow trench around the pool and simply tuck in the surplus material, making sure it is well anchored (Fig. 44).

Paving can now be laid to lap directly over the pool edge. Fitted tightly together, the slabs mask the liner and protect it from premature deterioration caused by ultraviolet light. Alternatively turf can be laid right to the water's edge. If this is allowed to actually touch the water it will not dry out. Otherwise, impermeable sheeting does not permit good rooting and establishment is difficult.

Concrete
Most people making a garden pool would probably choose concrete were it not for the heavy work involved. However, the finished job offers a great deal of satisfaction as an incentive to those who do decide to use this medium. When digging out the hole you must contemplate many extra trips with a wheelbarrow to obtain the extra 10–13 cm (4–5 in) depth and width required to accommodate the concrete. Also, unless the readymix lorry can chute the material straight into the construction, even more trips with a wheelbarrow will be needed. On the positive side, well-laid concrete has the greatest longevity of all the materials and should be selected if only for that reason.

Mixing
Concrete is made from a mixture of Portland cement, aggregate and washed sand.

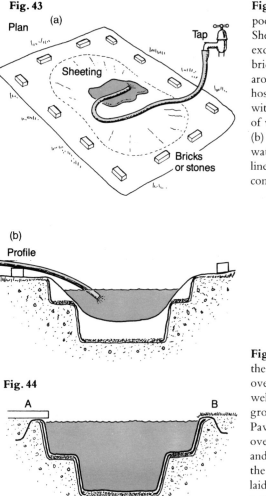

Fig. 43
Plan (a)

Fig. 44

Fig. 43 Fitting a pool liner. (a) Sheet laid out over excavated hole: bricks placed around the edge: hosepipe started with slow trickle of water. (b) Gradually the water pushes the liner to fit the pool contours.

Fig. 44 Finishing the edge. Liner overlap secured well into the ground. A: Paving laid to overlap the edge and help secure the liner. B: Turf laid right to water's edge.

The proportions of each material will vary according to the job. Portland cement is a standard material and can be bought in bags from most builders' merchants or D.I.Y. centres. Aggregate is made up of a mixture of varying sizes of gravel and should have an average particle size of 2 cm (¾ in). The sand should be washed sand, not the finer builders' sand which is used for mortar in brick laying. A general-purpose mix is recommended with the following proportions by volume:

1 part cement
2 parts washed sand
3 parts 2 cm aggregate

A waterproofing agent can be added in accordance with the manufacturer's recommended rate.

There are two methods of mixing concrete: by hand or machine. For a small pool hand mixing is most convenient since the cost of hiring a machine will be disproportionate to the job.

You will need to work close to the pool to avoid long-distance hauls with a wheelbarrow. Concrete should be mixed on a good hard surface. A heavy board or sheet of steel are ideal if you do not already have a concrete area. Water should be on hand, not only for mixing the materials but also for cleaning off tools and wheelbarrow immediately after use. If cement is allowed to harden on shovels, etc., it will never come off. Unless you have a good eye for measurements you will need two buckets of equal size. One must be kept dry for the cement. Similarly, two shovels will be needed to avoid wetting the cement still in the bag.

Measure the quantity of aggregate and sand on to the mixing slab, forming a neat conical heap. Pour the cement on top of this. Mix these together before adding water. Form a crater in the centre, pour in some water and mix by folding in the sides first. Add more water with a watering can and turn until you have a binding mixture which can be made smooth with the back of the shovel. The mixture should not be too sloppy.

The machine replaces the hard mixing surface and the heavy work of turning with a shovel. The mixing sequence is slightly different. First, after starting the machine, half the aggregate should be put in to mix with some water. Then, alternate shovelfuls of sand and cement, finally finishing with the balance of aggregate. This will give an even mixture and should take two to three minutes per mix.

Only in the construction of large pools is ready-mixed concrete going to be a practical proposition due to the minimum amount of mix that the companies are usually prepared to deliver. The essential requirement is to have everything absolutely ready for the delivery time. There will be little opportunity for adjustments to shuttering or levels that are not right. The lorry drivers are often working on bonus schemes for the number of deliveries per day and they will not want to hang around. Make sure you have plenty of wheelbarrows and willing helpers if access is difficult for a large heavy vehicle. A combination of ready-mixed and hand-mixing is often worth considering. The floor of the pool is a fairly straightforward operation and a delivery of ready-mixed would be ideal. For the sides, which are more time consuming, hand-mixing is often more appropriate.

Calculating the amount

It is important to estimate accurately the amount of material needed, particularly for ready-mixed concrete. The basic calculation is straightforward with the area × depth of material providing the answer. Metric measurements are necessary as they are used by the building trade. The material required for the side walls and shelves can be calculated independently using the same equation (Fig. 45)

For an informal pool with curves, measure in squares of a known size and where the shape only partly fills the square calculate the proportion as half, quarter filled, etc. (Fig. 46).

The procedure

Once the hole has been dug to the correct dimensions it should be lined with 500

Fig. 45

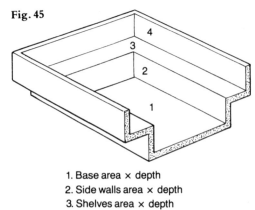

1. Base area × depth
2. Side walls area × depth
3. Shelves area × depth
4. Upper side walls area × depth

Fig. 45
Calculating amount of concrete for a pool.

(a)

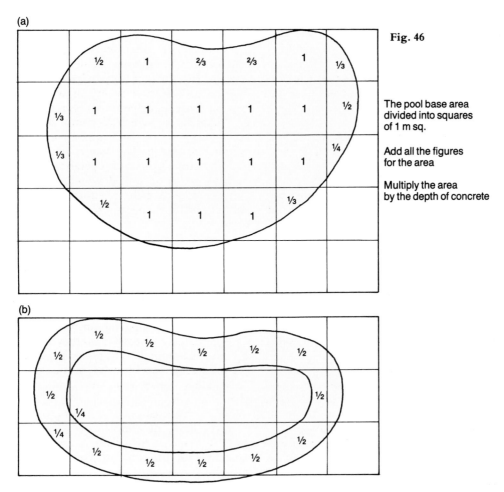

Fig. 46

The pool base area
divided into squares
of 1 m sq.

Add all the figures
for the area

Multiply the area
by the depth of concrete

(b)

Fig. 46
Calculating
amount of
concrete for
irregular shaped
pools. (*a*) The
base. (*b*) The
horizontal area
of the shelves can
be calculated
separately but in
the same way. For
the vertical pool
walls: (*i*) Measure
the inner
circumference
around the deep
area. (*ii*) Measure
the outer
circumference
around the whole
pool. (*iii*)
Multiply the
depth of the deep
area by the
circumference of
the area around it.
(*iv*) Multiply the
depth of the shelf
by the
circumference of
the whole pool.
(*v*) Multiply the
result of (iii) and
(iv) by the depth
of the concrete.
(*vi*) Combine the
two figures, (*iii*)
and (*iv*), to deduce
the volume of
volume of
concrete needed
for the vertical
component. Add
the volume
required for the
pool base and
shelves to (*vi*) to
ascertain the total
overall amount
needed.

gauge polythene or a damp-proof membrane of some kind.

Pool bottom
The first phase is basically a flat slab of concrete which is laid in one go. Any joints become weaknesses in later years. Large areas, over 3 × 5 m (10 × 16 ft), will need some kind of reinforcement. Usually steel rods or wire mesh are recommended and are put in as a sandwich filling about half way through the job.

Levelling the concrete in a 'pit' cannot be done in the normal way. Since pegs cannot be used an alternative must be found. One way is to span the pool with a straight-edge board resting on level pegs at ground level. From the straight edge hang several strings with weights at their ends to exactly the

same length: to the level required (Fig. 47). The concrete level can be brought up to these and by moving the plank around an overall level can be found.

Also more difficult is the job of tamping down the concrete, which is usually done by rocking a straight piece of timber from side to side. Since there is not room at the sides this has to be done by hand trowel or a wooden float. Initially using a shovel, then an iron rake, level the concrete as near as you can, firming in the corners with your feet and a wooden rammer as you work backwards. Check the level occasionally with your curtain of strings and finish with a hand trowel.

After an hour or two, before the surface has dried, make a key with a brush on the perimeter of the slab where the side walls

Fig. 47 Levelling
the concrete in the
pool bottom.

Fig. 47

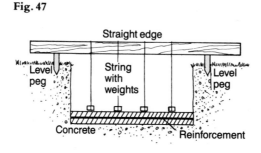

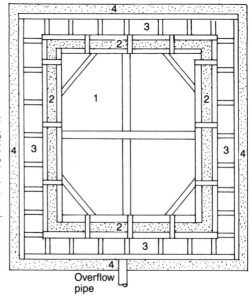

will join. Cover the whole thing with polythene to prevent drying out.

Pool sides
Construction of the sides must follow
within 48 hours. There are two techniques:
concrete formed into shape by shuttering
and concrete blocks faced with mortar.
Each method has good and bad points.
Your choice will depend on personal preference or a specific talent for one or the
other.
   Shuttering The first method involves
making timber shuttering to the internal
dimensions of the pool. It need not be
fancy carpentry, just strong, accurate and
sound. If you have shelves in your design
shuttering will have to be made for these
also (Fig. 48).
   The timber is there to hold the concrete

until it hardens. There are four phases for
the example illustrated, but variations can
be made depending on the design.
   Once the timber framework is in place
the concrete can be shovelled in, continually
tamping down hard with a wooden rammer
to exclude any air pockets. After a few
hours the concrete will have hardened sufficiently to 'stand' and the side shuttering
can be lifted out. To provide a key rough
up the wall with a brush at the point where
a shelf will join it. Care should be taken, as
the concrete is still not sufficiently hard to
withstand knocks. The inner shuttering can
be left for stability. Keep the polythene

Fig. 48
Shuttering for
concrete including
Stage 1. (*a*) Profile
(*b*) Plan. Although
this example
shows a formal
square, timber can
be bent to produce
curves and
irregular shapes.
The timber can be
nailed together:
fancy joints are
not necessary.

Fig. 48

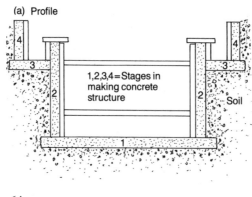

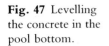

Although now crowded and in need of attention, this small pond continues to provide colour and interest. The plants should be divided in spring.

A water garden in a tub. A tangle of dwarf water lily with the miniature variegated sweet flag.

A demonstration of restrained planting. Interesting plants are grown in a tasteful manner, allowing the many qualities of the water itself to be enjoyed.

While plants are important in a water garden, the magic of moving water should not be overlooked.

Despite its clear–cut lines and rigid formality, this pool fits perfectly into its setting.

A water garden has many moods; during winter it exhibits beautiful reflective qualities and the absence of plants is a bonus.

The same pool during the summer is a tangle of interest and colour, the water being the means by which the plants can be grown.

Rich waterside planting at Wisley with *Trollius europaeus* in the foreground.

Contrasts of foliage
and form. The
rounded leaves of
Peltiphyllum throng
the waterside; spiky-
leaved *Orontium* in
the foreground.

This gentle stream
provides a haven for
a wide variety of
marsh plants. The
bold foliage of
rheum adds an
oriental flavour.

A lovely streamside with blue Siberian iris, variegated flag and the globular blossoms of the globe flower.

The giant leaves of the *Gunnera* are quite startling. A South American native that prospers in the bog garden.

Fig. 49

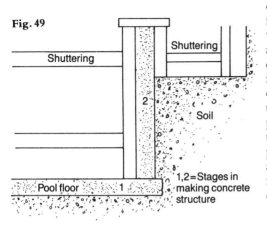

Shuttering

Shuttering

2

Soil

Pool floor   1

1,2=Stages in making concrete structure

concrete as before, taking care to leave the finished level at the correct height to receive whatever stonework or edging material you are using. Concrete shrinks a little when drying and this shrinkage must be taken into account. Do not forget to allow for an overflow pipe which should be connected to a soakaway of some sort. This should be positioned 2.5 cm (1 in) below the rim of the pool. Just above this point is an ideal place to secrete an electricity cable to power a pump or lighting, enabling the easy removal of these items without having to disconnect wires beneath water.

Concrete blocks The base and horizontal surfaces are constructed in the same way as described above. The sides are built with concrete blocks and backfilled with concrete. Follow the procedures outlined for providing a 'key', covering with polythene and levelling. A spirit level can be used to level the blocks which should be firmly cemented together using a mixture of 1 part cement to 3 parts sand. Build one course all round, tying in the corners to provide strength (Fig. 51). Do not backfill for at least 24 hours to allow for hardening of the cement.

The shelves should be built after the main walls and concrete backfill have hardened properly. The concrete blocks will provide a good key for the shelf concrete. The next day, the single course necessary for the outside wall can be built and the whole thing covered in polythene for 48 hours.

Fig. 49 Stage 2. Concrete rammed well down between shuttering and earth wall, making sure air is not trapped.

cover over the whole pool and start stage three within 48 hours (Fig. 49).

You will notice the walls are vertical, not sloping outward. Contrary to opinion, expanding ice will not damage a properly constructed pool; does not a swimming pool have perpendicular sides?

Stage 3 is laying the shelf area and is a repetition of the same procedures used to form the main pool floor, with string and plank techniques being adjusted to suit the level. Again, after a few hours, when the concrete has hardened, roughen the edge to make a key for the outer wall. Cover everything with polythene (Fig. 50).

Stage 4 is started by replacing the shuttering which will now be 10 cm (4 in) higher due to the concrete base. Fill with

Fig. 50

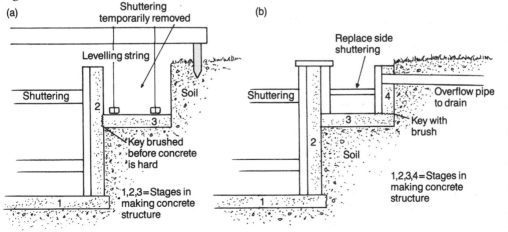

(a) Shuttering temporarily removed

Levelling string

Shuttering

Soil

2

3

Key brushed before concrete is hard

1

1,2,3=Stages in making concrete structure

(b) Replace side shuttering

Shuttering

Overflow pipe to drain

4

3

Key with brush

2

Soil

1

1,2,3,4=Stages in making concrete structure

Fig. 50 (a) Stage 3. Shelf floor. Trample the concrete when shovelling in, before finishing with a trowel. (b) Stage 4. Outer walls. Fill the outer wall with concrete, tamping frequently to prevent air pockets.

Fig. 51 Pool sides can be built with concrete blocks. Tying in the corners provides strength.

Fig. 51

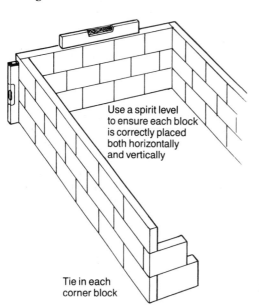

Use a spirit level to ensure each block is correctly placed both horizontally and vertically

Tie in each corner block

can be obtained by using a 1–200 by volume dilution of household vinegar. Retain this solution in the pool for three days before emptying, rinsing and refilling. A few plants and common fish should be introduced to test for any remaining toxicity. For the impatient, a 1–10 by volume solution of vinegar can be used to scrub the sides, followed by a thorough rinsing before introducing flora and/or fauna.

Alternatively, proprietary materials are available for neutralizing the free lime in concrete and acting as a sealant. One such sealant is applied by brushing it into the dry concrete surface. The crystals are first dissolved in water. Stocking the pool can take place immediately after use.

Plastic- or rubber-based sealants can be used for both new pools and repairing cracks in existing ones. They are obtainable in blue or grey.

Clay puddle

Naturally occurring clay is essential for this technique to be viable. A good-quality sample with a high degree of plasticity offers the greatest chance for success. The clay should have a smooth texture. It can be any colour: blue, yellow or orange. Puddling is an ancient craft and descriptions of pools and lakes made of clay appear in books dating back several centuries.

The principle of construction is simple and involves trampling and moulding clay into the shape of the pool. It is one of those delightfully mucky jobs that bring back childhood memories. That aside, it can be very satisfying and challenging to make a watertight basin without incurring huge costs and using artificial materials.

If you happen to live on clay the follow-

Do not attempt concreting or cementing in frosty weather (Fig. 52).

The block construction is no less versatile than shuttered concrete and contours can be easily achieved. It is therefore suitable for formal and informal pools.

Curing

Pools will need to have the free lime removed from the concrete before plants and fish can be introduced. For about a month after construction fill the pool and keep it full but totally change the water three times. After the third complete change the surface should be scrubbed down. A quicker result

Fig. 52

Fig. 52 When constructing a pool with concrete blocks, the shelves should be built after the main walls.

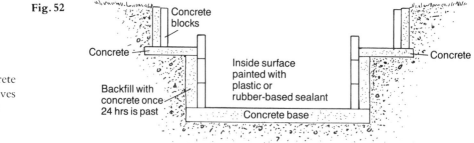

Concrete blocks

Concrete

Backfill with concrete once 24 hrs is past

Inside surface painted with plastic or rubber-based sealant

Concrete

Concrete base

ing construction points should be heeded. Digging out will be heavy work and when good-quality clay is reached it should be stored to one side. Stack the topsoil elsewhere. If the clay is not plastic-like, a little water should be added before trampling the base. Centuries ago this was done bare footed and no doubt a more consistant effect can be achieved that way. An occasional wetting with water will help. The object is to create a high level of compaction that will be impermeable.

The floor should be at least 30–45 cm (12–18 in) thick. To form the walls it may be necessary to 'shore up' with planks and pack clay down as hard as possible, using liberal sprinklings of water. The walls should be 30–45 cm (12–18 in) thick.

Once compacted the floor of the pool can be covered with 10–15 cm (4–6 in) of large-diameter gravel or pebbles which will provide easier access for attending to plants. The pool should be filled with water as soon as possible. To help clear the water, use a solution containing lime to settle the minute particles of clay that will remain buoyant.

A construction method used in the eighteenth century involved building a double wall of shards and rubble bound together with mortar made of one-third lime and two-thirds sand. This was occasionally annointed with oil or bullock's blood to prevent it cracking! The centre was then rammed hard with clay, producing a combined thickness of 1.2 m (4 ft). No doubt the idea could be used today were it possible to gain access to sufficient bullock's blood!

Raised pools

The success of a pool above ground is determined by its strength and ability to blend with or compliment other features. Only the soundest structures will survive, since water is such a heavy substance. The choice of construction materials is wide. Brick, stone and timber offer many potentially interesting designs. A watertight unit is best made with a flexible liner, butyl rubber being the most long lasting.

Where to start: brick and stone

When the materials have been selected the first constructive steps can be made. The earlier methods of marking out, levelling and making provision for water pipes and electricity cables should be checked and applied. Levelling is particularly important and a datum should be set 8–10 cm (4–5 in) below the finished level. If the ground slopes, make sure the datum is at the lowest level, otherwise the concrete footings will be visible (Fig. 53).

Because a liner is being used the floor of the pool can be roughly levelled in readiness for a covering of sand. Alternatively a concrete floor can be made. Unlike a sunken pool, the concrete can be levelled by using the much easier method of tamping with a plank rocked from side to side (Fig. 54).

Where a complete floor is not being made it is necessary to construct footings, 15 cm (6 in) deep and three times wider than the stone or brick, on which to build the walls (Fig. 55). Note the change in level which is used to step down on a sloping site and remember to leave a fairly rough surface to provide a good key for the mortar.

Before mixing the cement it is advisable, unless you are an experienced builder, to lay out the first course of bricks or stones to find the correct spacing between each one. When that is done fix a taut line along the length of the side to be built (Fig. 56). This should be level and will be moved up at the completion of each course. Use a spirit level to ensure each course it vertical.

The liner
Before the final capping is placed on the wall the liner should be put in place. Prior to fitting a few days must lapse to allow the

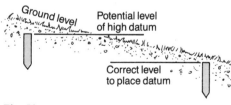

Fig. 53

Ground level
Potential level of high datum
Correct level to place datum

Fig. 53 Starting with a raised pool. The datum for the footings. If the ground slopes make sure the datum is at the lowest level, otherwise the concrete footings will be visible.

Fig. 54 Two people are needed to level concrete with a plank. A side to side sliding motion should be used with an occasional tamping down. If the shuttering is of the correct depth the plank can simply slide across from side to side. Otherwise the ends can be recessed as shown.

Fig. 54

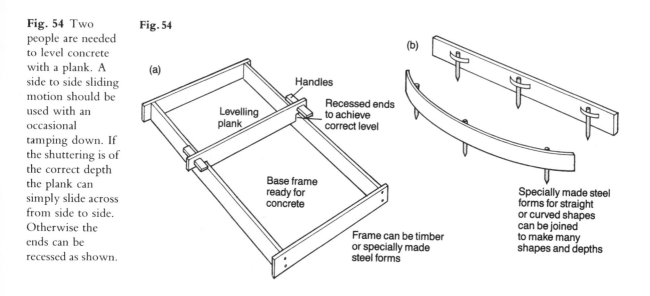

(a)

Levelling plank

Handles

Recessed ends to achieve correct level

Base frame ready for concrete

Frame can be timber or specially made steel forms

(b)

Specially made steel forms for straight or curved shapes can be joined to make many shapes and depths

Fig. 55 Concrete footings for building a raised pool. (*a*) Concrete footings stepped following the ground contours but always being 8–10 cm (4–5 in) below the finished level. (*b*) Concrete footings laid around the whole pool area. The central part can be levelled after the building is completed.

Fig. 55

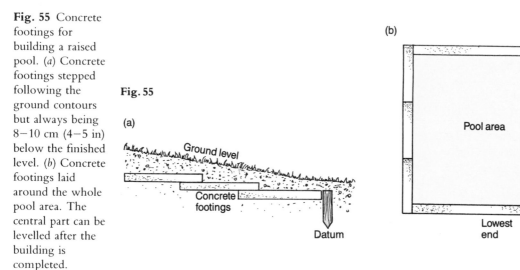

(a)

Ground level

Concrete footings

Datum

(b)

Pool area

Lowest end

Fig. 56 When building a brick wall stretch a taut line along each course to ensure a straight line.

Fig. 56

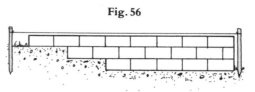

68

Fig. 57

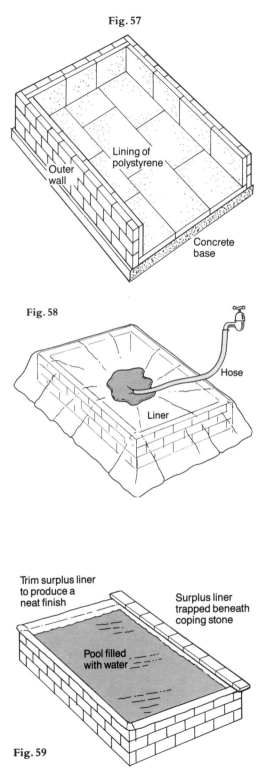

Outer wall

Lining of polystyrene

Concrete base

Fig. 58

Hose

Liner

Trim surplus liner to produce a neat finish

Surplus liner trapped beneath coping stone

Pool filled with water

Fig. 59

mortar to harden thoroughly. As a precaution against freezing an inner liner of expanded polystyrene can be fitted to the sides and base (Fig. 57). This will also act as a cushion, protecting the liner from sharp corners likely to cause punctures. Some alternative protection such as cardboard should be used if polystyrene is not available.

To ensure a good fit the liner should be draped like a tablecloth over the brick. As described in sunken pools, it is now allowed to fill with water, stretching it to fit the internal dimensions of the pool (Fig. 58).

The capping can now be fitted, trapping the surplus liner between it and the wall to make a neat joint (Fig. 59).

Joining with other pools of different levels
This idea has been discussed in the design section where water is circulated between two or more pools at different levels. Water then cascades from one pool to another (Fig. 60).

The basic construction is dealt with as described above and the shapes can be of your choosing. The circulating pump will be positioned in the lower pool. Details of pump types appear later in this chapter.

Timber
Old railway sleepers provide the best source of timber, which is long lasting, strong and attractive.

On average railway sleepers are 2.4 m (8 ft) long. They can be bought in varying qualities. The better grades should be chosen since they will not have splintered ends or misshapen sides. They will vary considerably in weight but little can be done about that.

When levels, etc., have been dealt with, an area long enough to accept the first sleeper should be prepared. A steel rake is ideal for this job. Foundations are not necessary and the first sleeper can be laid directly on the ground. Most sleepers have bolt holes where the railway track was fixed to them. A stout dowel or steel rod driven through these holes can secure their position (Fig. 61). Where the holes do not line up with each other on successive

Fig. 57 A raised pool can be lined with a flexible liner, such as butyl rubber, to make it watertight. But first line the pool with expanded polystyrene as a precaution against freezing.

Fig. 58 Fitting liner in raised pool. Take care liner does not snag on pool edges as water stretches it to shape.

Fig. 59 With a raised pool the edge of the liner can be trapped beneath the coping stones.

Fig. 60 Small raised pools less than 1 m (3 ft) across can be supported using marine plywood resting on strong batoning fixed to the walls. Larger pools will need stronger reinforcement with cross membering beneath plywood.

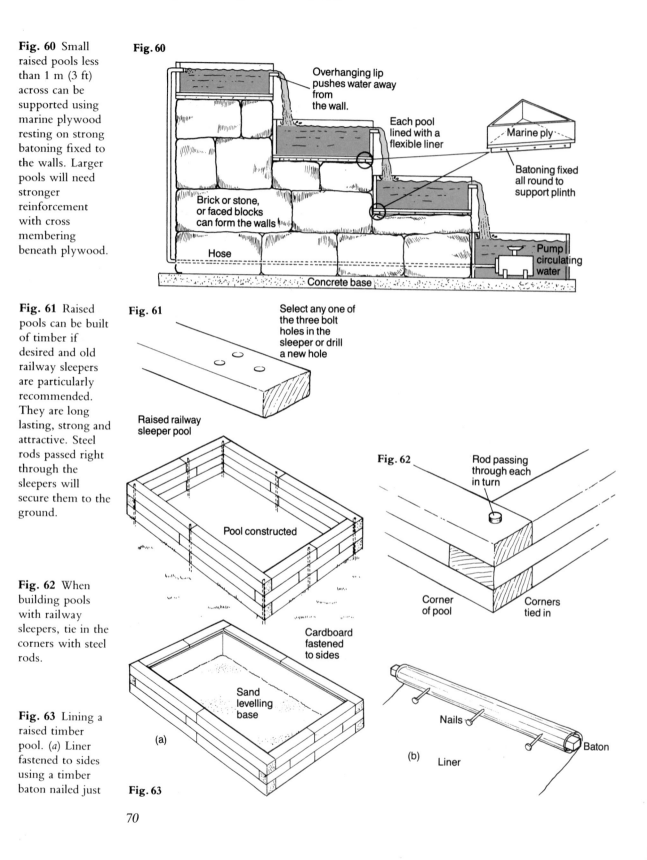

Fig. 60

Overhanging lip pushes water away from the wall.

Each pool lined with a flexible liner

Marine ply

Batoning fixed all round to support plinth

Brick or stone, or faced blocks can form the walls

Hose

Pump circulating water

Concrete base

Fig. 61 Raised pools can be built of timber if desired and old railway sleepers are particularly recommended. They are long lasting, strong and attractive. Steel rods passed right through the sleepers will secure them to the ground.

Fig. 61

Select any one of the three bolt holes in the sleeper or drill a new hole

Raised railway sleeper pool

Pool constructed

Fig. 62

Rod passing through each in turn

Corner of pool

Corners tied in

Fig. 62 When building pools with railway sleepers, tie in the corners with steel rods.

Cardboard fastened to sides

Sand levelling base

(a)

Nails

(b) Liner

Baton

Fig. 63 Lining a raised timber pool. (a) Liner fastened to sides using a timber baton nailed just

Fig. 63

70

courses, a wood drill will make amends and a securing rod can be passed right through. Build one course at a time and tie in the corners (Fig. 62).

It is also a good idea to use the sleepers in varying lengths. A handsaw or chainsaw is necessary to cut through them, but beware of ingrained grit and hidden nails that will ruin the saw teeth. Varying lengths will provide a more secure structure and a better appearance.

The liner
As before, a bed of sand should be spread over the base and cardboard fastened to the sides. The liner can now be fitted using water to stretch it to shape. Using a wooden baton nail the liner to the top sleeper to complete the pool (Fig. 63).

With imagination a variety of shapes can be produced in a series of different levels (Fig. 64).

Waterfalls

A wide range of materials can be used for constructing waterfalls. Stone is probably most commonly used, but timber and concrete are frequently seen, particularly in modern landscape constructions in public places. If you do not feel your talents or pocket will stretch to these mediums, plastic and fibreglass moulds can be fixed with relative ease and much less expense. The natural topography of your garden will

Fig. 64

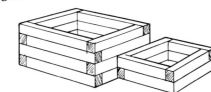

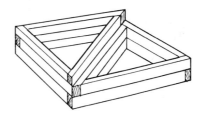

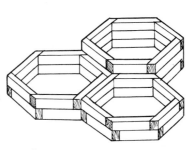

Fig. 63 *contd.*
inside the rim. (*b*) The liner should be wrapped around the baton once or twice to secure it properly.

Fig. 64 A selection of pool shapes is possible with railway sleepers. They can contain fountains or have water cascading between them (see also Fig. 26).

dictate how to tackle the initial stages of construction.

A natural slope
Should you be fortunate enough to have a naturally sloping garden then a waterfall can be blended easily into the landfall. If

Fig. 65 Waterfall on sloping ground. The concrete base must be large enough to accommodate the rocks if this method is used.

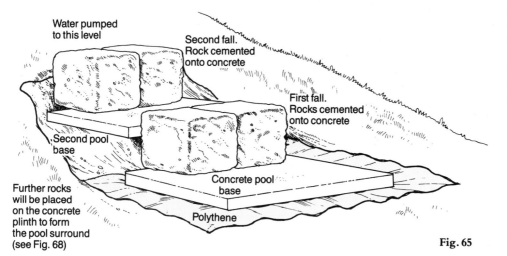

Water pumped to this level

Second fall. Rock cemented onto concrete

First fall. Rocks cemented onto concrete

Second pool base

Concrete pool base

Further rocks will be placed on the concrete plinth to form the pool surround (see Fig. 68)

Polythene

Fig. 65

Fig. 66 Waterfall on sloping ground. Polythene rolled out of the way during construction which can later be tucked out of sight.

your plan has been transferred into the ground with bamboo canes, as suggested in the design chapter, you will now be in a position to begin the first excavations.

Assuming the pool base is already constructed, the first phase of building will start at that point and work progressively upwards to the proposed water source. Where the fall is in more than one stage as opposed to a single level, each stage will be a repeat of the lowest one (Fig. 65).

Care must be taken to avoid puncturing the polythene sheeting during construction. It should be tucked neatly into the edge and rolled out only when soil is replaced behind the stones. Once the proposed water level is reached, the flap left over can be folded out of sight (Fig. 66).

A flat site

When dealing with a flat site an artificial mound must be made. The material used to create it will have to be imported. Alternatively, if the excavated material from the pool is reasonably easy to handle, it can be used. As there will be no planting behind the waterfall the soil need only be subsoil. In fact, a good stiff and stony marl is ideal since it can be firmed down readily and will be unlikely to sink. When building the mound it must be firmed regularly as any contraction will create problems later, lead-

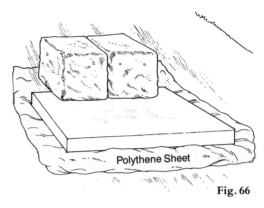

Polythene Sheet

Fig. 66

ing to leaking joints that have been created by ground settling unevenly. During this build up of soil, electric cables or water-flow pipes should be concealed (Fig. 67). Later they will be attached to a circulating pump.

Natural stone

Whatever stone you choose, in construction terms the principles are the same: good sound joints are essential and the angle or position of the rock critical to the finished appearance.

Assuming the waterfall is part of a natural pool included in a rock garden, the rocks will form the edge of the pool in places, emerging from below water to appear as natural as possible. Therefore the walls of the pool will be built with this in mind (Fig. 68).

A shallow pool, intended as a splash pool, will be built using a concrete base and stones will be the walls of the pool cemented directly onto it. A high waterfall should be built only on well reinforced concrete regardless of the overall size of the concrete base (Fig. 69).

In both instances it is important to make sure the surface of the rock cemented to the floor or its neighbour is clean and free from any soil or dirt it may have picked up en route to the site.

Handling rocks

Rocks can be manipulated by a variety of means depending on their size. Those small enough to pick up by hand are no problem,

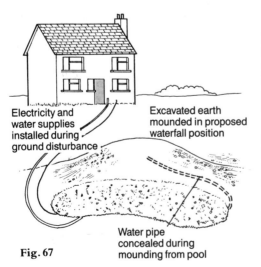

Electricity and water supplies installed during ground disturbance

Excavated earth mounded in proposed waterfall position

Water pipe concealed during mounding from pool

Fig. 67

Fig. 67 Building a waterfall on a flat site. An artificial mound has to be made.

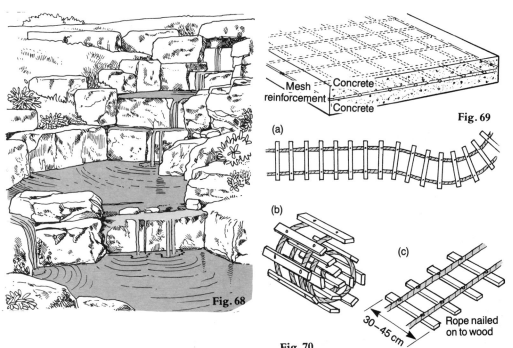

Fig. 68

Mesh reinforcement — Concrete — Concrete

Fig. 69

(a)

(b)

(c)

30–45 cm — Rope nailed on to wood

Fig. 70

but only rarely are these suitable even on the smallest scale. A sack truck is as versatile as any means for transporting all but the largest pieces. If the ground is uneven or inclined to be wet, a simple form of 'tank tracks' can be made from lengths of rope and 5 × 2.5 cm (2 × 1 in) timber. The timber should about 30–45 cm (12–18 in) wide, sufficient to accommodate the sack-truck wheels (Fig. 70).

Lengths of 3–4 m (10–13 ft) can be made up and simply rolled out wherever needed for the next load.

The sack truck should have pneumatic tyres to facilitate manoeuverability. A simple but useful addition is a length of rope about 2 m (6½ ft) long, attached to the front of the truck. It has two uses. Two people may be needed to move them along and a 'puller' on the end of the rope in addition to a 'pusher' can be most helpful (Fig. 71).

The second use for the rope is to hold the rock in position. This is especially useful if you happen to be working alone (Fig. 72).

If you are working to a scale with rocks too large to manhandle physically, 'sheer-legs' made of three poles and used in conjunction with winches are a good aid (Fig. 73).

Fig. 71

Fig. 72

Fig. 73 If working with rocks too large to manhandle physically, 'sheerlegs' made of three poles and used in conjunction with winches are a good aid.

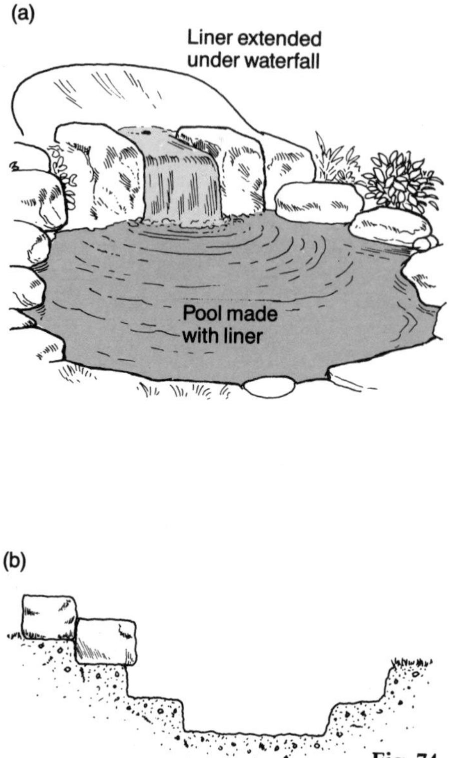

Fig. 74 Stone waterfall built on flexible liner. (*a*) The edges would be concealed as shown in Fig. 44. (*b*) Profile showing stones sitting on shelves created before the liner was fitted.

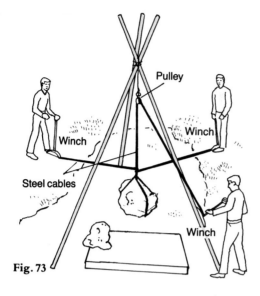

Fig. 73

(a) Liner extended under waterfall

Pool made with liner

(b)

Fig. 74

Large rocks that cannot be moved by hand can be located anywhere within the triangle by tightening or slackening the individual winches.

Liners

A stone waterfall can be constructed on a butyl rubber or other flexible liner. Stones can be stood on the liner surface taking care that there are no sharp edges to cut into it. Construct the pool as already described and allow an extra long flap where the fall will be. This will be tucked up behind the fall (Fig. 74).

Where possible, even when working with more than one level, lay out the whole area in one sheet. All the ground contours should be carefully shaped beforehand and the stones selected and tried in position or at least measured for size. Care must be exercised to ensure sufficient liner material is available to fit the finished area. Fill the lower pool as described earlier and then seat the waterfall stone in position before progressing to higher falls. With the sheet folded over this stone pack behind it with sand to minimize the gap which will later be filled with waterproof resin or cement (Fig. 75).

There are few worse sights than a waterfall with only a dribble of water trickling over the top and the areas around it gushing with leaking water. The sheet can then be pulled back over to its final position and filled with water to produce the final shape. If further falls are included, repeat the process.

When several falls are involved it may be easier to use separate sheets. Provided a good overlap is used to minimize leaks, this is an acceptable and satisfactory method (Fig. 76). This is considerably easier than the aforescribed, using one sheet throughout.

Preformed waterfalls

These waterfalls are designed as companions to the pool moulds. Masking the edges is difficult and requires imaginative planting to produce an acceptable finish. Fitting the shapes together is simply done and each mould can be set on a bed of sand.

The lower pieces should be positioned first, enabling those above to be seated at the correct level. Start by digging out a shape larger than the mould size. Then

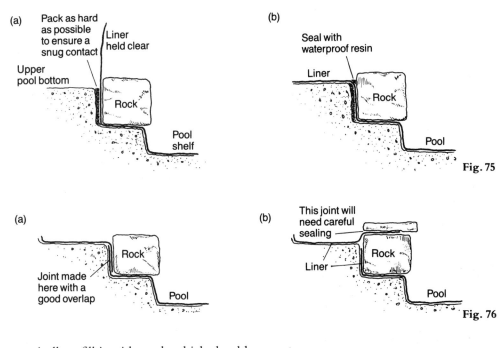

(a) Pack as hard as possible to ensure a snug contact / Liner held clear

Upper pool bottom

Rock

Pool shelf

(b) Seal with waterproof resin

Liner

Rock

Pool

Fig. 75

(a)

Rock

Joint made here with a good overlap

Pool

(b) This joint will need careful sealing

Liner

Rock

Pool

Fig. 76

Fill with soil right up to the edge

Settle onto sand

Fig. 77

Fig. 75 Constructing a stone waterfall on a flexible liner. (*a*) Packing with sand behind rock and (*b*) sealing the gap.

Fig. 76 When constructing several falls it is generally much easier to use separate sheets of flexible liner rather than one large sheet.

Fig. 77 Make sure preformed waterfalls are firmly established and do not rock, especially at the corners or around the edge.

practically refill it with sand, which should not be too wet. Roughly spread it to shape and sit the mould onto it. With a series of rocking, twisting and pressing movements manoeuvre the mould into its position. Make sure it is firmly established and does not rock, especially at the corners or around the edge. Soil can now be pushed into position around the mould ensuring the edges are well camouflaged (Fig. 77).

Streams

Of all the water features a stream is the most complex. It will embrace many of the construction techniques so far used and can be made of any of the materials described. It can be a very simple construction or a complicated one, incorporating a series of shallow waterfalls. Levels and distances must be carefully calculated and the flow of water judged correctly for a satisfactory result. If you are fortunate enough to have a natural stream, even a tiny trickle, this can easily be dammed and a series of pools created. A narrow overflow from one pool to the next is better visually than a wider one where the water will be spread more thinly, becoming less visible.

The fundamentals of construction vary only slightly from those used in pools and waterfalls. Modification of size, shape and depth are all that is needed.

Natural stream

To create a realistic stream all non–natural materials used in its construction must be hidden. The slightest chink in the disguise will ruin the whole effect. A stream of authentic appearance can only be made using natural looking man-made materials or genuine stone.

The stream should be made flat across its width and the overall width must be greater than that of the finished water course (Fig. 78). The reason for this is twofold. Firstly,

75

Fig. 78 A natural stream should be flat across its width and the overall width must be greater than that of the finished water course.

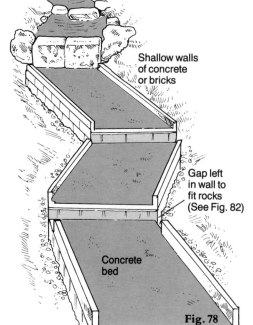

Shallow walls of concrete or bricks

Gap left in wall to fit rocks (See Fig. 82)

Concrete bed

Fig. 78

Fig. 79 (*a*) Stream bed constructed with a level base allowing deep enough areas for planting. (*b*) Stream bed on a sloping base. Suitable for steep gradients, especially in areas of strong subsoils where digging is difficult. The water feature shown in Fig. 78 was constructed in this way. (*c*) This is a compromise and provides deep water at the waterfall, giving the impression that the pool is deeper all through. The important objective is to retain water in each pool when the pump is switched off.

to allow the edges to be totally masked and, secondly, to provide some wet planting spaces. Despite the flowing water, a few plants will naturally establish themselves among the rocks. The water forget-me-not, *Myosotis palustris*, and an occasional *Iris laevigata* are appropriate examples.

Concrete

Prepare and construct the floor as described in the raised pool construction section. As already mentioned it will be made level across its width. The length of each section and the 'fall' on the floor will be determined by the lay of the land. The steeper the gradient the more waterfalls or sections there will be. The critical factor is that the top of any waterfall must be above the level of the bottom of the fall that feeds it, or is above it (Fig. 79).

Water need only be a few centimetres deep but the stream should always be full, whether or not the pump is circulating water, otherwise the source dries up.

The sides can be made using shuttering and will be no more than 10–15 cm (4–6 in) high (Fig. 80).

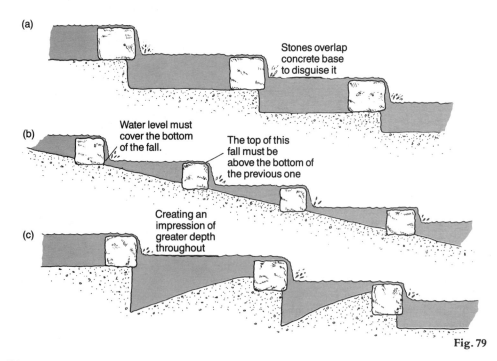

(a) Stones overlap concrete base to disguise it

(b) Water level must cover the bottom of the fall. The top of this fall must be above the bottom of the previous one

(c) Creating an impression of greater depth throughout

Fig. 79

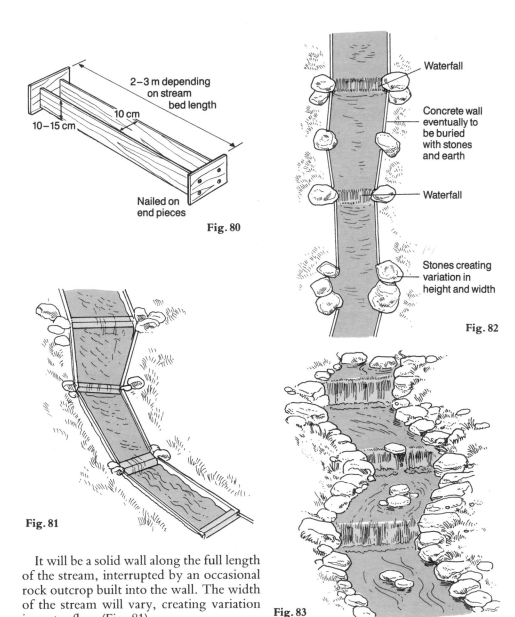

Fig. 80

Fig. 81

Waterfall

Concrete wall eventually to be buried with stones and earth

Waterfall

Stones creating variation in height and width

Fig. 82

Fig. 83

2–3 m depending on stream bed length

10 cm

10–15 cm

Nailed on end pieces

Fig. 80
Shuttering for concrete stream. Because this is to sit on concrete, the shuttering cannot be fixed with stakes in the usual way. Ensure a good 'key' has been provided in the appropriate places.

Fig. 81 Plan of stream width. At the narrow points the water will change tempo and be more visible.

Fig. 82 Each waterfall in a stream will need rocks to create naturalistic outcrops.

Fig. 83 This is the same water course as shown in Fig. 78 but completed. Note that the edges have been well masked.

It will be a solid wall along the full length of the stream, interrupted by an occasional rock outcrop built into the wall. The width of the stream will vary, creating variation in water flow (Fig. 81).

Similarly each waterfall will need other rocks to create naturalistic outcrops and stones will replace the wall here also (Fig. 82).

When the concreting and inclusion of rocks is completed soil should be banked up to hide the backs of rocks and level up to the side walls. Small stones of different sizes can now be distributed to mask the edges and provide the finishing touch (Fig. 83).

Flexible liner
Only the strongest butyl rubber is suitable due to the potential damage from sharp-edged stones. Use the same construction shape as described under concrete and apply the principles described under water-falls for the techniques.

Clay puddle
This is a less reliable method but a perfectly

Fig. 84 Natural water flow diverted around working area by guttering.

Fig. 85 A natural stream could be dammed to increase the water surface to allow more scope for planting. This is an initial test before a permanent dam is built.

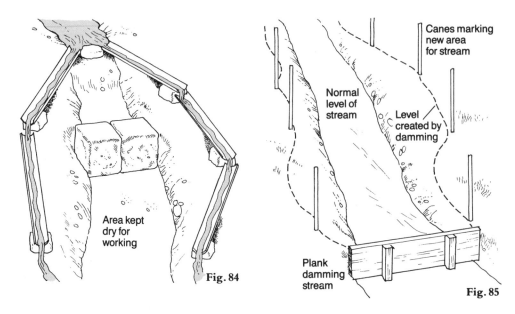

Area kept dry for working

Fig. 84

Canes marking new area for stream

Normal level of stream

Level created by damming

Plank damming stream

Fig. 85

functional stream can be formed where clay is abundant. The stream bed is made as described under pool construction. Rocks are settled into the clay along its length. Waterfalls need extra care around the edges where constantly flowing water is liable to erode the clay. Eventually the water will find an easier route around the rock, rather than over it.

Converting streams

There are special problems associated with the manipulation of natural water flowing through your garden. Temporarily diverting water while you are working requires a little ingenuity and may involve a visit to a scrap yard where water conveyancing equipment is often abundant. Old guttering is ideal and a series of lengths catching water from each other around your working area is remarkably simple and effective. They can be moved easily from place to place wherever a dry working space is needed (Fig. 84). With water out of the way construction can go ahead and any of the appropriate materials can be used to reconstruct or repair existing waterways.

Earlier, a brief comment referred to damming existing streams to increase the water surface to allow more scope for planting. The effect should be tested from several positions before embarking on a major undertaking. In selected places, use planks of wood to temporarily dam the existing stream. Soon this will indicate the potential each position has to offer as a dam site and the most suitable one can be chosen. Often the area flooded will give an idea of the natural shape you will need to excavate to widen the existing bed. Canes can be used to mark the outline before the water is allowed to subside (Fig. 85).

Creating a dam

A permanent dam can be made from stone or timber. Stone should be built onto a concrete plinth (Fig. 86). Notice in the figure the 'arms' extend well into the bank, preventing potential leakage through erosion.

Simple satisfactory dams can be made using railway sleepers. They should be dug well into the bank on either side and sealed with mastic to prevent seepage (Fig. 87). They can be stacked vertically or stepped to create different effects. Several holes can be drilled at the lowest level to allow for draining when further structural work or alterations may be necessary. The holes can be filled with corks or wooden bungs which

78

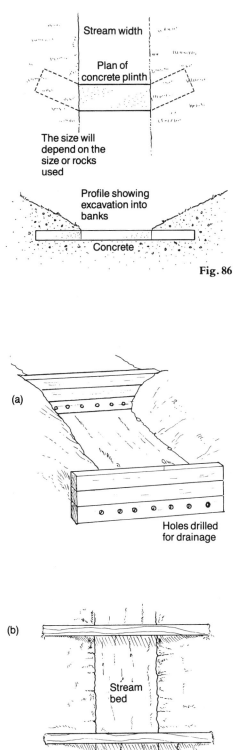

Stream width

Plan of
concrete plinth

The size will
depend on the
size or rocks
used

Profile showing
excavation into
banks

Concrete

Fig. 86

(a)

Holes drilled
for drainage

(b)

Stream
bed

Fig. 87

will be simple to remove when drainage is needed.

A sluice

To have absolute control of water flow a sluice must be built. Vertically grooved concrete blocks set on a plinth crossing the stream provide the framework. Hardwood timber planks are then slid in the grooves. The water level is adjusted by raising or lowering the planks (Fig. 88). This method is particularly useful for controlling a fluctuating water table. Boards can be added or removed according to the water level.

Circulating pumps

There are two types of pumps to choose from: submersible and surface. Both are designed to circulate water in the same way. Each consists of an electric motor operating an impellor which sucks water in and forces it out under pressure at the other end. The suction end has a strainer to prevent debris from entering the pump and clogging it. The outlet feeds into a pipe which is then fed to your waterfall or fountain. Large powerful surface pumps are

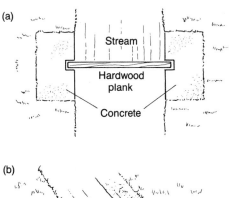

(a)

Stream

Hardwood
plank

Concrete

(b)

Planks can be
raised or lowered
according to need

Concrete

Fig. 88

Fig. 86 A permanent dam can be made from stone or timber. Stone should be built onto a concrete plinth.

Fig. 87 Dams can be made using railway sleepers. They should be dug well into the bank on either side of the stream: (*a*) shows a perspective view; (*b*) is a plan view.

Fig. 88 Constructing a sluice for control of water flow in a stream. (*a*) Plan. (*b*) Profile. Because timber expands when wet, the planks should be made with a generous fit.

required for big water displays or high waterfalls, while the smaller submersible ones are appropriate for a single fountain or moderately sized waterfall.

Power supply for a surface pump, or large submersibles

A permanent armoured cable should be used and switched at a point inside the house. It is wise to use an R.C.D. (residual current device) which isolates the plug socket if the cable is damaged or a short occurs. These can now be bought in simple plug form which fit into an ordinary 13 amp socket or special R.C.D. sockets can be fitted.

Advice on the cable and suitability of power should always be sought from a qualified electrician. Any type of electrical equipment used in the garden, particularly under water, is potentially more dangerous than in other domestic areas and extra care should be taken.

The cable should be laid in a trench at least 60 cm (2 ft) deep. It is best to bed it in sand to prevent damage. This depth may seem excessive and you may never want to dig so deeply. However, unless the cable is well buried other successive owners of your property may come across it unsuspectingly. Warning tape printed in red should be rolled out over the cable indicating potential danger. A plan of the route the cable follows is useful but be sure to make measurements from solid objects that are permanent.

The connection to the pump should be made using suitable outdoor fittings. Double headed sockets are available so that lighting can be operated from the same power source but switched independently. This extra socket is also useful for electrically powered hedge trimmers.

Power supply for small submersible pumps

Low-voltage pumps are very safe to use and need only light 24 volt cable wired through a transformer to operate them. The cable need not be buried and can be concealed among plants en route to the pump. A plastic conduit can be used to

cross under pathways or in other places where damage is likely to occur.

Selecting a pump

There is a wide selection of pumps available but not all of them are suitable for every application. At the smaller end of the market you will find submersible models suitable for tiny bubble fountains. At the other extreme surface pumps are capable of producing sufficient circulation to support huge columns of water.

Most stockists will provide performance tables showing flow rates for each pump and your selection will be based on the flow rate you require. The proper rate is not easy to gauge without practice and determining the amount of water that looks right coming over a waterfall is difficult. A wide fall is going to need more water than a narrow one to give an appearance of like volume. Therefore a large pump will be needed even though the 'lift' may be the same. A simple calculation can provide an indication of the pump size needed for a specific feature. Measure in pints the quantity of water which flows from a tap through a hosepipe into a bucket during a one-minute period. To produce gallons per hour multiply the quantity of water by 7.5. If you intend to have a waterfall of a known width, water from the hose can be run over a piece of wood or any object of the same width. You can then judge whether more or fewer gallons per hour (than in your test) will be needed (Fig. 89).

Fig. 89 To help you choose the right circulating pump for a waterfall of a known width, water from a hosepipe can be run over a piece of wood. You can then judge whether more or fewer gallons per hour (than in your test) will be needed. The wood beading can be quickly removed and repositioned at varying widths to judge the flow rate required.

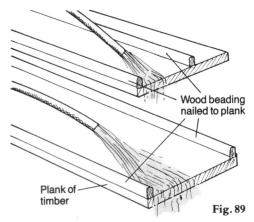

Wood beading nailed to plank

Plank of timber

Fig. 89

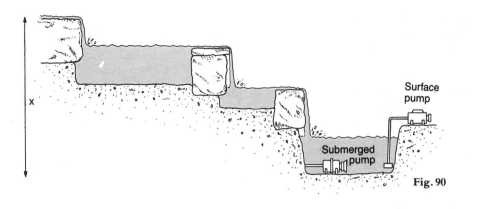

Surface pump

Submerged pump

Fig. 90

For a combined effect of more than one waterfall, or a waterfall and fountain, you must include a calculation for each item. In the performance tables the height of each water display will be given in addition to the flow rate and before a pump is selected the fountain and/or waterfall height should be measured. Take into account the difference in level above the submerged pump and the foot of the waterfall. This is especially important if a stream and several small falls are involved before water returns to the pool (Fig. 90).

When buying a water flow delivery hose be sure that your measurements allow for ground curvature and undulations. Kinks, caused by turning corners too fast, will impede the flow of water and reduce the pump's efficiency.

Submersible pumps
Pumps that are submerged in the pool are capable of operating a wide range of equipment and the more powerful ones compare favourably in output with some surface pumps. Unless capacity in excess of 4545 l (1000 gal) per hour at a head of 6 m (20 ft) is needed, the ease of installing a submersible pump favours its selection. On the other hand, some of the more powerful submersible pumps can be more expensive than a surface pump of the same capacity.

Most fountains can be operated by a submersible pump with the more powerful models capable of lifting water in excess of 3 m (10 ft). In association with the fountain, coloured discs are available which rotate above a sealed light, creating special effects

after dark. This lighting technique is not available with surface pumps.

Positioning the pump. When only a waterfall is being operated the pump can be placed at almost any convenient, deep part of the pool where it will be continuously submerged (Fig. 91). A similar position is also appropriate when a second pipe from the pump leads to a fountain head.

When a specific fountain pump is installed it may require a plinth beneath it to bring the fountain head just clear of the water's surface (Fig. 92).

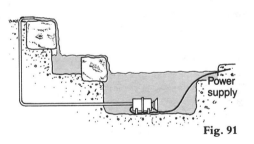

Power supply

Fig. 91

Surface pumps
The position for a pump of this kind has been discussed briefly in the siting chapter. Following on from that, the position should be as close as possible to water level, or even below it. The performance of the pump will be markedly reduced the higher it has to lift water from the pool.

A surface pump should be provided with well ventilated dry housing where it is easily accessible. When not in use during the winter it should be disconnected and stored in a dry shed. A surface pump is more versatile than a submersible one and can

Fig. 92 When a specific fountain pump is installed in a pool it may require a plinth beneath it to bring the fountain head just clear of the water's surface.

Fig. 93 When a surface pump is sunk below ground a foot valve is not necessary because the pipe will be constantly full of water.

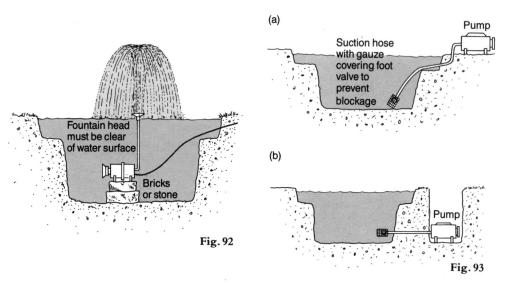

Fig. 92

Fig. 93

sustain a larger output for longer periods. It also has a longer life expectancy. Depending on its output, a pump can operate several separate waterfalls or fountains.

Water is pulled from the pool via a pipe fitted with a filter to keep out debris. Unless the pump is located at (*a*) or below (*b*) water level a foot valve will be needed to prevent water returning by gravity to the pool when the pump is not in use (Fig. 93).

A single fixed outlet leads from the pump. Where there is only one waterfall this will feed a single pipe leading directly to the waterfall head. When more than one display is planned a T connection can be fitted and on each outlet a gate valve installed. Water naturally follows the easiest route. This results in one feature benefit-

ing from more water than another. Adjustable valves provide the opportunity to balance the water in each fall or fountain (Fig. 94).

In addition, an extra outlet is always useful even in the absence of an immediate use. During drought periods, watering a valuable plant can be done without contravening local by-laws and a few centimetres' reduction in the pool level rarely causes problems to plants or fish. Another benefit is at pool cleaning time when the pump can be used to empty the water quickly without disturbing fixed pipes to waterfalls or fountains.

Fountains

Rarely does one construct a fountain as such. Building a suitable receptacle to contain a fountain is no different from building one to contain fish or grow water lilies. There is a vast range of single and multi-jetted fountain heads available and these are simple to attach to a pump.

Bubble fountains

A little imagination can produce results of individuality and character beyond those possible using only commercially available fountain heads and statuary.

Fig. 94 With surface pumps it is important to control each outlet independently with a valve.

Fig. 94

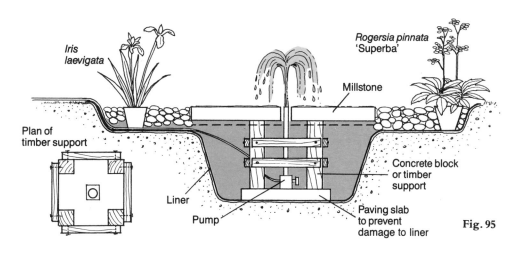

Iris laevigata

Rogersia pinnata 'Superba'

Millstone

Plan of timber support

Concrete block or timber support

Liner

Pump

Paving slab to prevent damage to liner

Fig. 95

Millstone fountains

If you are fortunate enough to own an old millstone, water can be pumped through the hole in the middle providing not only an attractive display but also one safe for children. If not, manufacturers have now produced a realistic looking fibreglass version which is almost as good, but it could cost as much as, if not more than, the genuine article. The main advantage of fibreglass is that it is lightweight which makes handling easy.

The method. You will need a low voltage submersible pump which can run from a 24 volt supply via a transformer. Dig a hole about 45 cm (1½ ft) deep and about the width of the diameter of the millstone. The hole can either be lined with a pool liner, using the described method for larger pools, or, if you can find a stout plastic bucket of adequate size, that could be used.

A frame is needed to support the stone. This can be made from either timber or concrete blocks and should be soundly constructed (Fig. 95). To prevent uneven pressure on the liner, the structure should be built on a paving slab. However the support is built, it should allow for a hosepipe to pass unimpeded from the pump up through the hole in the millstone. The pump will sit on the paving slab.

The millstone should be made to sit steadily on its support so that it does not rock. Large pebbles or beach stones will complete the effect and mask the edge of the liner. In addition, an occasional distinctive moisture loving plant can be planted. Rogersia and iris are good examples with *Houttuynia cordata* 'Chameleon' winding its way between the stones, providing colour at a lower level.

Barrel fountains

These days it is fairly easy to obtain old half whisky barrels which make excellent planters. If you can buy one before the holes are made in the bottom, it can be used to make a simple but effective fountain container.

Use a similar pump to that described for a millstone fountain. It can stand in the bottom of the barrel. Saw a piece of 2 cm (¾ in) thick timber so that it fits flat across the barrel about half way up. It need not be a neat fit, just as long as it is firm. A hole large enough for a hosepipe should be made

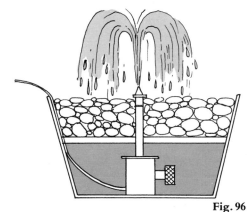

Fig. 96 A barrel fountain. A half barrel contains a low-voltage submersible pump fitted with a fountain jet and a layer of large stones or beach pebbles supported with timber.

Fig. 96

Fig. 97 All pools will need to be topped up or lose excess water from time to time and will therefore need to be equipped with an inlet and overflow, which can be fitted through flexible liners. Use special adapters with watertight fittings. The two nuts tighten the washers against each other, trapping the liner between them.

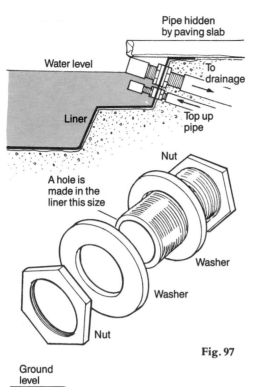

Water level

Pipe hidden by paving slab

To drainage

Liner

Top up pipe

Nut

A hole is made in the liner this size

Washer

Washer

Nut

Fig. 97

in the centre. One of the great variety of fountain jets can be fitted to the hose, depending on the effect you choose. The barrel can now be topped up with large stones or beach pebbles. The fountain head will need to be just on the surface for best results (Fig. 96).

Lighting

The installation of pool lighting requires the same care and attention described earlier on pump installation. Both direct power and transformed systems are available. Although the same circuit can be used it is wise, from a practical and safety point of view, to have them switched separately.

Overflows and inlets

Due to evaporation and heavy rain all pools will need topping up from time to time and a means of losing excess water. A hose pipe, leading from the domestic supply and secreted underground, is easy to operate by the turn of a tap. An overflow pipe of a

Fig. 98 It is possible to top up a pool automatically by using a simple ballcock cistern fed from the main water supply. The cistern must be filled absolutely level with the pool water level. The same system can also be used to drain surplus water from the pool during heavy rain by means of an overflow pipe fitted above the inflow level.

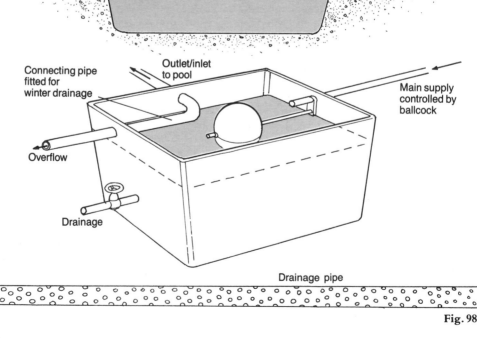

Ground level

Water level

Position of cistern in relation to pool

Connecting pipe fitted for winter drainage

Outlet/inlet to pool

Main supply controlled by ballcock

Overflow

Drainage

Drainage pipe

Fig. 98

larger diameter than the inlet pipe and fitted just above it will feed directly into a soak-away or drainage system (Fig. 97).

Fitting such pipes through flexible liners can be done using special adapters with watertight fittings.

Turning valves can be a chore and often evaporation and heavy rain occur when you are away on holiday. It is possible to top up and drain automatically by using a simple ballcock cistern. The cistern must be filled absolutely level with the pool water level and be set on gravel. Water is fed into the cistern directly from the mains tap which remains open at all times. Link a pipe to the pool through one side of the cistern. As the water level drops in the pool it will fall simultaneously in the cistern tank which in turn will cause the ballcock to fall and call for more water (Fig. 98). The ballcock could be used directly in the pool but it would be difficult to disguise.

The same system can also be used to drain surplus water from the pool during heavy rain. An overflow pipe is fixed above the inflow level. High water levels will then flow out through the same pipe and drain into a perforated pipe buried in the gravel beneath the tank. The drainage pipe will feed to an appropriate drain elsewhere.

It is important to make a bypass pipe for winter use when the cistern and inlet pipe will be drained down to prevent frost damage. A connecting pipe can be fitted easily between pool and cistern outlets which can be removed the following spring (Fig. 98). Modern plastics have virtually eliminated metal pipework, but just in case you happen to have some spare copper pipe left over from another job, do not be tempted to use it. The combination of copper and water will produce a toxicity which kills fish.

Bog gardens

A bog can be created separately or as part of a pool. The objective is to provide a place for plants that do not tolerate dry soil during their growing cycle. Almost all the plants suitable for a garden of this kind are herbaceous by nature.

While the plants have a high moisture requirement few of them will tolerate waterlogged conditions. A stable environment is called for, with little fluctuation in moisture levels and temperature.

Observance of conditions in a natural bog can provide clues to those that are needed in a garden. It is almost impossible to duplicate them because of the many subtleties inherent in any natural ecosystem. Most bogs have developed over many thousands of years and the soil is made up of partly decomposed vegetable matter. In many instances this is peat. Some bogs support only a spartan plant life due partly to the high level of acidity present and the near anaerobic conditions.

Familiar plants, such as the lovely candelabra primulas, are not found growing naturally in a soil that is sodden throughout the year. They do, however, occur in areas of high rainfall. The monsoon rains of the Himalayan mountains coincide with the growing and flowering periods of many well-known garden plants. Once the rains finish these perennial plants fade, in preparation for their long winter dormancy under snow. The surface water drains away to leave the plant in relatively dry surroundings, very different from those in most gardens.

You will not be surprised to learn that the most successful primula gardens are located in cooler moister areas. Where humidity and rainfall decrease, more creative gardening techniques are needed for success. These are within reach of the average gardener. Only a few specialized plants will need extra treatment beyond the descriptions that follow. It is really impossible and unnecessary to produce fluctuating soil conditions similar to those of the Himalayas.

The best compromise, and one that works for most plants, is to create a wet subsoil under a friable, open-textured topsoil. Incorporate large amounts of humus into the topsoil to achieve the desired texture. Peat is ideal for this purpose but well-composted garden refuse is even better, or a combination of the two. The question remains, how to retain this essential soil moisture.

Fig. 99 Creating a bog garden adjacent to a pool. The pool liner will extend into it.

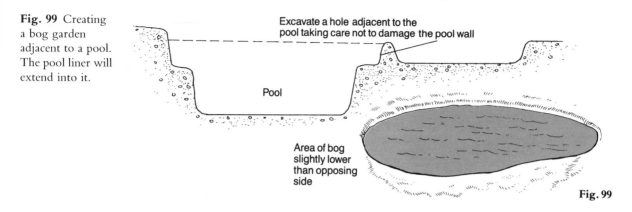

Excavate a hole adjacent to the pool taking care not to damage the pool wall

Pool

Area of bog slightly lower than opposing side

Fig. 99

Bogs adjacent to pools

The most natural place to find moisture-loving plants is adjacent to a pool or stream. Earlier, under pool construction, mention was made of providing extra overlap of the flexible liner. This additional liner material can now be used.

The method

Immediately adjacent to the pool edge the soil should be removed to a depth of 30 cm (12 in). Take care to avoid damaging the level pool wall (Fig. 99). Where the bog is on only one side of the pool the opposing side needs to be a few centimetres higher. This can be done gradually or in a concealed step, depending on your design.

The area dug out will correspond to the amount of liner you have allowed. The excavation should have a reasonably level bottom and slightly sloping sides. Use a rake or the back of a fork to break up the lumps. Spread a 1–2 cm (⅜–¾ in) layer of washed grit over the area. When it is laid out puncture the sheeting at approximately 1–2 m (3–6 ft) intervals with a sharp spike. The objective is to allow drainage and prevent stagnant water collecting in the liner, while retaining a continuously moist

Fig. 100 The area you have dug out for the bog garden should correspond to the amount of liner you have allowed. The liner is sandwiched between layers of washed grit.

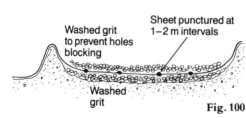

Washed grit to prevent holes blocking

Sheet punctured at 1–2 m intervals

Washed grit

Fig. 100

soil. When the sheet is in place a layer of washed grit, similar to that put beneath the liner, can be spread over it. This will help prevent the holes from becoming blocked (Fig. 100). The liner is now ready to be filled with soil.

The growing media

The quality of soil in your garden will determine how much amending is necessary. Any reasonably fertile soil will be suitable with the addition of peat, grit and a little fertilizer. A good mixture consists of 7 parts garden soil, 5 parts moss peat (medium or coarse grade) and 2 parts washed grit (lime free). Fertilizer can be added just before planting in the form of 60 g per m^2 (2 oz per sq yd) of fish, blood and bone meal.

Before putting this mixture into the liner a layer of well-rotted compost or farmyard manure (not pig or chicken) should be put in to cover the grit. This will not only be good for plant growth but also will help to retain moisture. The soil mixture can now be shovelled in. It should be mounded above the intended level to allow for settling. With weight resting on your heels, trample the mixture evenly, using a shuffling motion. This will help to firm the soil. The area is now ready for planting.

Controlling the moisture

The importance of maintaining constant moisture in the bog during the growing season has already been stressed. This can be done by adjusting the pool level. The normal overflow pipe should be blocked.

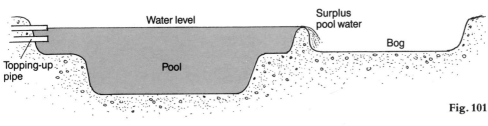

Fig. 101

Fig. 101 The moisture in a bog garden adjacent to a pool can be controlled by blocking the overflow pipe during summer and opening it during winter.

This will allow surplus water to escape via the only alternative route — over the side and into the bog. During dry weather the pool can be topped up regularly, allowing water to flood into the bog. When winter comes the overflow pipe can be brought back into use again, allowing the bog to become a wetter than normal border (Fig. 101).

By installing the ballcock and cistern system described on p. 84 you can automatically control water levels.

An island bog
The same principles of installation described for a bog attached to a pool are applicable. The only real difference is the lack of direct access to water. This can be supplied by a buried hosepipe fitted to an outside tap. Again the ballcock and cistern will work but with some modifications.

The method
Lay the sheeting as usual, making sure it is level. This need not be expensive butyl

rubber. Cheaper and almost as durable is 500 gauge black polythene. Do not puncture holes in the bottom. Adjacent to the bog dig a hole to accept the cistern, which should be in a well-constructed chamber that has a drainage pipe leading from it to disperse surplus water. The cistern should be positioned to accept the 5 cm (2 in) perforated plastic pipe which runs through a hole in the plastic into the bog. The plastic sheet and pipe should be sealed together with special glue (Fig. 102).

Fig. 102 An island bog can be kept moist by means of a buried perforated hosepipe fed from the mains water supply via a cistern fitted with a ballcock valve.

Fig. 103 The installation of the perforated hosepipe in an island bog garden. The plan shows a bed wider than 3 m (10 ft).

Fig. 103

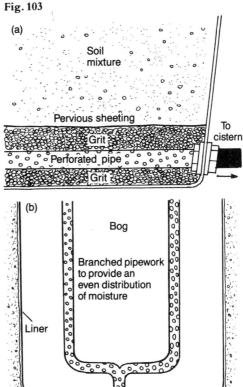

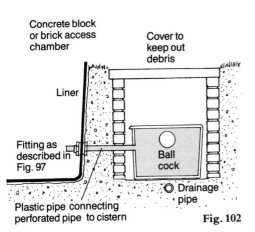

Fig. 102

The pipe should be laid along the centre of the bog on a bed of washed grit 1–2 cm (⅜–¾ in) deep. Then cover the pipe with just enough washed grit to conceal it (Fig. 103). A pervious mat can be laid above this to prevent root penetration. The soil mixture is then filled in as described earlier.

The water level will be maintained as a reservoir at the bottom of the bog, allowing ample scope for capillarity to pull moisture up to where the plant roots are growing. During the winter the system can be drained down to prevent frost damage and stagnation of the soil. For beds wider than 3 m (10 ft) a second pipe will be necessary to provide even distribution of water.

A simpler but less controllable bog can be made by laying polythene sheeting on a prepared hollow, puncturing it as before, and allowing nature to control the moisture. In this situation it is still possible to increase moisture, but not to decrease it.

A bog on clay soil

If you have made a pool by puddling clay, this type of bog is appropriate. You will need a number of stakes 8–10 cm (3–4 in) in diameter and about 1 m (3¼ ft) long. Ideally they should be of a good hardwood such as oak or sweet chestnut. The stakes form the pool perimeter and once the floor has been soundly puddled they are driven in at intervals of 8–10 cm (3–4 in). Wire mesh or heavy duty black netting can then be nailed to the stakes around the periphery (Fig. 104). The soil mixture already described can be used to back fill to the top of the stakes. Once the water is let in it will permeate through the soil making a permanently wet area. The back of the bog can be made impermeable either with clay or a sheet of plastic.

There are many possibilities for bog-garden construction. Ideas on the preceding pages hopefully will stimulate more.

Fig. 104 A bog garden constructed on clay soil adjacent to a puddled pool. (*a*) The overall appearance. (*b*) Stakes and wire mesh separating pool and bog. (*c*) The water from the pool permeates the bog garden soil, making a permanently wet area.

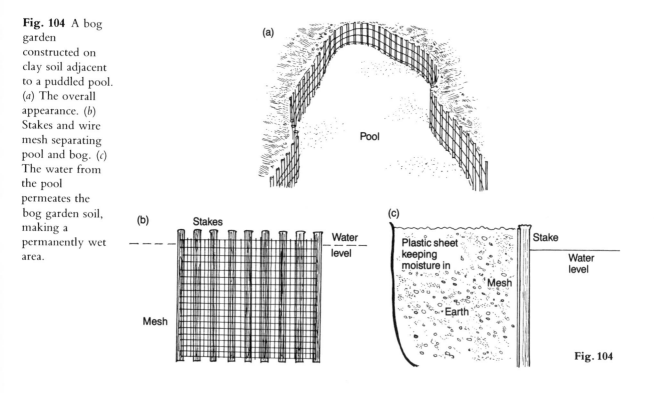

PART 2

PLANTING

INTRODUCING FISH

MAINTENANCE

PROPAGATION

POND PROBLEMS

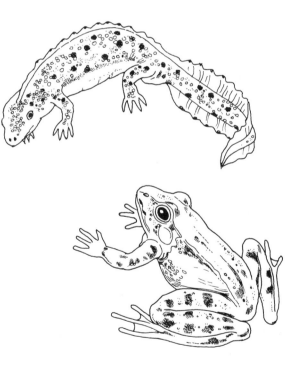

CHAPTER 5
Planting

Aquatic plants of all kinds are ideally planted during the spring and early summer. This is not always possible, especially if pool construction has not started until the spring. Planting is then often delayed until late summer. While the plants are still actively growing they can be successfully transplanted. The problem is that the plants are rather unwieldy, untidy and need cutting back severely. It is not until the following spring that they start to look respectable.

With the exception of floating aquatics, which are merely tossed onto the surface of the water, all other water plants require planting. They should all be treated in a similar manner to their terrestrial counterparts, for all demand a suitable growing medium. It is useful to bear in mind when planting a water lily that in many ways it is the equivalent of planting a tree. The water lily probably costs almost as much and has a similar life expectancy, so a comparable amount of care should be afforded to it.

Water lilies and deep-water aquatics
There are two planting methods advocated for water lilies and other deep-water aqua-

tics. Either the pool floor can be covered with a generous layer of prepared compost and the plants grown directly in this, or they can be planted in containers. The wise pool owner will adopt the latter method as then there is more control over plants. They can be easily removed for inspection or division and on occasions when the pool needs to be cleaned out.

Specially manufactured water lily baskets are the most suitable containers to use and are readily available from most garden centres (Fig. 105). They are made of a heavy gauge rigid polythene or plastic material and of a design that will not easily become over-balanced. As they have lattice-work sides it is advisable to line them with hessian before planting to prevent any compost spillage into the water, especially when the soil is rather light.

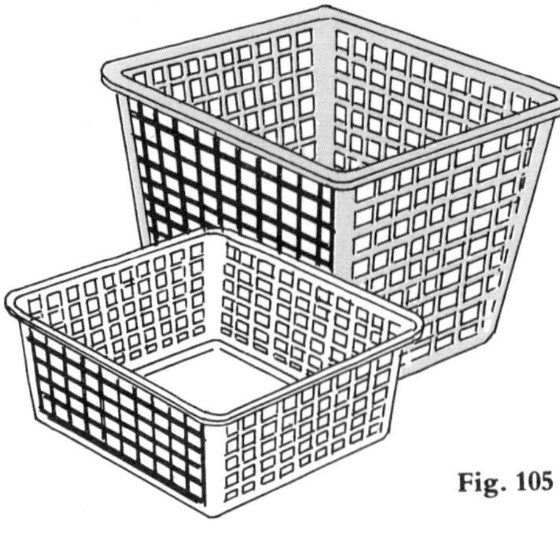

Composts
The most suitable compost to use for water lilies and other deep-water plants is good clean garden soil from land that has not recently been dressed with artificial fertilizer. This should be thoroughly sieved and care taken to remove twigs, pieces of old turf, weeds, old leaves, or indeed anything that is likely to decompose and foul the water. On no account should soil be gathered from wet low-lying land or natural ponds and streams as this will often contain the seeds of pernicious water needs which may be difficult to eradicate once they become established in the pool.

The soil having been prepared, a little coarse bonemeal can be added. Allow about a handful for each basket to be planted and mix it thoroughly into the compost. As an alternative a coarse grade of hoof and horn fertilizer may be used, but only sparingly. It must not be fine and powdery or it will cloud the water and may even prove harmful to fish and other livestock. In the early

Fig. 105 Aquatic planting baskets are usually made of tough plastic with lattice-work sides and a broad base to provide stability.

Fig. 105

days of water gardening rotting turf and animal manures were recommended for water lily culture. While they certainly promoted vigorous growth, they also encouraged the proliferation of green water-discolouring algae.

In recent years specially prepared composts for aquatic plants have become available. These vary widely in quality, but the more popular brands seen in garden centres are likely to be perfectly adequate. The tricky ones are those produced by individual companies for their own customers. These vary from exceptionally good and superior to the popular branded types and downright awful. Before purchase you should, if possible, take the opportunity of examining the medium. It should be of a fairly heavy consistency, preferably smearing when rubbed between finger and thumb, and free of all extraneous material. A good heavy potting compost, in fact.

The compost should be dampened so that when squeezed in the hand it binds together, yet is not so wet as to allow water to ooze through the fingers.

Planting techniques

Before planting look carefully at the roots of water lilies. Those of *Nymphaea odorata* and *N. tuberosa* and their varieties are long and fleshy and should be planted horizontally about 2.5 cm (1 in) beneath the surface of the compost with just their crowns or growing points exposed. The *N.* × *marliacea* and *N.* × *laydekeri* hybrids, together with most of the other popular garden varieties and the nuphars, have bulky log-like root stocks with fibrous roots arranged like a ruff immediately below the crown. These are planted vertically, or at a slight angle, with the crown just protruding above the planting medium.

With both water lilies and pond lilies it is advisable to remove all the adult foliage just above the crown before planting (Fig. 106). This may seem rather drastic, but it usually dies anyway, and when planted intact the leaves often serve as floats, thus giving the plants buoyancy and lifting them right out of the baskets.

The fibrous roots should also be cut back

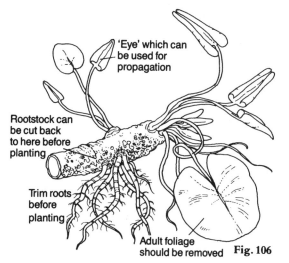

'Eye' which can be used for propagation

Rootstock can be cut back to here before planting

Trim roots before planting

Adult foliage should be removed **Fig. 106**

Fig. 106 An adult water lily has a fleshy root stock The non-growing end should be cut back to sound tissue before planting.

to the root stock and any dead or decaying area of the rhizome pared back with a knife to live tissue and dressed with powdered charcoal or flowers of sulphur to help seal the wound and prevent infection. If a rootstock takes on a gelatinous appearance and is evil-smelling do not let it come into contact with sound varieties. These symptoms are a certain indication of infection with water lily crown-rot.

It is important when planting (Fig. 107) that the compost is packed as tightly as possible into the container. If not it becomes full of air spaces and decreases in volume as the water drives the air out. Roots of newly planted water lilies can be left completely exposed following this sinking effect. Where the roots have had insufficient time to penetrate the compost the whole plant will come floating to the surface.

Water newly planted water lilies like pot plants prior to placing in their permanent positions. This helps to settle the compost and drives the air out. A layer of washed pea shingle 2.5 cm (1 in) deep should be spread over the surface of the planting medium to discourage fish from nosing in the compost in their quest for aquatic insect larvae and clouding the water.

In a newly constructed pool the planted baskets should ideally be placed in their final positions with enough water run in to cover the crowns. As the young foliage starts to grow the water level can be slowly

Fig. 107 (*a*) It is prudent to line the basket with hessian before introducing soil. (*b*) Half-fill the basket with soil or compost and trim off the excess hessian. (*c*) Plant the water lily firmly in the soil or compost. (*d*) Fill the basket to within 3 cm (1¼ in) of the top. Cover with a generous layer of pea shingle.

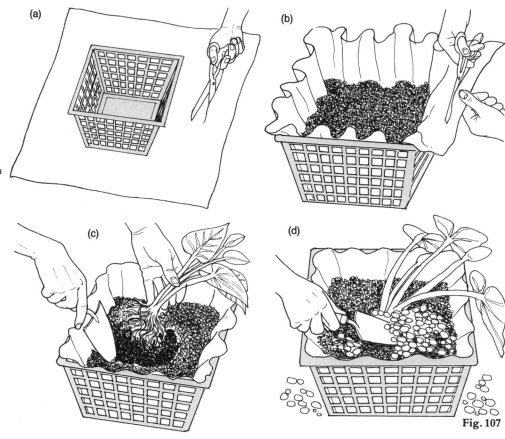

Fig. 107

raised. When adding a water lily to an established pool this procedure can be reversed: the basket being stood on a pile of bricks and gradually lowered by removing the bricks one at a time as the growths lengthen.

When baskets have to be placed in a tricky position in the centre of the pool, lengths of string can be threaded through either side of the basket. Two people are then needed, one each side of the pool, the basket being gently lowered into place (Fig. 108).

If there is a good reason for planting directly into compost on the pool floor then all the same general advice applies as far as is possible. One of the greatest potential hazards associated with this method

Fig. 108 When it is difficult to place the water lily in the pond, get the help of a friend and lower the basket using strong strings.

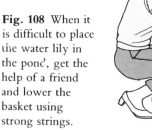

Fig. 108

concerns the filling of the pool with water. It follows that if a hosepipe is placed directly into the pool and turned on, the stream of water will stir up the soil and the pool will become cloudy. By placing the end of the hosepipe on a large sheet of polythene and allowing the water to trickle over the edge this is prevented. As the water level rises the polythene is lifted and trapped beneath the end of the hosepipe which, if the sheet is large enough, will also be gradually raised until the water is at the desired level.

Natural ponds
Water gardeners with a natural pond have to adopt different planting techniques. The major problem is that a natural pool is rarely easily emptied and so planting has to take place through the water. Use the kind of growing medium described earlier and plant on squares of hessian. The four corners of the hessian are then lifted and tied just beneath the crown. These wrapped roots can then be gently placed into the water and allowed to sink to the bottom. The hessian will eventually rot, but by that time the plants will be well established in the compost and will almost certainly have penetrated the surrounding soil on the pool floor.

Positioning water lilies
The positioning of water lilies in the pool must be carefully considered if they are to prosper. Attention must be paid to the depth of water available. This will determine, within limits, the varieties which can be successfully accommodated.

Moving water restricts the number of plants which can be safely accommodated, for few water lilies will tolerate even the slightest movement of the water. In such circumstances nuphar and other deep-water aquatics like aponogeton have to be considered. This particularly applies in pools where a fountain is constantly playing.

Sunlight is also vital, the plants being placed in positions where they can receive the maximum amount. If the pool is badly placed and this is difficult to arrange because an area is shaded for much of the time, then

of the deep-water aquatics only pond lilies are likely to flourish.

Marginal plants and submerged aquatics
Marginal aquatics require the same kind of compost as water lilies and other deep-water aquatics and should be treated in much the same way. Plant in containers as if potting any other plant, but be sure to firm the compost well and water thoroughly to drive out all the air. Cover the surface with a generous layer of pea shingle to prevent fish from poking about. Always plant a single species or variety in one container. Never entertain mixed plantings as these end up in a frightful tangle.

Some marginal aquatics can be planted as single plants in individual baskets, but usually two or three small plants of a kind are to be preferred. These bulk up quickly and give a speedy effect.

It is always preferable to purchase pot-grown marginal aquatics. These invariably establish more rapidly and are absolutely essential when planting takes place into a soil-covered marginal shelf, or more especially when a natural feature is being planted and the marginals are going directly into a waterside bank. Bare-rooted plants in these situations are often almost impossible to hold down. They just keep floating out and steadily deteriorate. Pot-grown plants rarely present such a problem.

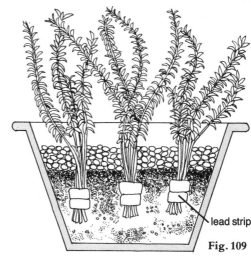

lead strip

Fig. 109

Fig. 109 Be sure that the lead strip on submerged plants is buried or else it will rot through the stems.

Submerged aquatics

Submerged aquatics are those that we affectionately refer to as water 'weeds' or oxygenating plants. They are highly perishable and should either be kept in a bowl of water or wrapped in polythene prior to planting.

When received from the nurseryman they usually appear as a bunch of cuttings fastened together with a lead weight, although there are occasional submerged plants, such as the hair grass, *Eleocharis acicularis*, which are purchased as clumps. These are planted in exactly the same way as marginal aquatics. But those that come as cuttings need to be left in their bunches and then planted so that the lead weight is buried (Fig. 109). If the lead is exposed it will rot through the stems and the tops of the cuttings will float away. Cover the surface of the compost with pea gravel in exactly the same way as for deep-water aquatics, water thoroughly and then place in position on the pool floor.

Planting indoors

Relatively few gardeners have the opportunity to construct an indoor pool. For those who have, a brief account of the planting of tropical water lilies is included under caring for the indoor pool. It is more likely that the gardener with an interest in tender aquatics will grow them in an aquarium.

Planting an aquarium

Planting an aquarium can be likened to creating a miniature garden, for the overall effect should be an underwater landscape. Thus the taller plants for the most part will occupy the back of the picture, or frame it on either side, while the shorter occupants will fill the foreground. The positioning of various plants in an aquarium should be as natural as possible and must consist of numbers of the same species rather than multitudes of different kinds.

For the average aquarium no more than half a dozen different species is necessary. These should be planted in a mass, but with an irregular outline so that small stands of plants project into the foreground and other

allied species intermingle quite naturally.

It should be remembered when selecting suitable species that they must not only blend into the general scheme and be complimentary to one another visually, but have approximately the same cultural and nutritional requirements. This latter aspect should not be neglected, as ill-chosen companions will be clearly seen to suffer.

Growing medium

The growing medium selected is a matter of personal choice, for there are many mysterious and wonderful mixtures recommended for the aquarium.

While there are specific composts for aquarium plants, the following combination works well for most tender submerged aquatics. A 2.5 cm (1 in) layer of finely sieved peat is spread over the tank floor and covered with about 2 cm (¾ in) of fine silver sand topped off with a covering of washed shingle or multicoloured dyed grit which is sold specifically as aquarium gravel. Coloured glass chips which have been sand blasted to smooth off the sharp edges, or even a layer of children's marbles, can be used to similar effect.

Certain fish, notably cold-water catfish and loach, are not really at home with gravel on the floor of their tanks and for these an additional depth of soft sand is advisable.

However, no matter what finish is desired it must not only be used to disguise and beautify the surface of the growing medium but extend down the side against the glass and hide the compost cross-section from view.

Rockwork

With the growing medium prepared and undulations created to give the appearance of aquatic terrain, rockwork can be introduced. Well-placed natural rocks do much to enhance an underwater scene, but just like a rock garden it is essential that the strata be placed in the same plane and pieces of uniform depth and texture are used. Clashes of colour should be avoided; for example, red Mendip stone and white spar never coming together nor black Devon rock and red or green granite.

Establishing a balance

Establishing and maintaining a balance within a pool is very important. Unfortunately it is rarely fully understood by water gardeners and is considered something of a mystery. One of the greatest misunderstandings is that if the pool is well oxygenated the water will always remain clear and balanced. Therefore if a fountain is introduced to the pool it will be a cure for all maladies, the water droplets falling into the pool and picking up oxygen on the way down. The droplets will be well oxygenated, it is true, and on warm sultry days the fish will delight in their cool spray, but the presence of oxygen is no guarantee of water clarity.

This misconception has been inadvertently created because it is submerged oxygenating plants which have the greatest influence on the condition of the water. However, it is not the oxygen that the plants produce that creates clear water and a healthy balance, but the competition that the plants provide for the green water discolouring algae which invade the pool as soon as the water is warmed by spring sunshine. Algae are primitive forms of plant life and flourish in water that is rich in mineral salts. Only when competition is provided by more sophisticated plants for these mineral salts is there any chance of them coming under control.

When there is sufficient underwater plant growth to utilize all the mineral salts that are present, then the water will be clear. Only when there is an abundance of plant foods available will algae and submerged plants live alongside one another.

Shade

Shade also helps to reduce the occurrence of algae. Not shade that is going to restrict the growth and development of the plants, but that which prevents sunlight from penetrating the water. It is undesirable that the entire surface of the water is covered with foliage, for both practical and aesthetic reasons, but for an even balance to be achieved from the outset at least one-third of the surface area should be covered either with the floating foliage of water lilies or free-floating aquatic plants.

In assessing the area to be covered ignore that occupied by the shallow marginal shelves and then permit one-third of the remainder to become colonized. When calculating the number of submerged oxygenating plants to be included, allow one bunch for every 0.093 sq m (1 sq ft) of surface area. That is not to say that the plants must be distributed evenly over the pool floor: it is the specific quantity required for the given surface area. Most submerged oxygenating plants are sold as bunches of cuttings fastened together with a lead weight and the formula assumes this typical plant material.

Submerged plants benefit the fish as a source of oxygen and when fine-leafed kinds are grown these serve as a suitable place for the deposition of spawn. Floating leaves offer shelter and some respite from bright summer sun. Some species like the starworts or calli-triches also provide green matter, an essential part of the diet of all cold-water fish, while the fish reciprocate by depositing organic matter rich in plant foods and in addition control many aquatic insect pests, especially mosquitos.

The numbers of fish that can be introduced into a pool varies and is not so critical for clear water. A maximum stocking rate is 15 cm (6 in) to every 0.093 sq m (1 sq ft), but a more sensible figure is 5 cm (2 in) to the same surface area. Snails and freshwater mussels can be introduced liberally, their progeny being controlled naturally by the fish.

Filling and planting

Construction having been completed the aquarium can be filled with water. A bowl or jug of water upended over a carefully laid aqua-scape will obviously leave it in ruins, so a more gentle method must be adopted. The simplest method is to fill a bucket with water and siphon it out by means of a narrow plastic tube on to a sheet of polythene spread over the gravel. By doing this disturbance of the growing medium is minimal and as the level of the

Choosing aquatic plants

Selecting a variety of plants for a pool is one thing; being sure that you have purchased good-quality plants is another. Unlike trees and shrubs where there is a reasonable means of visually assessing quality, knowing how good your aquatic-plant purchases are is a different matter.

Submerged plants

Purchasing from a specialist is almost always the best way of obtaining plants, although for some submerged aquatics, like *Lagarosiphon major*, the local pet shop maybe just as good. This plant is sold in large quantities for goldfish bowls and is consequently turned over quickly. Submerged oxygenating plants for the pool are by and large bunched plants. These are bushy kinds which are sold as bunches of cuttings secured with a thin strip of lead around the base. Although seemingly clinging precariously to life, these unrooted cuttings quickly become established when planted.

When selecting bunched plants always reject those of a 'tired' appearance and with flaccid stems. Look rather for individuals with bright perky foliage. Always inspect the lead strip, for although useful in the plant's formative life it can cause damage to the stems if the bunches remain unsold and unplanted for a week or so. Black marks on the stems in the vicinity of the foliage indicate that the plant has been bunched for at least a week and that the lead strip is probably causing the stems to rot at the point where they are held together. This can only be rectified by removing the lead and the lower portion of the plant and rebunching, although by this time the stems will have doubtless deteriorated and become brittle. A further indication of the age of an unplanted bunch is the preponderance of succulent white roots which sprout indiscriminately from leaf axils at irregular intervals along the stem. In newly planted healthy stock most of the roots ramify the growing medium and only an occasional one is to be seen elsewhere among the foliage.

A number of submerged plants grow in what one might term a conventional manner.

That is, they consist of a mass of fibrous roots, a stem and individual leaves. Often the stem is very short and consists of nothing more than a base from which leaves arise, or is a solid gathering of embryo foliage. Most oxygenating plants that fall into this class are delicate and require careful handling; any showing signs of browning or bruising at the base of the foliage or stem should be avoided. The root system should be inspected and plants with withered or badly damaged roots discarded. With these plants it is always better to select good small specimens.

Marginals and water lilies

For marginal plants and water lilies it is best to purchase pot-grown plants. Never be tempted by water lilies or other water plants that are floating loosely around in a tank of water. Deterioration has already set in.

Similarly it is unwise to choose prepacked aquatics. These are often encountered in pet shops and small nurseries hanging from pegboards. These will start to suffer after the first couple of days and should definitely be avoided. The ideal plants should be growing in shallow tanks of reasonably clear water. They should preferably be growing in pots and certainly be free from any insect pests. Look out for cylinders of jelly attached to the leaves. These contain the eggs of the freshwater whelk, a snail that delights in grazing on succulent aquatics. Many newcomers to water gardening mistake the eggs for fish spawn and leave them on the plants when they are introduced to the pool. The resulting population of snails is at the very least a nuisance and is not easy to eliminate. Before putting new plants into the pool always inspect for snail eggs and remove any that are found, except the small flat pads of jelly which belong to the desirable algae-eating ramshorn snail.

Finally, always purchase plants from a nursery: never be tempted to gather wild aquatics. Apart from the fact that it is likely to be against the law, there is a strong chance of introducing a pest or disease to the relatively sterile environment of the pool when plants are taken from the countryside.

This generously planted poolside features *Iris sibirica*, spiky needle rushes and the bold and beautiful candelabra primulas.

Despite its shady
location, this water
feature is full of
diversity. Hostas,
trollius and ferns all
tolerate such
apparent adversity.

This tastefully planted pool is well integrated into the garden. The glyceria in the foreground provides a colourful foliage highlight.

A pool bristling with plant life. The fountain adds movement and sound without dominating the scene.

Nymphaea 'Froebeli', one of the best red–flowered kinds for the small or medium sized pool. Free–flowering and easy.

Nymphaea 'Gonnere' is undoubtedly the finest water lily to be produced by the French hybridizer Marliac.

Nymphaea ×
marliacea 'Carnea',
one of the finest
water lilies for the
medium or large
pool. Easy-going
and very free-
flowering.

Nymphaea 'Rose Arey' is the loveliest pink-flowered water lily with a long season of colour and a rich aniseed fragrance.

Orontium aquaticum is a member of the arum family, often known as the golden club. A reliable plant for early flowering.

Nelumbo nucifera is more popularly known as the sacred lotus. One of the finest tropical aquatics for greenhouse or tub culture.

water rises so the sheet is lifted until it reaches the top of the tank and is then easily removed. The aquarium is then ready to receive the plants.

Most growers, however, prefer to plant a tank when it is half full of water as then the finished picture can still be seen as planting progresses, but the shallower water allows more comfort and greater manoeuverability for the planter.

Planting sticks are most useful and can be purchased from any aquarist's shop or made from a strip of wood 45 cm (18 in) long with a V-shaped notch cut in the end. Two of these are used, holding the plant between the notch and pushing it into the growing medium. Then with one stick holding the plant firmly the other spreads out the roots and covers them with compost and gravel. Bunched plants are often easier planted with the fingers.

Once planted, the tank can be filled with water of roughly the same temperature as that present. Topping up a warm tank with cold water from the tap will cause chilling of the plants and retard growth.

Planting a tub
Whatever kind of tub is used it is important that it is absolutely clean. Spread about 8 cm (3 in) of soil over the bottom, avoiding old leaves, pieces of turf or indeed any organic matter as this is likely to pollute the water. So will soil that has been recently dressed with artificial fertilizer, the abundance of mineral salts encouraging a persistent algal bloom which will be impossible to disperse until the fertilizer has been exhausted. Nowadays specially prepared aquatic-plant composts are available and these can be used if you can justify the expense. Whatever medium is used, it should be mixed into a muddy consistency by adding a little water. The container is then ready for planting.

Planting ideas
Planting can be undertaken at any time during the spring or early summer choosing a miniature water lily such as the yellow-flowered *Nymphaea* × *pygmaea* 'Helvola' or its white cousin *N.* × *pygmaea* 'Alba' as a centrepiece. Alternatively the tiny form of the brandy bottle or yellow pond lily, *Nuphar pumila*, can be exploited.

Around the edge the attractive miniature form of the familiar 'bulrush' or reedmace, *Typha minima*, with tiny brown poker heads, can be planted together with the slender powder-blue *Mimulus ringens*. *Myosotis scorpioides* (water forget-me-not), *Eriophorum angustifolium* (cotton grass), *Calla palustris* (bog arum) and *Mentha aquatica* (water mint) may also be tried, although the latter may need controlling towards the end of the season.

Several bunches of one of the less-vigorous kinds of submerged oxygenating plants like *Fontinalis antipyretica* (willow moss), *Callitriche verna* (starwort) or *Tillaea recurva* can be introduced to help keep the water clear, although in a small volume of water with widely fluctuating temperatures this is not always easy.

After planting, but before water is added, the entire exposed soil surface should be covered with a generous layer of pea shingle to prevent fish from stirring up the soil in their quest for aquatic insect larvae. The end of a hose pipe used for filling the tub can be placed in a polythene bag on the bottom and the water turned on. By using a polythene bag in this way any turbulence that is likely to disturb the soil and gravel is avoided and the water remains clear. The bag is removed, together with the hosepipe, when the required water level has been achieved.

Final touches
A couple of portions of floating plants like *Azolla caroliniana* (fairy moss) or *Hydrocharis morsus-ranae* (frogbit), half a dozen ramshorn snails and two or three small goldfish are added and the miniature water garden is complete.

Routine maintenance is exactly the same as for an ordinary garden pool, although the fish should winter indoors. There is always a question-mark over their survival during a severe winter in such a small volume of water, but their presence in the summer is essential for the control of mosquito larvae.

CHAPTER 6
Introducing Fish

When a pool has been planted there is a great temptation to introduce fish. This should be resisted for four or five weeks so that the plants can become established. If fish are put into a freshly planted pool they nose among the plants, disturbing them and retarding their growth. Even a generous layer of pea shingle covering the surface of the compost will not prevent this from happening.

How many?

There is no minimum number of fish necessary for a pool, although without any fish at all it will become a nursery for mosquitoes and there will be little chance of controlling aquatic insect pests. Even if you have no interest in fish it is prudent to introduce half a dozen merely to control insect life.

Most gardeners find fish as important as plants, particularly those who have a young family. It is with the children that the danger lies, for it is so easy to persuade dad to overstock. While there is no minimum requirement, there is a maximum number which should not be exceeded.

The most satisfactory stocking rate is 5 cm (2 in) of fish to every 0.093 sq m (1 sq ft) of surface area. This is not of the total surface area of the pool but of open water uncluttered by marginal plants. This rate of stocking permits growth and development of the fish and makes natural breeding likely. The calculation of the length of fish in this formula is based on the total length, nose to tail. Therefore if a total length of 90 cm (3 ft) is calculated, the fish population may consist of three fish each 30 cm (1 ft) long, six fish 15 cm (6 in) long, or any combination of each that results in a total figure of 90 cm (3 ft). Some enthusiasts stock more heavily than this, but an absolute maximum is 15 cm (6 in) to every 0.093 sq m (1 sq ft) of surface area.

Choosing healthy fish

A well-balanced mixture of healthy ornamental fish is essential if a pool is to be a success. Most retailers of cold-water fish keep them in large aquariums, fibreglass tanks or pools that are devoid of plant life but supplied with air from a pump. This may seem a very unhealthy manner in which to maintain stock, but it is the most satisfactory method from both the customer's and retailer's point of view. The purchaser has a good clear view of what is being offered and the vendor can easily keep tanks scrupulously clean when they are devoid of plant life.

The only time to be concerned is when one tank is connected to another, or when fresh water is being constantly introduced and the surplus drained away via an overflow. In the first instance there is likelihood of disease being spread rapidly from one tank to another and in the second the constant introduction of fresh turbulent tap water leads to the breakdown or reduction of protective body slime on the fishes. This means that they are wide open to disease, particularly fungal infections. The reason for adding fresh water constantly to a tank of fish is usually to help prevent the build-up of troublesome white spot disease by washing away the free-swimming stage of its life-cycle.

The most reliable purchase can be made from a static tank of fish in which an air pump is running and where the water has a matured amber look.

Imports

Almost all the pond fish sold in Britain today are imported, most coming from much more equitable climates where they breed more freely. This does not mean that they will be vulnerable to a cooler climate, because all adapt readily. However, it is the wise pool owner who enquires of the retailer how long the fish have been in the country, for they are often rushed from airport to wholesaler to garden centre in two or three days and could be swimming in your garden pool a week after leaving their country of origin.

This is undesirable, so if you are in any doubt look at the colours, particularly of the goldfish. Those that are bright red, orange or yellow are recent imports, for once removed from a stock pond into a selling tank they lose their brightness. This takes three or four weeks, bright red fish fading to salmon-pink and bright yellows mellowing to ochre. Such fish can be purchased with confidence, as they have been effectively quarantined against everything except white spot disease. When reintroduced to a pool they quickly regain their vivid hues.

A guide to health

A good guide as to whether a fish is in satisfactory health is the condition of its fins (Fig. 110). A stout upright dorsal fin and well-expanded ventral fins indicate good health and this can be confirmed if the eyes are clear and bright as well.

An obvious consideration when choosing fish is their liveliness. However, while a lively fish is likely to be a healthy fish, it could equally well be a very hungry one. It is common practice to keep fish hungry in dealers' tanks so that they swim and dart about in search of food and therefore appear livelier than they would ordinarily. An added bonus is the reduction in the fouling of the tank.

With small fish it is important to see that there are no damaged or missing scales as exposed tissue is very susceptible to fungal infection. The same applies to larger specimens, although it is not so critical, and the likelihood of finding a large fish that has no scales missing is fairly remote. If an otherwise healthy fish has a few scales missing, then dip it in one of the proprietary fungus cures based on methylene blue or malachite green. It is prudent in any event to treat all newly purchased fish in this way, giving them a dousing with a solution of either as a precaution before introducing them to the

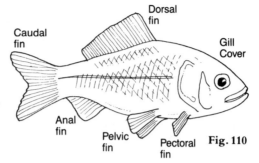

Fig. 110

Fig. 110 Goldfish are typical of ornamental pond fish. All have similar requirements and associate well together.

pond. It cannot be over-emphasized that the manufacturer's instructions regarding the dilution rates are carefully followed.

Sometimes white spots, rather like tiny raised pin heads, will be seen on the bodies of the fish. These are invariably associated with white spot disease, which although curable takes a long time to overcome. Never purchase any fish from a retailer who has fish with this disease on the premises.

However, it is important that this is not confused with the nuptial turbucles which appear in profusion on the gill plates, head and sometimes front or pectoral fins of normal healthy male fish during the breeding season. While looking like the pustules of white spot they are mostly concentrated around the head area. The fins will have an upright stance and the fish a bright eye, which is a complete contrast to a white spot infected specimen in which the eye will look misty and the dorsal fin will sag.

There are few other points to consider, for the ideal colour, shape and conformity of the fish are a matter of personal taste. Some species have their own shortcomings and a number are afflicted by maladies that are specific to them. One of the most serious is the condition in carp known as 'big head'. This manifests itself as an enlarged and distorted head, but is also characterized by a pinched body which reinforces the belief that this is some tubercular infection. When selecting carp it is essential to avoid any that appear to have larger heads than normal. And while considering physical defects one must not overlook the strange crooked backbone deformity that is not infrequently seen in tench.

99

Introduction to the pool

When the pool owner purchases fish they will be packed in heavy-gauge polythene bags which are usually blown up with oxygen. Fish travel happily this way under normal circumstances, but it is advisable to ensure that large specimens are packed individually. If the weather is hot or thundery resist the temptation to purchase fish such as golden orfe which have a high oxygen requirement, for the chances are that they will succumb on the way home.

Freshly purchased fish should be introduced to the pool gradually. If the bag has been blown up with oxygen allow it to float on the surface of the pool for a short time so that the temperature of the water inside becomes equalized with that in the pool and then gently pour the fish out. If the fish have been purchased by mail order and have travelled overnight by rail the same procedure should be adopted.

A meal shortly after their arrival is desirable as the fish will have been starved for a couple of days before despatch to ensure they do not excessively foul the water in the bag while in transit. New arrivals are often nervous for a few days, lurking among the submerged plants and hiding among the water lily foliage, but confidence soon develops and after a couple of weeks they are usually active and more noticeable.

Making a choice – ornamentals

All the ornamental cold-water fish which are described here live happily together, with the exception of the catfish. Even young fishes, once they are past the fry stage, will mix happily with all sizes and both sexes of the varieties discussed.

Fish of all kinds grow in accordance with their surroundings; thus a goldfish that has been confined to a bowl for a number of years will remain small, yet once introduced to a pool will grow quickly and attain sizeable proportions.

Bronze carp

This is a collective name used by the water-garden trade for any bronze coloured carp-like fish, but usually refers to uncoloured goldfish. Bronze carp are cheap and useful fish for stocking large volumes of water, but cannot be recommended for a small pool, particularly when goldfish breeding is envisaged as both forms will obviously interbreed and the dominant bronze colour will be prevalent in the young.

Common carp

The common carp is a fairly dull yet lively fish which is useful in a large pool, but more of a nuisance in a smaller water garden. It is usually a silvery or bronze colour with a chubby meaty body, narrow tapering head and four pendant barbels. It delights in nosing and probing in the plant containers for aquatic insect larvae, disturbing the compost and causing clouding of the water.

The Chinese red carp or Higoi is a coloured variation. A salmon or orange-pink fish of handsome proportions with a slightly more depressed head and typical pendant barbels. Of similar appearance, but of bronze colouration, the scale carp is another variety that often makes an appearance. Other carp with different proportions of visible scaling are the mirror, leather and band carps. All these are available from time to time and while attractive in a tank or aquarium, are not so appealing when in the amber waters of a garden pool and should therefore be introduced with caution.

Crucian carp

Not unlike the common carp, but this fish is without the pendant barbels and depressed head of that species. It is deep bodied with a rich chocolate and bronze colouration, lightening to gold or greenish yellow on the belly. Again a fish that does not have a high level of visibility in a pool compared with the brightly coloured goldfish varieties.

Dace

Although the dace can seldom be satisfactorily kept in a small pool owing to its large oxygen requirement, it is an attractive fish for larger pools. It is a handsome fish, steely grey in colour with a large head and long cylindrical body.

Goldfish

The goldfish is unquestionably the best loved cold-water fish: an easy-going character that is available in red, pink and orange through yellow to white.

Apart from obvious differences in colour, the most striking divergence from the true goldfish is the transparent-scaled variety which is known popularly as the shubunkin. In this the body appears to be smooth and scaleless and in a much wider range of colour combinations. Red, yellow and shades of blue and violet intermingle and are often and variously splashed and blotched with crimson or black. Certain of the specific colours and colour combinations have been line bred so that now there are strains which have been given names. Two of the most popular of these are the Cambridge Blue Shubunkin and the Bristol Blue Shubunkin. The Cambridge Blue has an even base colour of soft powder-blue overlaid with violet and occasional patches of ochre, while the Bristol Blue is typified by a blue base which is heavily overlaid with violet and mauve and liberally splashed with crimson.

One of the most popular variations of both goldfish and shubunkins is the comet-tail. This is a sleek-looking fish with a long flowing tail, often as long as the body. Fantails and moors are further variations, but these have bodies which are short and rounded as well as handsome divided tails. The fantails are goldfish in every other respect, while the moors are characterized by bulbous telescopic eyes. Typical goldfish-like fantails are refered to as red or red and white fantails and the shubunkin types as calico fantails. The moors are sub-divided as well, the shubunkin types being known as calico moors, goldfish kinds as red telescopes and the variety with a velvety black body as the black moor.

There are also double-tailed goldfish of the same general appearance as fantails, which are known as veiltails. Developments from these are the oranda, which has a strange strawberry-like excrescence on its head, and the lionhead which has a similar but exaggerated growth which calls to mind a lion's mane. However, the most amazing

diversion of all is the celestial: a typical goldfish in most respects but with a flattened head that bears two upward pointing, staring eyes.

All goldfish and shubunkins are hardy in their natural forms, but most of the fancy kinds are short-lived if not given some protection during the winter. This need merely be sufficient depth of water in which to overwinter, for while the common kinds will tolerate being frozen in the ice for a day or two, their fancy counterparts will not. A minimum depth at one point in the pool of 45 cm (18 in) is the minimum depth required, but this is no guarantee of safety and most goldfish fanciers prefer to bring their charges inside in a cold-water aquarium for the winter.

Koi carp

The Koi or Nishiki-koi are the most outstanding members of the carp family (Fig. 111). Colours vary from red, orange, yellow and pink through glowing metallic bronze and steely blue to grey, violet and white. Some selections have been named and increasingly these are available for purchase by name. Among the better named kinds currently available are Shirogen, pure white; Sanke, white with red and black; and Ki-ogen, a lovely yellow selection. In shape they are like all the other carp varieties, being strong and meaty with a well-formed head and usually short pendant barbels.

Fig. 111

Fig. 111 Koi carp are particularly prized by fish fanciers, but they are boisterous and should be introduced sparingly.

Orfe

This is a handsome fish for the medium sized and larger pool (Fig. 112). As with other shoaling fish it should be introduced in quantity for the best effect. As it is very energetic the water must be oxygenated

Fig. 112 Orfe are very fine surface swimming fish which delight the gardener with their lively antics.

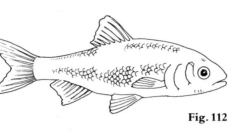

Fig. 112

properly. Orfe love nothing better than leaping in the spray of a fountain or waterfall. The common species is known as the silver orfe, a long slender fish with a small blunt head, but the one most frequently offered to the water gardener is the salmon-pink variation, the golden orfe.

Rudd

While the common rudd is seldom available for purchase at garden centres, its lovely silver and golden variations are frequently encountered (Fig. 113). Like the orfe they tend to keep close to the surface of the water and are generally seen swimming around in groups. The silver rudd has something of a metallic look about it and conspicuous red fins, while the golden variety is of a coppery hue rather than a solid yellow or orange colour.

Fig. 113 Rudd are much loved fish with a healthy appetite for filamentous algae.

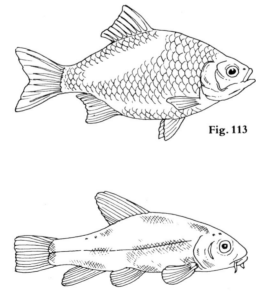

Fig. 113

Fig. 114 Green tench are the most popular scavenging fish for the bottom of the pool.

Fig. 114

Making a choice – scavengers

There is a common misconception that a pool will not function satisfactorily without scavenging fish. This has been brought about by the belief that the scavengers will act as animated vacuum cleaners and clear up all manner of debris, mud and stones and completely clear the pool of slime and algae. This is completely untrue. What scavengers do is clear up any uneaten goldfish food which falls to the bottom of the pool, thereby preventing it from decomposing and fouling the water. In a well-balanced pool where the goldfish are *not* regularly fed the scavenger is largely unnecessary.

Catfish

Retailers of cold-water fish use the collective name catfish for a number of different species. All are similar in appearance, having long barbels or whiskers and similar habits. These habits are mostly undesirable and any pool owner contemplating introducing cold-water catfish should be aware of their mode of life. While it is true that they will scavenge and devour uneaten fish food from the pool floor and prey upon aquatic insect life, once they have reached adulthood they usually turn their attention from worms and insects to young fry and the tails of fancy goldfish. Those of fantails, moors and comets are frequently shredded beyond recognition. Therefore the use of the species referred to loosely as catfish can only be considered when other large fish are involved and breeding is not intended.

Green tench

This is the most usual scavenging fish, a sleek fellow with short broad olive-green body and narrow tapering head (Fig. 114). Like other scavenging fish, once introduced to the pool it is seldom seen, preferring to lurk among accumulated debris on the bottom in which it searches for gnat larvae and similar delicacies.

Other livestock

Apart from the fish there are other livestock like snails and mussels that can be introduced to the garden pool and will contribute to the maintenance of a healthy balance.

There are others, like frogs, toads and newts which will appear naturally. These sometimes cause the novice pondkeeper concern, but they are all part of the natural ecology of the water garden and rarely cause any problems. Indeed, the home gardener's pool is often the last refuge of threatened amphibians like the great crested newt.

Snails and mussels

Snails can be useful additions to a garden pool as they devour rotting vegetation and algae, especially the soft filamentous species that cling to the pool walls, planting baskets and foliage of submerged plants.

Snails are also good indicators of the condition of the water in a pool. In strongly alkaline water their shells are smooth and lustrous, whereas in acid water they become brittle and badly pitted.

Mussels also assist in ridding the pool of suspended algae, acting as filters by sucking in water and then blowing it out again, at the same time retaining the algae.

Great pond snail

Although frequently offered for sale as a garden-pond snail, this species has a voracious appetite for aquatic plants and should never be knowingly introduced, for while it does feed to some extent on algae it much prefers the succulent floating pads of the water lilies which it reduces to unsightly scraps. When established in a pool it can be controlled by floating lettuce leaves or an old cabbage stalk on the water over night. In the morning all the pond snails in the vicinity will be clinging on and can then be removed and destroyed.

Great pond snails are easily recognized by a tall spiralled and pointed shell 2.5 cm (1 in) or more high and a fleshy greyish cream body (Fig. 115). They lay their myriad eggs in long cylinders of jelly which can often be detected on the undersides of water-lily leaves and the foliage of submerged aquatic plants. Removal of these at an early stage helps in the control of the species.

Ramshorn snail

This is the only species of snail that can be

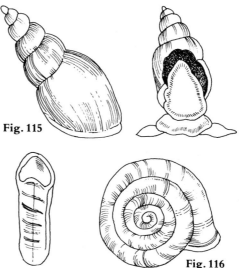

Fig. 115 The great pond snail is often mistakenly introduced to a pool. It can be captured by floating fresh lettuce leaves on the water.

Fig. 116 The ramshorn snail helps considerably in the battle against algae.

unreservedly recommended for a garden pool (Fig. 116). It is a handsome fellow with a flattened shell which the creature carries in an upright position on its back. The shell may be likened to a small catherine wheel and is not likely to be confused with any other common species. There are red-bodied and white-bodied varieties in addition to the common species which is all black. All three are perfectly hardy, despite the fact that the coloured forms are often used in tropical aquaria.

If the various colours are introduced to a pool for the sake of variety, black will ultimately dominate. Black is the dominant colour and during the course of breeding will swamp the other varieties. Snails are hermaphrodite, but rarely fertilize themselves. One mating by a snail is sufficient for several batches of eggs, so the colour of the progeny for some time will be dependant on the colour of the original male element. Eggs of the ramshorn snail are laid on submerged plants in flat sticky pads of jelly about 12 mm (½ in) in diameter. They are much-loved by all pond fish who regard them as something of a delicacy, so over-population is unlikely to occur.

Painter's mussel

Although not the most efficient or spectacular of the freshwater mussels, this interesting creature is used by enthusiasts as

Fig. 117 Painter's
mussels serve as
algae filters in the
pool. They should
not be introduced
until the pool is
established.

Fig. 117

the host for the progeny of the bitterling,
a fish which some fanciers introduce to
their ponds (Fig. 117). The mussel has a
yellowish green shell conspicuously marked
with brown growth rings.

Swan mussel
This is the mussel that is most frequently
available and certainly the most useful for
the garden pool. However it is not advisable
to introduce it to very small volumes of
water for it enjoys cool conditions and a
liberal accumulation of debris on the pool
floor through which it can crawl. Of pleasing habit and appearance, it frequently attains a length of 10–12.5 cm (4–5 in) and
has an oval brownish green shell which
contains a white fleshy body.

Fig. 119 (*Right-
hand column*)
Newts spend the
breeding season in
the pool. They are
of great benefit,
devouring all
manner of
troublesome
insect life.

Common frog
This is a very popular and welcome creature
to the garden pool (Fig. 118). It breeds
during spring and early summer. Both
males and females enter the water and
remain there for several days, the male
embracing the female from behind and
hugging her tightly. When amplexus, as
this process is known, has finished the
female deposits her spawn into the water,
whereupon the male ejects his sperm into
the mass.

Once fertilization has been completed the

Fig. 118 The
common frog is a
welcome addition
to the pool,
associating
happily with fish
and snails.

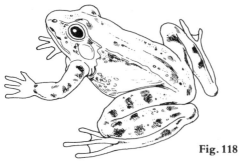

Fig. 118

jelly-like masses with tiny black spots are
slowly transformed into tiny tadpoles.
These at first feed on algal growth, but as
they start to change visually they become
carnivorous. Around this time their tails
begin to disappear and tiny legs develop.
After three or four months they resemble
tiny versions of their parents. In a couple of
years they start to breed.

Common toad
Toads live in much the same way as frogs
and breed in a very similar manner. They
are not generally as appealing in a garden
pool for they have a tough brownish warty
skin, an ungainly walk and are mainly nocturnal, but they are among the gardener's
greatest friends, for they feed almost exclusively on slugs, snails and other garden
pests.

Newts
Common newts are small lizard-like creatures which spend part of their life cycle in
a pool and the remainder in the surrounding
damp areas where they feed on all kinds of
insects (Fig. 119).

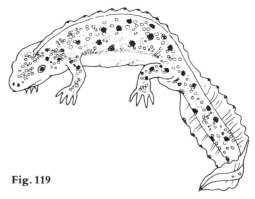

Fig. 119

They are most interesting for the pool
owner when they start their spring-time
courtship dances in the pool. During these
the male contorts his body and flicks his tail
violently for several minutes before depositing a spermatophore which is taken up
by the female. The sperms from this then
make their way along to fertilize the eggs.
These are released individually and wrapped

Choosing a breeding pair

Selecting a good pair of breeding fish from a retailer is not difficult. Health is obviously of prime importance and all the usual characteristics of a healthy fish should be present in those intended for breeding. Colours and conformation are also prime considerations and any scaling or other desirable features must be taken into account.

Sexing fish in the spring is relatively easy. A female fish (Fig. 120) when viewed from above has an oval or elliptical body shape while that of a male (Fig. 121) is slim and pencil-like. The male is further enhanced by white pimple-like nuptial tubercles which are liberally scattered about the gill plates and head. Large females with distended bodies that look full of spawn should be avoided as having been kept in restricted surroundings they may be suffering from the disorder known as spawn binding (see p. 128).

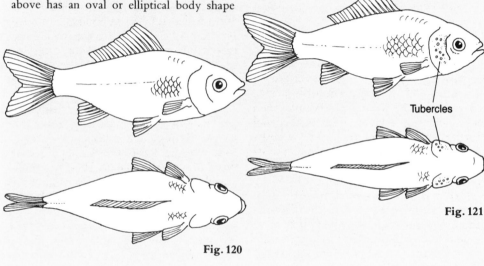

Tubercles

Fig. 121

Fig. 120

Fig. 120 A female fish has a distinctive, broadly elliptical, shape in the spring when viewed from above.

Fig. 121 A male fish is slim when viewed from above and has conspicuous white nuptial tubercles on the gills and head.

into individual leaves of submerged aquatic plants. Breeding continues well into the summer, then the parents leave the water to spend the autumn and winter on land.

The female is of a brownish or olive colour, but the male displays a wavy crest along his back and a bright orange patch on his belly.

The palmate newt is of similar habit and appearance to the common newt except that both male and female are much smaller and the male has a much lower, straighter crest and webbed toes.

The great crested newt is usually a much more persistent aquatic species than its smaller relatives, extending its stay in the water until well past the breeding season. It is a handsome creature 15 cm (6 in) or more long with a long tapering crest and black body with contrasting bright yellow belly.

CHAPTER 7
Maintenance

As with other features in the garden, a pool, its inhabitants and immediate surroundings need regular attention if they are to give of their best. Maintenance is generally minimal, but must be carried out regularly if major problems are not going to ensue.

Spring cleaning the pool

It is a fallacy to believe that a pool must be cleaned out every spring. If it is disturbed too much it is unlikely that a healthy balance with clear water will be achieved until well on into the summer. A thorough spring clean will be necessary only every five or six years, otherwise it is merely a case of lifting and dividing overgrown plants and replanting them in fresh compost.

When it is necessary to clean out a pool completely this will be indicated by a substantial accumulation of organic debris on the pool floor and difficulty in keeping the water absolutely clear. An oily scum will appear on the surface, sometimes accompanied by an unpleasant smell. Plants will have become crowded and merely lifting and dividing a few will not substantially alter the general lack-lustre appearance of the pool.

Emptying a pool

Before spring cleaning can begin the pool must be drained. Older concrete pools often have a drainage plug, but most gardeners have to resort to siphoning or baling out the water. Siphoning presents no problem if some of the surrounding ground is lower than the pool. A length of hosepipe is filled with water and while one end is submerged in the pool with a thumb over it, the other end is simultaneously removed to a lower area. As long as this is done in sequence and the end of the hosepipe outside the pool is lower than that in the pool, gravity will withdraw the water.

If the pool has been constructed in a lower part of the garden and this is impossible then the water will have to be laboriously baled out with a bucket. Great care should be taken to ensure that fish and snails are not thrown out with the water. Most fish will linger in the mud and debris on the pool floor and are then readily captured. When emptying a pool it is a good idea to have one or two buckets of water nearby to quickly accommodate rescued fish.

Fish that have been removed should be placed in as cool a place as possible while spring cleaning takes place. A garage or outhouse are ideal, the fish being put in containers of water with as large a surface area as possible. Snails should be kept separately in a jar or bucket. When put with fish in a confined space they are likely to be sucked out of their shells and devoured by the hungry fish. Remember, too, that fish swimming around in a bucket will have little natural food to eat, even if generous quantities of pondweed are put in with them. So a pinch of standard fish food every day is essential.

Aquatic plants also need careful attention, especially the submerged types. These dry out very quickly if exposed to the air. Ideally some of the best material should be placed in buckets of water in a cool but light place. When ready for re-planting it can be bunched up as cuttings fastened together with a lead weight or a short piece of wire. Water lilies will last for some days merely wrapped in a generous sheet of polythene, while marginal plants are mostly happy for a week or so if kept in a cool light place. Some of the submerged foliage might shrivel, but the plants will not really suffer.

Dividing plants

Most years, though, such extensive spring

cleaning is unnecessary. There may be replacements to be made for losses sustained during winter and, of course, some plants will need lifting and dividing if they are to retain their vigour. As a rule marginal plants should be lifted and divided every two or three years, but it is undesirable to lift large numbers of plants at one time. This leads to 'fat' and 'lean' years as newly replanted aquatics always look rather sparse early on, but conversely if they all need dividing together, by the time this is necessary the whole pool looks overcrowded. A policy of lifting certain groups of plants each year is the most sensible and ensures an acceptable appearance throughout.

Water lilies do not need attention so often. The third year after planting is an appropriate time to divide vigorous varieties, while some of the more restrained kinds will last for four or five years without attention. The need for division will be apparent in any case. The plants will make a preponderance of small leafy growth in the centre of the clump, often accompanied by diminishing flower size.

Submerged plants can often be left for a number of years without attention, although the stringy winter growth of semi-evergreen kinds like the curled pondweed should be removed each spring to allow fresh growth to break from the bottom. If a basket of submerged plants is not prospering it is a good idea to shake out the soil and replant healthy young cuttings in fresh compost.

When dividing marginal plants treat them rather like herbaceous perennials. Separate tough roots by inserting two hand forks back to back and then lever them apart. Always replant material from the outer edge of the clump as this is young and vigorous.

Water lilies can be treated similarly, except that most will need to be separated with a knife and therefore care should be taken to see that any wounds are dressed with powdered charcoal to prevent infection. The crown of a healthy mature water lily consists of a main fleshy root, which was the one originally planted, together with a number of side branches. It is these side growths that should be retained as they are young and vigorous. The original crown is discarded, but each severed branch will produce a plant provided it has a healthy terminal shoot.

Routine summer care

During the summer little attention needs to be paid to the plants although, as in a herbaceous border, dead flower heads should be regularly removed to prevent plants from exhausting themselves by setting seed. With a number of marginal plants this also prevents the haphazard distribution of seed around the pool, which in the case of plants like the water plantain or alisma, would potentially cause a nuisance with rapidly germinating seedlings.

Feeding plants

Otherwise little needs to be done, except for feeding plants that have not been repotted in fresh compost. Modern aquatic plant fertilizers are available in perforated sachets. These are pushed into the compost next to the plants and release plant nutrients at the roots rather than into the water where a higher level of plant foods would encourage the rapid development of algae (Fig. 122). This form of feeding aquatic plants is excellent, but somewhat more expensive than using traditional bonemeal 'pills'. These are made from coarse bonemeal rolled into balls of clay. Each serves in a similar way to a sachet of fertilizer, a ball being pushed into the compost of each planting basket close by plants that have not recently been repotted.

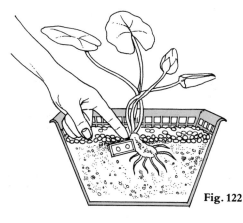

Fig. 122

Fig. 122 A sachet of special aquatic plant fertilizer should be pushed into the soil next to the root. It causes no pollution.

Feeding fish

In an established pool feeding fish is generally unnecessary as there are always sufficient aquatic insects around to satisfy the most voracious appetites. However, most pool owners enjoy feeding their fish and derive considerable enjoyment from the fish swimming to the surface at the sound of a footfall or in response to a shadow falling across the water. Regular feeding at the same place in a pool encourages such antics. Feeding fish can be likened in many ways to feeding plants, for not all varieties have the same requirements. Overfeeding can be both wasteful and, in a small pool, dangerous as any uneaten food is likely to decompose and pollute the water.

Balanced fish foods are available in three different forms. The conventional crumb food usually comes in a multitude of colours from white and ochre to red and vivid yellow. This is often the by-product of biscuit manufacture. The flaked foods are also multicoloured, but take the form of thin flakes rather like a much-refined breakfast cereal. Then there are floating pellets which are brownish in colour. All have their advocates and each their drawbacks. Both pelleted and flaked foods float for a considerable length of time. This is an obvious benefit, but on windy days the flakes may be carried on the breeze and end up out of the reach of the fish in the tangle of marginal plants at the poolside.

It does not matter too much which food is used, or even if a combination of diet is arranged, for fish adapt readily to a change of diet and will continue to thrive provided all their nutritional requirements are satisfied.

Fish, like people, appreciate variety in their diet. Dried flies, daphnia, shredded shrimp and ants eggs are freely available, although the nutritional value of the latter, once dried and packaged, is open to question. Fish generally prefer the real thing and while not advocating a search for fresh ants eggs, if you happen to stumble across a nest in the garden it is worth setting up a trap in which to gather the eggs. Take a small box like a match box and cut a tiny hole out of it to provide an entrance. Invert

the box and place it close by the ant hill which should then be disturbed to ensure that the eggs will be transported from the main nursery to a safe depository. On seeing the inverted box with the tiny hole the ants believe that this is a safe refuge and start to move their eggs into it. Once the removal is complete, the box can be lifted and the eggs taken away.

Live foods are much appreciated by all fish. Gnat larvae, mosquito larvae and daphnia or water fleas are occasionally found in water butts and similar receptacles and can be netted with a fine-mesh net and fed to the fish. Daphnia can be cultured to provide a constant food supply throughout the summer. A tub of rainwater is set up with 2.5 cm (1 in) or so of soil in the bottom and allowed to settle. A net full of live daphnia is added. Reproduction will be so rapid that a small harvest of succulent insects can be gathered each week.

The feeding of conventional packeted food, when a pool is established, depends on the weather and the time of year as to the amount given and frequency. Throughout the summer the equivalent of a pinch of food for each fish on alternate days is adequate. Pay regard to the speed at which the fish clear the food. Any that remains after 20 minutes should be netted and the rate of feeding reduced until a happy balance is achieved.

Breeding a few fish

If fish start breeding in a garden pool it is an indication that all is well. For the newcomer to pond-keeping it can be a time of concern. Here swimming in the water are myriad young fish which are being preyed on each day. The instinct to save every individual is strong, but should be resisted, for it is natural for the smaller and weaker individuals to perish and provide nourishment for other inhabitants. Sufficient fry usually escape to grow into young fish and then take their place alongside their parents in the general rough and tumble of the pool. It is likely that the water gardener with a good natural balance in his or her water garden will produce a few youngsters each year without needing to do anything.

Artificial spawning (stripping)

Many pool owners are satisfied with natural spawning of their fish and are happy to let nature take its course. However, those who take a particular interest in fish may well wish to make specific unions between male and female. This demands an artificial method of union known as stripping. Although this can be done at any time during the breeding period, mid-summer is the best time, when females which have not spawned already are in a suitable condition to do so.

A chubby female with the desired characteristics should be carefully netted and examined. If the vent is slightly reddened and distended the fish should be in a suitable condition for stripping. This involves holding the fish in wet hands and applying gentle pressure to the sides of the body, slowly progressing towards the vent. The fish is held over a flat-bottomed dish containing a little water. When stroked rhythmically the eggs will cascade into the dish and can be easily distributed by moving the fish backwards and forwards.

The desired male then has to be selected.

Great care must be taken during netting so that premature emission of his milt is not induced by his thrashing about in the net. Gently stroking the flanks should result in the emission of the milky-white milt or sperm-bearing fluid which should be distributed as evenly as possible over the waiting spawn. Successful stripping can only be undertaken with firm and confident handling. Pinching and squeezing could well damage the fish.

Fertilization takes place between the milt and eggs in the dish and will have been completed about 20 minutes after stripping. The spawn can then be gently rinsed with luke-warm water to reduce the incidence of fungal attacks. It is possible to hatch the eggs in the dish, but an aquarium is preferable. After three or four days the fry will be seen developing like tiny pins clinging to the submerged plants. After two or three weeks they will become recognizable as fish, sometimes transparent, sometimes bronze, but all in due course attaining the bright colours and proportions with which we are generally so familiar.

Most pool owners regard the breeding of a few fish as an integral part of pool management. Those intent on doing this usually select pairs of breeding fish from the start and ensure that there is sufficient underwater foliage to provide cover and for the deposition of spawn. The breeding season lasts from late spring to late summer and is triggered by the intensity of light and the warmth of the water. Most goldfish are capable of breeding during their second year, although any fish 8 cm (3 in) or more in length should be sexually active.

While most fish in a garden pool will be of the carp family, not all breed readily in this country. Like breed with like, although some of the true carp and goldfish will on occasions interbreed.

Male fish can be distinguished from female fish by their more slender body shape and the presence during the breeding season of nuptical tubercles on their gills and heads. These look like tiny white spots

which disappear entirely for the winter.

Spawning is the mating of fish in the open water, the female being chased around a pool by a male who will knock and brush against her in an effort to get her to release her spawn. When this has happened the male will deposit his milt or sperm-bearing fluid over the eggs and fertilization will take place. When this has happened the spawn and the plants on which they were laid should be transferred to a bucket of pool water. This will be of the same chemical composition and temperature and few problems should be encountered with the emerging fry. The spawn can take its chance along with the hungry adults in the pool, but few will survive. Taking fry from the pool ensures a good yield of young fish.

If the spawn removed from a pool is placed in a cool place with an even temperature, after three or four days the fry will begin developing. To start with they are difficult to see, looking much like tiny translucent pins in the water clinging to the submerged plant foliage. Two or three weeks later they become recognizable as fish, sometimes transparent, sometimes bronze, but all eventually attaining their adult colour.

Goldfish sometimes remain bronze for several years and then suddenly change colour. This delay in complete colour change is associated with water temperature at spawning time. The lower the water temperature at spawning, the longer it takes for full adult colours to develop.

Fry that usually live freely in an open pool soon find their own food, but in the sterile conditions of a large bucket this is not very likely. Special baby fish foods that resemble tubes of toothpaste are available, but an equally successful food can be made

from scrambled eggs. Feeding in a container should continue until the fry are 2.5 cm (1 in) long when they can be fairly safely returned to a pool.

Preparing for the winter

Most gardeners tend to forget about their pools once the last water-lily blossom has faded. The dull wet days of autumn descend and they take to their fireside, thinking that little is happening in the pool. This is a mistake, for more trouble can ensue from neglecting a pool in the autumn than at any other time of the year.

The first problem to be dealt with is falling leaves from surrounding trees. Even a small accumulation in the bottom of a pool can be dangerous, particularly if, like horse chestnut, they are toxic as well. A fine-mesh net placed across a pool is absolutely essential until trees are bare.

Marginal aquatics must be cleaned up as soon as frost has turned the foliage brown. Reduce them by about two-thirds of their height. Never cut them below water level for some aquatics have hollow stems and will die from being completely submerged. However, it is important they are all tidied so they do not become a winter refuge for insect pests like water-lily beetle.

Water lilies need no winter preparation as they are hardy and die down naturally without fuss. Only the pygmy kinds, when grown in a rock pool or sink, are at risk of being damaged by severe weather. The best method of protection is to drain the water and give the roots a liberal covering of straw protected by a frame light. They survive well like this and can easily be started into growth again in spring by removing the straw and frame light and adding water.

Floating plants disappear as the days shorten, retreating into winter buds or turions which fall to the pool floor where they remain until the spring sunshine warms the water again. It is useful to collect some of the over-wintering buds and keep them in jars of water with a little soil in the bottom. If stood in a light frost-free place they start into growth much sooner in the spring and are an invaluable aid in the

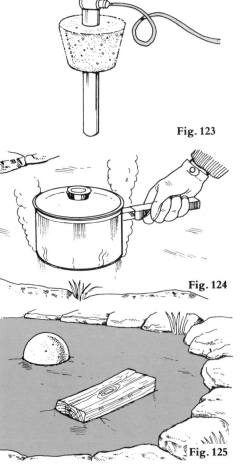

Fig. 123 An electric pool heater with a polystyrene float will keep a small area of water open during the coldest weather.

Fig. 123

Fig. 124 A pan of boiling water stood on the ice will create a hole without causing distress to the fish.

Fig. 124

Fig. 125 A rubber ball or piece of wood floating on the water prevents ice exerting pressure against the sides of the pool.

Fig. 125

battle against algae. By being well advanced they provide surface shade a good few weeks before those that are resting naturally on the pool floor.

Fish should be prepared for winter by the careful feeding of daphnia, ants eggs and other delicacies on days when the weather is warm and bright and they are seen to be active. Precautions for their winter welfare should be taken at this time with the introduction of a pool heater or other means of maintaining an ice-free area.

The pool in winter

The pool in winter is an inhospitable place and often causes concern to the new water gardener. Worries about the safety of the fish are natural, but provided sensible precautions are taken the fish rarely come to any harm. The only ones likely to succumb in severe weather are those that are weak and sickly, together with a few of the later-hatched fry. This is a normal form of natural selection.

Most decorative cold-water fish are extremely hardy. During the winter their metabolism slows down much in the same way as a tree which becomes dormant. Therefore, being inactive, they feed less. So feeding is totally unnecessary during winter. Uneaten fish food will just fall to the floor of the pool and decompose.

This semi-torpid state is particularly useful, for it enables most fish to be frozen more or less solid in the ice for a few days without apparently coming to any harm. A prolonged period with a layer of ice over the surface of a pool is likely to cause far more casualties than mere cold because of the build up underneath of noxious gases. In a well-maintained pool the problem of gases is not so acute as there is much less organic debris to decay. But when a layer of ice has formed there is no way of knowing exactly what is going on beneath and it is a wise precaution to keep at least a small area free from ice.

The simplest method of doing this is by installing a pool heater (Fig. 123). This consists of a heated brass rod with a polystyrene float which can be connected to the electrical supply which operates the pump.

Even in severe weather this creates a small ice-free area. If electricity is not close at hand the safest way of obtaining a similar effect is by standing a pan of boiling water on the ice and allowing it to melt through (Fig. 124). Never strike the ice with a heavy instrument as this will concuss and often kill the fish.

However, not only are the fish vulnerable to the effects of severe weather, but so too is the pool, particularly if made of concrete. The pressure ice can exert against the walls is often sufficient to cause cracks to appear. To overcome this float a child's rubber ball, or even a sizeable piece of wood, on the water (Fig. 125). These are capable of expanding and contracting with the pressure of the ice and should alleviate any trouble.

Looking after an indoor pool

Few water gardeners regard the cultivation of aquatic plants under glass as a serious

Growing nelumbo

The cultivation of the sacred lotus or nelumbo is not difficult where cool greenhouse conditions can be provided. The whitish banana-like roots are available during early spring. These should be planted in round tubs, for then if the root comes into contact with the edge it will travel around in a curved fashion. In a square tub or pool, should the fleshy rhizome meet a flat uncompromising wall it will often perish.

A good heavy loam compost liberally enriched with coarse bonemeal suits nelumbos best. They should be planted horizontally 2.5 cm (1 in) or so beneath the surface of the compost and then about 7.5 cm (3 in) of water added. As the young foliage emerges the level of the water can be gradually raised until it is about 25 cm (10 in) deep.

Throughout the summer a watch should be kept for aphid attacks and occasional support given to foliage that becomes top heavy. Then as autumn approaches the water level can be progressively reduced until the foliage dies away. The roots should then be carefully lifted and overwintered in a box of damp sand in a cool frost-free place.

proposition, for most tropical kinds look too exotic and vigorous to be accommodated in the average greenhouse or sun porch. While it is true that those like the giant Victoria water lily will remain with the parks departments and botanical gardens, there is a host of others of easy culture which can be happily cultivated in a small pool, tub or aquarium.

A pool can be constructed by any of the methods outlined earlier, but without one needing to be concerned about frost damage or the pool in proximity to other features. Within a greenhouse or conservatory there is the freedom to do almost anything. The most satisfactory is likely to be a raised pool with a walled surround so that on a warm summer day it is possible to sit on the edge and dabble the fingers in the water as brightly coloured goldfish laze among the lily pads.

The less affluent can consider the possibilities of tub culture. Indeed, for the keen grower of tropical water lilies and lotus this is probably the best method of cultivation. Most tubs that become available are second-hand barrels which have been sawn in half and made watertight. Old wine or vinegar casks are ideal. So are beer barrels, but those which have contained fats, oils, tar or wood preservative should be avoided, as any residue is likely to pollute the water, forming an unsightly scum on the surface.

Before attempting to plant anything in a newly acquired tub, give it a good scrub with clear water and then rinse it out. Never use detergent for cleaning as it is difficult to know when all traces have been removed. Tubs that have been used before often become coated on the inside with a thick growth of slime and algae, and where it is felt that water alone is insufficient to remove this, the addition of enough potassium per-

manganate to turn the water a violet colour will usually have the desired effect.

The plants

Planting an indoor pool is very similar to one outside except that water lilies are likely to have been pot grown and be much larger and better established than their hardy counterparts. Small sprouted tubers often have great difficulty in becoming established under pool conditions, whereas a large plant removed from its container with rootball intact will hardly realize that is has been transplanted and will grow away vigorously.

Such plants need little attention during the summer except for a periodic check for pests and diseases. When the plants are growing in tubs ensure these are topped up regularly with fresh water.

As autumn approaches the water should be gradually lowered and the mud allowed to dry out. Container-grown plants should be removed and dried out slowly. This causes the top growth to die away and ripens the tubers, which are then lifted for storing. Damp sand is the most suitable material in which to store tubers and should be contained in a vermin-proof box and kept in a frost-free place. An old bicuit tin or cake tin is ideal, the tubers being sandwiched between 2.5 cm (1 in) deep layers of sand. The tubers will keep very well for the winter without any attention and should not be disturbed until planting time the following spring.

Some water gardeners never bother with storing tubers and treat the plants as annuals, purchasing fresh stock each spring. This has much to commend it, for fresh young tubers are often more active and grow into far better plants than older woody ones.

CHAPTER 8
Propagation

One of the most enjoyable aspects of gardening is propagation. It is so rewarding to be able to produce your own plants. For the majority of water gardeners any extensive efforts at propagating aquatic plants are impractical. Unlike the vegetable grower and the raiser of bedding plants, the water gardener does not have ready access to propagation material, especially seed.

Aquatic facilities also have to be found and these are not always easy to arrange on a small scale. However, the enthusiastic water gardener with a close interest in plants does have an opportunity of raising some plants, using little more than a few pots of compost, an old aquarium or a washing up bowl of generous proportions. With care, even some of the better water lilies can be propagated under such spartan conditions and progress can certainly be made with a number of marginal plants both from division and occasionally seed.

Hardy water lilies

All the commonly grown hardy water lilies, with the exception of the tiny *Nymphaea* × *pygmaea* 'Alba', can be readily propagated from 'eyes'. These are tiny growing points which occur with varying frequency along the roots of mature plants. Mainly they appear as smaller versions of the parent plant, each with juvenile foliage seeming ready to burst into growth. However, with *N.tuberosa* and its hybrids they take the form of brittle rounded nodules which are easily detached.

Established plants are carefully lifted during early summer and the eyes removed with a sharp knife. The wounds of both eye and root should be dusted with powdered charcoal or sulphur to prevent fungal infection and the adult plant returned to the pool. The severed eyes can then be potted into small pots using good clean loam or standard aquatic planting compost and

stood in a shallow container of water with the growing points just submerged. As most of the eyes are very small it is wise to give them the protection of a cold frame or greenhouse during their early stages of growth.

As the petioles of the young plants lengthen the water level can be raised. When the plants fill their pots with roots they can be transferred into progressively larger pots. When sufficiently large they can be moved into baskets and placed in a pool in their permanent positions.

Raising seeds

Nymphaea × *pygmaea* 'Alba' does not produce eyes and therefore has to be increased from seed. This must be freshly collected from ripened seed pods and not have been allowed to dry out. If harvested in its correct state the seed will be embodied in a gelatinous mass which should be sown with the seed. Attempts to separate the tiny individual seeds are futile.

A good loam soil or standard aquatic planting medium is perfectly adequate. Shallow pans can be filled with this and the seed and jelly spread as evenly as possible over the surface. A light sprinkling of fine compost is necessary to cover the seeds and a gentle soaking from a watering can fitted with a fine rose will settle the compost (Fig. 126). The pans should then be stood

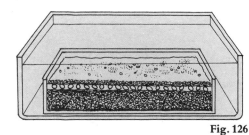

Fig. 126

Fig. 126
Water-lily seed should be sown in a good, clean heavy loam and then stood in a container just covered with water.

Fig. 127
Water-lily
seedlings are very
fragile. They
should be
transplanted as
soon as they are
large enough to be
handled.

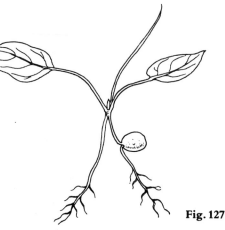

Fig. 127

with a fine rose will settle the compost.
The pans should then be stood in a bowl or
aquarium with the water just above soil
level and maintained at room temperature
in a greenhouse or on a window ledge (Fig.
126).

After two or three weeks the first seedlings should appear. They will have tiny
translucent lance-shaped leaves and look
rather like liverworts. From the time they
germinate, and indeed for the first few
months of their life, filamentous algae are
likely to be a nuisance, becoming entangled
with the fragile juvenile foliage of the
seedlings. A good proprietary algaecide
correctly administered will alleviate this
problem, but any dead algae should be
removed promptly before fermentation
begins and causes rotting of the water lily
foliage.

Water-lily seedlings are very fragile.
When the first two or three true floating
leaves come to the surface of the water the
plants should be pricked out (Fig. 127). Lift
them in clumps and wash them thoroughly
to remove all the soil. Then gently tease
them apart. A plastic seed tray is the most
useful container in which to prick out the
seedlings, immersing it so that the compost
is about 2.5 cm (1 in) beneath the surface of
the water. The water level can be raised as
growths lengthen and become stronger.
After six months or so the plants will become crowded and the compost exhausted,
at which time they may be carefully lifted
and potted individually. They can then be
treated in the same way as water lilies reproduced from eyes.

Marginal plants

All popular marginal plants, and deep-
water aquatics other than water lilies, are
propagated by one of three ways: seed,
division or cuttings.

Division

Divisions are produced in a similar way to
herbaceous plants. An established plant is
divided into several portions, each with a
strong shoot and root of adequate size to be
capable of an independent existence.

Some marginals like typha and scirpus
have creeping roots. In this case division
involves removing a length of root with a
terminal shoot attached and planting it
separately.

When such plants are divided it is usual
to trim the tops. However, take care not to
replant with the cut ends of the stems below
the surface of the water. Being hollow they
fill with water and the plants rot.

With clump-forming plants such as iris
and caltha the individual divisions are more
like small plants and are pulled away from
the main plant by hand or with a small
fork. The plantlets can then be potted individually and stood in a bowl or tray of
water. When potting divisions select those
from the outer part of the clump. These
have the vigour of youth and become much
more rapidly established than old woody
central portions.

Creeping aquatics like *Menyanthes trifoliata* (bog bean) and *Calla palustris* (bog
arum) are easily increased by the division of
their scrambling rhizomes. Menyanthes is
merely chopped into small sections of stem
each with a latent bud, and preferably a
vestige of root attached, and then planted
in plastic seed trays filled with mud until
established and sprouting. Bog arum can
be increased the same way, but dormant
buds that arise along the rhizome can be
detached readily and planted out independent of the old stem.

It is a similar process for *Butomus umbellatus* (flowering rush). With this, tiny bulbils
appear in the axils of the leaves where they
arise from the hard woody rootstock. If
planted in trays of mud they rapidly turn
into healthy young plants.

Stem cuttings

Some creeping aquatics are better increased from stem cuttings taken during the spring when the shoots are about 7.5 cm (3 in) long (Fig. 128). These include *Mentha aquatica* (water mint) and *Veronica beccabunga* (common brooklime). *Myosotis scorpioides* (water forget-me-not) can be increased from cuttings with a little root attached, or by division, while the improved variety 'Semperflorens' can be raised from seed.

Seed raising

Seed raising is an obvious method of propagation for many aquatic plants. However, it is a slower process and plants will take several months longer to attain plantable size. Seed raising of aquatics is still something of a hit and miss affair, for little research has been done on the subject and no two species seem to require identical conditions.

Pontederia cordata (pickerel weed), must be sown while still green, whereas, *Alisma plantago-aquatica* (water plantain) will grow if the seed is 12 months old. *Aponogeton distachyos* (water hawthorn) will grow either if sown immediately it ripens or if kept until the following year, but it loses its viability if allowed to dry out completely.

The sowing of aquatic-plant seeds and the subsequent care of the seedling is exactly the same as recommended for water lilies from seed.

Submerged aquatics

Almost all submerged aquatics are increased from cuttings. Only *Eleocharis acicularis* (common hair grass) should be increased by division. This looks rather like a dense mat of seedling grass and is lifted and divided into small clumps, the separate portions being parted by hand.

Otherwise healthy young shoots are removed, prepared as bunches of cuttings and fastened together around the base with a strip of lead or wire. The cuttings are then planted in their bunches directly into the growing medium in a basket. Most bunches should consist of half a dozen separate stems no longer than 10 cm (4 in). When planted these must be put into the compost at such

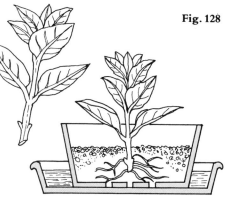

Fig. 128

Fig. 128 Short, non-flowering pieces of stem make excellent cuttings. They root freely in a pan of very wet mud.

a depth that the lead strip is buried. If exposed it will rot through the stems and the cuttings will float to the surface. Cuttings removed like this during the active growing periods of spring and summer will root within a week or 10 days.

For a number of submerged aquatics the regular renewal of the plants by cuttings is of great benefit, especially for the various species of myriophyllum and potamogeton.

Bog plants

Growing from seed

While the technique for raising most true aquatics from seed is little understood and not widely practised, the seed raising of bog-garden plants is the most frequent way of growing these lovely moisture-loving subjects. Even though some, like primulas, germinate best when sown directly after collecting from the parent plant, most bog-garden plants, unlike true aquatics, have a reasonable period of viability and can be sown the following spring, or often during early summer when pressure on greenhouse and frame resources is less.

The business is not so messy either, for although bog garden plants often grow in viscous mud or even standing water they can be propagated in standard potting compost. Indeed, it is preferable that they are. Never be tempted to use ordinary garden soil for seed raising. Even if it looks suitable, for it will be full of pathogens and will cause innumerable problems later on.

The seed that you receive has only one purpose in life and that is to germinate, so provide it with the best conditions that you can. Seed is very precious, so do not skimp on the cost of a tray full of good compost. Plants reflect directly the medium in which they are growing.

However, it is very important to be selective about the compost used. Proper seed composts have few nutrients in them and are a perfect medium for germination. This lack of nutrients ensures that the compost is unlikely to damage tender seedlings and that the growth of moss and liverworts is impaired.

Soil-based composts are theoretically suitable for all plants, but quicker results and better initial plants can often be raised in a good soilless compost. The all-peat soilless compost needs treating with a little reserve as it has large air pockets in it. Unless great care is taken to ensure a smooth even surface, fine seed like that of primula or perennial lobelia can get lost in an air void in the surface of the compost. All-peat composts are excellent for larger seeded subjects like irises and rheums, while smaller-seeded plants will make a better start in a soilless compost consisting of a peat and fine sand mixture.

It is always desirable when selecting a seed compost to choose a well-known branded kind rather than mix your own. The components of home-made compost can be very variable and the results unexpected. The small extra cost involved in purchasing properly mixed scientifically balanced compost is a first-class investment.

Pans and trays should be filled almost to the top with a suitable compost. If this is soil based, then it should be firmed down and tamped level. If it is a soilless type it should be merely put into the tray or pan and tapped level. Never firm soilless compost. This excludes all the air and causes problems for emerging seedlings. It is often difficult to wet, particularly if it has been allowed to dry out for an hour or two. With all kinds of composts it is important to firm the corners and the edges of the seed tray with the fingers. This prevents the otherwise inevitable sinking of the compost around the edge and the irritating prospect of all the seeds being washed to the sides where they germinate in a congested mass.

Seed compost should be watered from above prior to sowing. This is particularly useful for soilless composts, as they settle and the undulations can be levelled with a pinch of compost before sowing takes place.

Sowing and germinating

Seeds of most bog-garden plants should be sprinkled thinly over the surface and a fine layer of sifted compost scattered over the top. Large seeds like irises, which can be handled individually, can be placed at regular intervals so that the later pricking-out process is minimized. A light covering of compost gently tamped and watered then completes the operation. The covering of seeds with compost, except very fine ones, is a necessity, but should not be carried to extremes. A good general rule is to cover the seed by its own depth with compost.

Very fine seeds, such as those of primulas and mimulus, look almost like pepper and are therefore very difficult to handle. Their even distribution over the surface of the compost can be helped though by mixing the seed initially with a little silver sand. If this is poured into the seed packet and then shaken the seed should become fairly evenly distributed through the sand. This can then be scattered with the seed. Apart from acting as a carrier, the sand serves to indicate the area over which the seed has been distributed. The tray or pan, once sown, can be stood in a bowl of water and moisture allowed to soak through. This is very useful for all subjects, for watering from above, even from a watering can fitted with a fine rose, can redistribute or disturb the seeds on the surface and cause all kinds of problems.

Trays or pans of seeds benefit from being stood on a warm heating cable if available. Warm compost promotes rapid germination of most seeds. In a cool greenhouse the combination of soil-warming cables and a sheet of glass over the pan or tray can create a very effective microclimate. Similarly, a sheet of newspaper placed lightly over a seed tray will act as perfect insulation and still allow sufficient light to pass through. It is important to remove glass and newspaper immediately germination takes place. When the seedlings are emerging maximum light is vital to ensure that they develop into stocky plants.

Some subjects on germination quickly keel over with a disease called damping off, even though the plants are naturally moisture-lovers. It is associated with the close atmosphere created by emerging seedlings that have been sown too thickly, or even by too warm and humid conditions. Certain plants are more prone to this malady than others: among the most likely to succumb are mimulus and primulas.

Prevention is better than cure, so immediately seedlings are seen to be actively growing a routine watering with Cheshunt compound or, once the seedlings have emerged, a modern fungicide with benomyl as the active ingredient, is a necessary precaution. It is wise to repeat the treatment every 10 days until the plants are well established.

Pricking out

When seedlings are large enough to handle they should be pricked out. This involves lifting and transplanting them into trays so that they can develop as individuals. Most standard seed trays accommodate 35 plants, although some smaller-growing plants like mimulus can be planted at a greater density.

Ideally the seedlings should have their seed leaves or cotyledons fully expanded and the first rough leaf in evidence. Great care should be taken in handling seedlings as they are very delicate and brittle. Never hold a seedling by its root or stem; always take hold of it by the seed leaf. Holding a tender seedling, such as that of a primula or trollius, by the stem is likely to result in the appearance of the damping-off disease.

Plant the seedling slightly lower than it was in its original tray or pan: indeed, in certain circumstances it can be planted so that the seed leaves are at compost level. This applies only if the seedling is short-jointed strong and healthy. Deep planting will rarely turn a drawn and elongated plant into a short healthy one. If planted too deeply such a seedling will rot off and die.

If seedlings are pricked out into potting compost they are unlikely to require feeding before being planted out or potted. However, if planting or potting is delayed and the trays become absolutely full of roots it is useful to give a general liquid feed to maintain their vigour. Apart from this little special care is required during the development of the young plants provided they have plenty of light, are watered regularly and an eye is kept open for pests and diseases. Apart from greenfly and mildew, few troubles are likely to be encountered in a well-organized greenhouse or frame. Both of these problems can be controlled by the use of systemic insecticides and fungicides.

Hardening

The most important part of seedling care, once they are successfully established in seed trays, is hardening. This is the process by which plants are weaned from the artificial environment of a greenhouse or window sill and prepared for the reality of life in the open garden. This even applies to plants that are perfectly hardy, but have been raised under 'soft' conditions.

A cold frame is invaluable for hardening, for in chilly weather the frame cover can remain on, whereas if the weather turns warm it can be removed. What has to be achieved is a gradual transition over a period of two or three weeks. First of all the frame cover is lifted to give ventilation. This is gradually increased until the cover can be removed entirely for the day. It is then lifted slightly at night to allow ventilation. Eventually the cover is removed both night and day.

If a frame is not available and the plants have been raised in the house or sun lounge the same effect can be provided by taking them out during the day and standing them in a sheltered place, returning them to the house for the night. The weaning process can continue in just the same way until the plants take on a hardy appearance. This is indicated by a stiffness of foliage, often associated with a darker green colour. If the plants have turned bluish-green the weaning process has been too swift and the plants are checked. They will eventually grow out of it, but it does slow up their development, so gradual hardening is vital.

Potting

While many plants like mimulus can be grown right up to the planting stage in trays, others are better finished in pots. Indeed, primulas, trollius and even iris seem to make much better plants and transplant more readily when pot grown.

Soilless composts are quick acting, light and easy to handle, young plants advancing quickly in all respects. It should be remembered, though, that peat is an organic material that eventually decomposes, the process being hastened by regularly feeding with liquid fertilizer. With peat forming the entire or bulk of the compost this decomposition can create problems if repotting is not regularly undertaken or the plants are not moved on into their permanent positions. Apart from the hostile airless conditions which develop in the compost and restrict proper root development, mosses and liverworts invade the surface and sciarid flies take up residence. These are irritating little characters that, although predominantly consumers of decomposing organic matter, will destroy vital nutrient-transmitting root hairs.

Soil-based composts, while not yielding such rapid growth, do offer more stability. Watering is easier to get right with a compost which contains a significant proportion of soil, this also acting as a buffer against the breakdown caused by liquid feeding. The presence of soil in a compost allows for a greater margin of error when watering, for it permits the percolation of surplus moisture through the compost much more rapidly than if it were composed entirely of moisture-retaining peat. Indeed, it is the excessive moisture-holding capacity of peat, together with the relative difficulty of wetting it when it has been allowed to dry out, that makes soilless composts less popular with newcomers to plant raising.

So use soil-based potting compost for all actively growing plants and if you have the option use clay pots. These are not any better for the plants, but it is well known that the moisture content of the compost in a clay pot can be more easily recognized than when confined by a plastic pot. Take a short length of dowel rod, or a stick of similar substance, and tap the pot. If a dull thud results the compost is damp, but if a ringing sound is heard then it is dry. With soil-based compost and clay pots the gardener has little excuse for failure.

Cuttings

Unlike true aquatic plants, which when amenable to being propagated from cuttings root almost without question and an ease that defies description, when dealing with bog plants that are reproduced in this manner great care is needed.

A number of the bog plants that are raised from seed can also be increased from short spring stem cuttings, but these are usually species. Named forms rarely come true from seed and this is where cuttings are invaluable, particularly for cultivars of aconitum, lythrum and some of the more shrubby mimulus species, particularly *M. cardinalis* and *M. lewisii* which should be overwintered as rooted cuttings from a late-summer 'take' to cover for the possibility of root kill of the parent plants during a severe winter.

However, it is during early spring that most bog garden plants are increased from stem cuttings, just as growth is pushing through the soil. Succulent shoots no more than 10 cm (4 in) long, preferably slightly less, should be removed with a sharp knife. Be sure that each cutting is solid, for hollow shoots rarely root.

Preparation and rooting

Having taken the cuttings trim off any lower leaves that are likely to touch the rooting medium and cause decay. At the same time these will continue to transpire and may cause excessive loss of moisture and wilting. A detached cutting needs a balance between stem and foliage. Even after removing the lower leaves it is usually necessary to reduce the overall leaf area that remains.

The base of the stem should be cut just below a leaf joint to expose the maximum concentration of active cambium cells and

Tropical water lilies

Unlike hardy water lilies most tropical *Nymphaea* species can be successfully grown from seed in the same way as *N.* × *pygmaea* 'Alba' (p. 113). However, they will require a temperature of 23–27°C (75–80°F).

When the first floating leaves have developed the plants should be potted into small pots and kept at the same temperature in full sunlight for the winter. Young plants should not be allowed to fade as autumn approaches for if induced into dormancy they will almost certainly rot in the damp compost. Gathering the tiny tubers in the autumn is virtually impossible as they are so very small.

Equally it is almost impossible to overwinter the large tubers which many varieties of tropical water lilies make. Fortunately most of these form a tiny tuber, about the size of a chestnut, at the base of the main crown and this can be successfully stored in sand. Nocturnal varieties and hybrids derived from the rare species *N. colorata* bear masses of small tubers or 'spawn' on the surface of the parent as well as beneath and these should be treated in the same way.

During early spring young tubers can be potted about 5 cm (2 in) deep in a sandy compost and the pots stood in water at a temperature of around 21°C (70°F) in a sunny position. After about two weeks the young leaves will start to appear. When the first true floating leaves have developed locate the stem-like growth connecting the young plant to the tuber with thumb and forefinger, and follow this growth down to the tuber, pinching it off just above the tuber. Remove the young plant with its root intact, but leave the tuber in its pot. The young plant should be potted straight away and placed in a heated aquarium at a temperature of 21–23°C (70–75°F). After another two or three weeks the original tuber will send up another plant, which can also be removed and potted. This

can be repeated several times before the tuber is allowed to retain what you consider should be its final plant.

The live-bearing or viviparous group of tropical water lilies are those which bear young plants in the leaf sinus (Fig. 129). As these young plantlets develop roots they can be removed and potted into small pots of sandy compost. These are stood in water which is maintained at a temperature of 15–18°C (60–65°F), potting them into progressively larger pots as necessary. They should grow strongly throughout the first winter and may even flower.

Sometimes multi-headed plants will occur following this method of propagation and these will generally have smaller flowers than the single-headed plants raised from tubers and will produce irregularly placed clumps of foliage on the surface of the water. When well established little can be done about this condition but if spotted early enough the hasty division of the dividing crown will solve the problem.

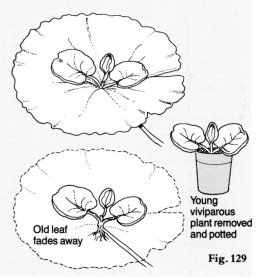

Old leaf fades away

Young viviparous plant removed and potted

Fig. 129

Fig. 129 Some tropical water lilies produce plantlets on their leaves. These can be detached and grown on individually.

thus enhance rooting. If the cut is made at an angle an even greater potential rooting zone is exposed. Hormone rooting powders or liquids are invaluable aids to propagation as they encourage the initiation of

root-forming cells and at the same time provide a degree of protection from fungal infections.

After the end of the cutting has been dipped in the hormone preparation it can be inserted in the rooting medium. The choice of material is wide, but a mixture of equal parts peat and coarse sand has proved to be very satisfactory, although in recent years many gardeners have turned to perlite as a clean and successful alternative to sand. Shallow pans are the most useful containers to use, the cuttings being inserted around the edge. Nobody has discovered why, but all cuttings seem to root better when inserted around the edge of a pot or pan.

A moist atmosphere is desirable and this can be provided by inverting a large jar or plastic bag over the pan. Rooting times vary according to the subject, but when the growing point shows signs of growth the cuttings must be removed and potted. It is preferable to pot cuttings as soon as they produce roots. Allowing them to become entangled leads to losses when they are lifted. The roots are extremely brittle and easily broken.

Potting
Pot rooted cuttings individually in small pots. As they do not have a rootball great care needs to be taken to see that a pot of sufficient size is used to accommodate the existing root system and is in-keeping with the aerial parts of the plant. One of the commonest errors in potting rooted cuttings is to put them into too large a pot with the idea that they will not require potting on. This is a grave mistake, for what usually happens is that the large body of compost around each plant becomes very wet and stale. The young roots come into contact with this and then die back.

When placed in a pot each plant should be held firmly and the compost gently poured around the roots. The young plant should be at the same level in the compost in the pot as it was in the pan in which it was rooted. Do not firm the compost, not even if using a soilbased kind, but allow the first watering to settle it.

Root cuttings
Root cuttings can be taken of a number of bog-garden plants, notably primulas. These are removed from plants that are lifted during the dormant winter period. The best roots are those filled with the vigour of youth which are substantial enough to exist on their own, without desiccation, yet are no thicker than a pencil.

If this kind of material is cut into sections 2.5 cm (1 in) or so long, laid horizontally in trays of good potting compost and placed in a cold frame, young plants will be in evidence by late spring. These can then be lifted and treated as seedlings, being potted individually in small pots and planted out the following winter.

Division
Many herbaceous bog plants can be propagated by division in early spring, using the technique described for marginal plants in Chapter 7.

Shrubby bog plant propagation
There are relatively few woody plants that are suited to the water garden or streamside, but the salix or willows and coloured-stemmed cornus are among these, and important they are, too, particularly as when stooled they provide the only winter colour at the waterside. It is this technique of stooling — cutting back the growths annually — that provides the material for their propagation: hardwood cuttings. Ideally cuttings of this kind should be taken during the autumn or early winter, but if prunings are depended upon for winter colour reasonable success can be obtained during early spring.

When choosing suitable cutting material avoid any shoots that are thin and likely to dry out before rooting, but also any that are thicker than a pencil, as these are likely to be of wood that is too old to root easily. Trim the cuttings to a leaf joint and then push them into well-prepared soil to about half their length. Some gardeners take out a trench and put sand in the bottom before lining out the cuttings and backfilling. This is unnecessary with salix or cornus as both root freely when merely pushed into the soil.

Cuttings inserted during autumn will be well rooted by the spring, but those taken during the spring will have to remain undisturbed until the autumn.

CHAPTER 9
Pond Problems

As with all other garden features a pond is not without its share of problems. However, there are few of these that cannot be overcome by good hygiene and routine maintenance. For most gardeners the watery environment and its inhabitants are unfamiliar and it is this which can make the potential difficulties seem greater than in the general garden. In reality a pool and its inhabitants are subjected to far fewer problems than the average allotment.

Pests and diseases of plants

Fortunately few pests and diseases of plants need cause any great anxiety, although it must be appreciated that even mild infestations create difficulties beyond those encountered in the open garden. Insecticides and fungicides cannot be used in or around a pool where fish are present and so often more traditional manual means of control have to be resorted to.

Common plant pests
Brown China mark moth
This is a common pest in the garden pool, cutting and shredding aquatic plant foliage and making a shelter for itself prior to pupation by sticking down pieces of leaf in which it weaves a greyish silky cocoon (Fig. 130). The damage to plants is often extensive, chewed and distorted leaves crumbling towards the edges and surrounded by pieces of floating, decomposing foliage.

Eggs are laid during late summer in neat rows on the floating foliage of aquatic plants. Within a few weeks the tiny caterpillars emerge and burrow into the undersides of the succulent foliage, later making small oval cases out of the leaves. The caterpillars continue to feed in this manner until late autumn, hibernating for the winter but re-appearing in the spring to continue their trail of destruction.

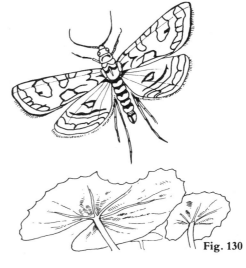

Fig. 130 Brown China mark moth. This has caterpillars that can destroy aquatic plant foliage.

Fig. 130

Small infestations can be hand picked and all pieces of innocent-looking floating leaf should be netted and discarded as these often have cocoons attached. When damage is widespread it is best to defoliate all aquatic plants with floating leaves and consign the debris to a compost heap. All the plant species likely to be affected will rapidly regenerate healthy growth.

Caddis flies
Most species of caddis fly to some extent have larvae which feed on the foliage of aquatic plants (Fig. 131). Many are totally aquatic at their larval stage and swim around inside little shelters made from sticks, sand shells and pieces of plant.

Caddis flies visit pools in the cool of the evening, depositing up to 100 eggs at a time in a mass of jelly which swells up immediately it touches the water. It often becomes hooked around submerged foliage in a long cylindrical string, or attached to a waterside plant so that it can trail in the water. The larvae hatch out after about 10

Fig. 131 All the larvae of the caddis flies damage aquatic plants.

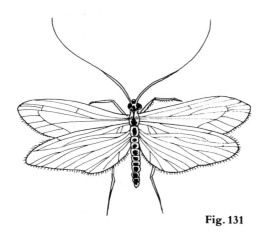

Fig. 131

days, immediately starting to spin their silken cases and collecting debris and plant material with which to construct their shelters. At this time they feed voraciously on aquatic plants, eating leaves, stems, flowers or roots. They eventually pupate in the pool or among reeds and rushes at the water's edge. The emergent adults are dull coloured moth-like insects with greyish or brown wings.

Chemical control is impossible, as the pests hide themselves in their protective shelters, but an adequate stock of fish will help to keep the population under control.

False leaf-mining midge

In most gardens this is not a serious pest of

Fig. 132
Water-lily aphis are as destructive to aquatic plants as black bean aphis are to broad beans.

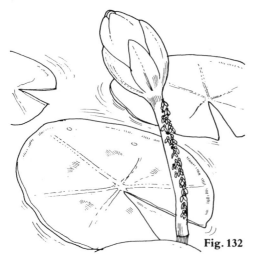

Fig. 132

aquatic plants. It is most irritating, though, the tiny larvae eating a narrow tracery of lines all over the surface of the foliage of floating leaves. The eaten areas begin to decay and large areas of leaf become detached and decompose.

Forcible spraying of the foliage with a strong jet of clear water provides some measure of control.

Water-lily aphid

A widespread and troublesome pest of water lilies and other succulent aquatic plants (Fig. 132). It attacks leaves and flowers with impunity, having the same effect on aquatic plants that black bean aphid has on broad beans.

Eggs from the late-summer brood of adults are laid on the boughs of plum and cherry trees during early autumn for over-wintering. These hatch the following spring and the winged female adults fly to the plants. Here a sexual reproduction takes place, the females giving birth to live wing-less females. These continue to reproduce every few days. As autumn approaches, a generation of winged males and females is produced. These unite sexually and then fly to the plum or cherry trees to deposit their eggs.

During the summer the only effective control is to forcibly spray the foliage with clear water from a hosepipe and hope that the fish will clear up the pests as they fall in the pool and before they have an opportunity to crawl back onto the foliage.

Much can be done to reduce the over-wintering population by spraying all the plum and cherry trees in the garden with tar-oil wash during the winter when the trees are completely dormant. This effectively breaks the life cycle.

Water-lily beetle

This is a very difficult pest to deal with (Fig. 133). Water-lily leaves become stripped of their surface layer by shiny black larvae with distinctive yellow bellies. The leaves then begin to decompose.

The tiny dark brown beetles hibernate during the winter in poolside vegetation and migrate to the water lilies during early summer. Here they deposit eggs in clusters on the leaf surfaces. A week or so later the larvae hatch. These feed on water-lily foliage until pupation occurs, either on the foliage or surrounding aquatic plants. Under suitable warm conditions as many as four broods may be produced in a season.

Spraying forcibly with a jet of clear water to dislodge the pests is the only remedy, although the removal of the tops of marginal plants during early autumn will do much to prevent the adults from hiding in the vicinity of the pond and hopefully dissuade them from launching such a vigorous attack the next season.

Common plant diseases
Water-lily leaf spot
This appears as dark patches on the leaves of water lilies, eventually rotting through and causing their disintegration. It is particularly prevalent in damp humid weather. As soon as noticed, affected leaves should be removed and destroyed.

A similar species causes the foliage to become brown and dry at the edges, eventually crumbling and wasting away. Removal and destruction of all diseased leaves is the only effective cure, although a weak solution of Bordeaux mixture sprayed over the foliage can be recommended for checking its spread in the absence of fish.

Water-lily crown rot
The crown rot common to water lilies is believed to be caused by a relative of potato blight. Water lilies with dark or mottled foliage, especially yellow cultivars, appear to be the most susceptible. The leaf and flower stems become soft and blackened and the rootstocks take on a gelatinous appearance and are foul-smelling.

Affected plants must be removed immediately and destroyed before they infect their neighbours. When other water lilies are in danger of becoming infected and it is possible to remove the fish, impregnating the water with copper sulphate provides some protection. The crystals should be tied in a muslin bag attached to a long stick and dragged through the water until completely dissolved.

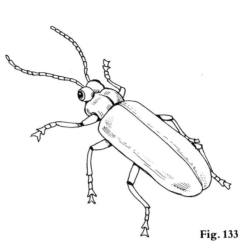

Fig. 133

Fig. 133
Fortunately the water-lily beetle is of local occurrence, but where it has become established it causes extensive damage.

In recent years a very virulent form of this disease has become established in commercial stocks of water lilies. This does not respond to treatment and infected plants should be destroyed and the pool sterilized with sodium hypochlorite.

Pests and diseases of fish
Common pests of fish
Anchor worm
This pest is not technically a worm but a crustacean (Fig. 134). It is a destructive little creature with a tiny slender tube-like body and barbed head which embeds itself into the flesh of its host causing unsightly lesions and tumour-like growths.

Control can only be effected by capturing the host fish, holding it in a wet cloth and then touching the parasites with a brush dipped in a solution of potassium permanganate or ordinary household paraffin.

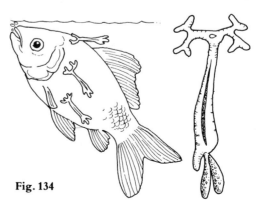

Fig. 134

Fig. 134 Anchor worm is an unpleasant pest of fish, but is not difficult to control.

This kills the parasites which can then be withdrawn with tweezers and the open wound dressed with a mild antiseptic disinfectant solution.

Dragonfly

All the common species of dragonfly have naiad or developing stages which are predatory on fish. Naiads can vary in their period of development within species and between species from one to five years. They are unpleasant-looking creatures resembling small scorpions and varying in colour from green and brown to grey. All their young life is spent in the water clinging to submerged and partially submerged aquatic plant life awaiting suitable prey to pass by.

When likely prey is seen, the naiad shoots forward a 'mask' from beneath its chin. This mask is like a pair of jaws with strong hooks which grip the prey and then retract, bringing it back to the naiad's mouth. Although dragonfly naiads can seldom eat a fish at one go, they are capable of causing very unpleasant injuries and should be removed from pools whenever noticed.

Fish louse

Fish lice are parasitic crustaceans which cling to the bodies and gill plates of all kinds of ornamental pool fish (Fig. 135). They have a somewhat flattened shell-like carapace with a small abdomen projecting, and strange feelers at the anterior end that are used for attachment to their host.

Males and females look identical, but it is only the females that are parasitic. These can be easily dislodged if the affected fish is held in a wet net and the parasites are

dabbed with a drop of paraffin from a child's paint brush. As the tissue beneath may have been damaged the fish should be dipped in a solution of malachite green as a precaution against fungal infection before being reintroduced to the pool.

Great diving beetle

Both adults and larvae of the great diving beetle prey on young fish. The adult beetle is a handsome fellow with a hard, oval shaped, chitinous body of dark brown with a distinctive golden border up to 5 cm (2 in) long. The larvae are of similar appearance to dragonfly naiads but seldom more than 3.8 cm (1½ in) long. Being wonderful fliers, the adults can spread quickly from pond to pond.

The only control is to net them whenever they are seen and before they have an opportunity to reproduce.

Great silver diving beetle

The hideous-looking larvae of the great silver diving beetle can create havoc in a pool, devouring small fish, tadpoles and water snails. The larvae are seldom less than 5 cm (2 in) long, more or less sausage shaped, of a dark brown colour and have three pairs of legs just behind the head which are used to drag it along.

Control is very difficult as the beetles can travel freely from one pond to another. The netting and disposal of adults is all that can be recommended.

Hydra

These strange little creatures are of octopus-like appearance and spend their lives attached to submerged plants. They capture their prey by means of stinging tentacles which paralize the victim. Their usual diet consists of worms and water fleas, although severe infestations can decimate the fish fry population.

Control is difficult as they are so very small. Hand picking is not practical, for while they are visible to the naked eye, once the plant that they are clinging to is touched, they virtually 'dissolve' into an indistinct gelatinous mass. Only when they are being particularly troublesome is it

Fig. 135 The fish louse is a parasitic crustacean which can cause severe damage if left unnoticed.

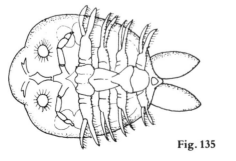

Fig. 135

124

worth while using a chemical control. This involves removing the fish and adding an ammonium salt to the water and then emptying and refilling the pool with fresh water.

Leeches

All leeches are harmful in varying degrees to both fish and snails, but it is only the fish leech which really makes itself a nuisance (Fig. 136). In common with other leeches it has numerous blind sacs within its body for storing blood which it sucks from its unfortunate victims. One gorging can last for a couple of weeks, during which it lingers harmlessly among the water plants digesting its meal. Most leeches are hermaphrodite, sometimes mating in pairs, but self-fertilizing as well. They generally attach their eggs to aquatic plants, although at least one of the minor species carries its eggs around with it.

Control is difficult, but where there is a severe infestation a piece of raw meat suspended in the water from a length of string will attract considerable numbers which can be removed and destroyed. Fish with leeches attached should be held in a wet net or cloth and a dab of salt placed on the tail of each leech. They will then detach themselves.

Water boatmen

These insects feed chiefly on other aquatic insects, tadpoles and fish spawn, but are capable of inflicting nasty wounds on large fish and killing small fish outright. The commonest species is a small roughly oval creature with a black belly and pale brown back with a conspicuous triangular mark in the centre. Its legs appear like oars and propel it on its back through the water at great speed.

Control is not easy and is restricted to regular netting and disposal.

Water scorpion

This is a vicious aquatic creature with a strong pair of front legs with which it grabs its prey, and a hideous mouthpiece which it uses to pierce and suck its victim dry. It sits motionless for hours among aquatic plants

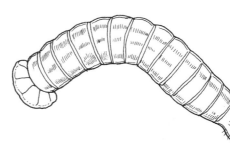

Fig. 136

or on the floor of a pool waiting for suitable prey to pass by. Breeding takes place during the spring, its eggs being deposited among decomposing plant remains and blanket weed.

General pool hygiene deprives them of suitable places to breed and forms an important part of their control. Hand picking is also possible when they can be seen.

Water stick insect

This relative of the water scorpion has similar unpleasant habits. It is slightly larger than its cousin, but with a very thin body. Although not so frequently encountered, it can cause trouble if not discouraged by good pool hygiene.

Whirligig beetle

These are the remarkable little black rounded beetles which swim in fast spirals or circles on the surface of water. During spring and early summer they deposit eggs on the roots and submerged foliage of aquatic plants. The eggs hatch into small yellowish white larvae, roughly cylindrical in shape, and with three pairs of legs and several pairs of feathery appendages. They feed predominantly on other aquatic insect life, but also attack small fish and fry.

Control of the larvae is impossible and while hand picking of the adults is time consuming it is the only effective means of keeping the population within bounds.

Common diseases of fish
Dropsy

The condition known variously as dropsy or scale protrusion is understood to be of bacterial origin. Afflicted fish generally become distended with their scales standing out from the body and their internal organs filled with fluid. Although it is possible to have this drawn off with a hypodermic syringe, it is not an operation to be considered lightly. Most pool owners destroy affected fish.

Fin rot and tail rot

A number of bacterial infections have been blamed for this unpleasant condition, although the main culprit is still unknown. A fairly common disease, it usually appears first on the dorsal fin, spreading to others and quickly reducing them to short stubs. The first sign of the disease is a whitish line along the outer edge of the fin which gradually advances downwards. This leaves the outer margin badly frayed owing to the disintegration of the soft tissue between the hard rays of the fins. If infection creeps as far as the flesh the fish will almost certainly die.

However, if an affected fish is noticed in time, the badly frayed tissue can be removed with a pair of sharp scissors and the fish dipped in malachite green. The infection is likely to be checked and much of the lost tissue will regenerate.

Fungus

Every time a fish damages itself in any way it becomes open to attack from one of many fungal diseases (Fig. 137). Apart from attacking living fish, some of these can be seen on fish spawn and uneaten goldfish food. This indicates the potential value of scavenging fish and the importance of pool hygiene. When a large fish becomes infected with fungus it is a relatively simple matter to clear it up. However, with fry and small fish it is almost impossible and any tiny fish

that become infected should be humanely destroyed as soon as the disease is noticed.

There are many fungus cures available, mostly based on malachite green or methylene blue. These are used as dips into which diseased fish are immersed. A salt bath is often recommended and while this can be beneficial it is a slow and unreliable method of treating this ailment. If salt must be used ensure it is rock or sea salt, not iodized table salt.

When the fish has been dipped in a proprietory fungus cure, the cotton-wool-like growth of the fungus should fall away. After the fish has been re-introduced to the pool keep an eye open for re-infection as the raw areas of tissue will still be vulnerable.

Gill flukes

Gill flukes are minute creatures that are invisible to the naked eye. However, they can have a devastating effect on their hosts, causing them to swim in a violent and irrational manner, banging against the walls of the pool and periodically rushing to the surface of the water as if having a fit. The rate of breathing of an infected fish is greatly increased and the fins twitch constantly.

Various cures based on mild disinfectants and formalin have been tried with varying success in the past, but as at least half the fish treated die in any event, it is better to kill the fish humanely as soon as flukes are suspected.

Red pest

Although this is not particularly common, it is a very infectious bacterial disease. Affected fish become sluggish and constantly rise to the surface of the water. Rusty red patches appear on the sides and bellies and sometimes on the fins as well. It is best to destroy the entire stock of fish unless very choice individuals are involved. These can be kept in a tank of running water for several weeks, the constant flow of fresh water giving them hope of survival.

However, as fresh tap water also destroys their body mucilage, it is questionable as to whether the danger of red pest can be eliminated before fungal infection takes over.

Fig. 137 Fish fungus diseases are very common, but with modern medications are easily controlled.

Fig. 137

A pool in which the fish have suffered from red pest should remain fishless for several months before restocking, and if possible thoroughly scrubbed using sodium hypochorite.

Slime and skin diseases

A number of single-celled organisms cause skin disorders and slime disease. Afflicted fish can often be seen swimming against the edge or bottom of a pool as if they are trying to scrape themselves and relieve an irritation. They usually have folded fins and become covered in a bluish-white slimy deposit which would appear to be a combination of natural slime and parasites. Badly diseased fish must be destroyed, but mildly infected individuals can be bathed in a solution of acriflavine for two or three days with a reasonable expectation of recovery.

White spot disease or itch

This is a widespread and destructive disease. It is much more prevalent in the warmer temperatures of aquaria, but is a not infrequent assailant of pool fish, often having been introduced with freshly purchased stock that has spent a period of time in warmer and more amenable surroundings. In a garden pool, where the water temperature is invariably lower, the life cycle is slowed down and treatment can be given before too much damage is caused.

The white spot protozoan is a tiny organism, scarcely a millimetre across, but its presence for at least part of its life-cycle bedded in the skin of a fish does have a considerable effect on the host. Fish that have become badly infested look as if they have white measles, take on a pinched appearance and swim in an ungainly manner.

Severe attacks are difficult to cure and such fish are best destroyed from the outset. If a light sprinkling of spots is noticed on the tails or fins of a fish then this is generally curable, unless the fish is very tiny. Certainly fry that show infection should be destroyed.

White spot disease has several phases of development. In the initial stages the 'spores' or 'swarmers' bore their way into the skin of a living fish. Here they feed on their host until of an adult size and recognizable to us as white spots. The mature parasite leaves the fish through a puncture in the skin and then becomes free-swimming, eventually encysting. Inside the cysts they divide into upwards of 1000 spores — which leave the cyst in search of a host.

It is at this swarming stage that the disease can most effectively be controlled. The white spots which give the disease its common name are visible, but inaccessible until they rupture. The higher the water temperature, the shorter the period the swarmers have to locate a host; thus in warm water this period can be as little as two days. Therefore if infected fish are placed in tanks at a relatively warm temperature the swarmers will be released more quickly. If water is constantly flowing into the tanks these swarmers will be regularly washed away. When a pool is known to be infected it may be several weeks at a warm temperature before fresh fish can be safely introduced without fear of infection.

Apart from attempting to wash away the free-swimming stage or starving the infection of a host, there are various chemical treatments that can be tried. Most are based on an acriflavine solution, or else quinine salts like quinine sulphate or quinine hydrochloride, and mixtures such as methylene blue and acriflavine. The fish are kept for a period in a solution of one of these chemicals, the free-swimming stage being killed as it emerges. The fish can be re-introduced to a pool when the white spots have disappeared completely.

Apart from the cures prescribed, there are other ways to fight the disease. The most useful is prevention, for white spot can be easily introduced on plants and fish purchased from a local garden centre. Fish should receive a quarantine period before being placed in an established pool and if part of this treatment involves being treated with a white spot disease cure, then problems are unlikely to be encountered.

Other disorders

Cataract

An infrequent problem but one which is

readily spotted. Affected fish develop a white film over the eye. This starts with the pupil and eventually envelopes the whole eye. A mixture of one part by volume of iodine to nine parts glycerine dabbed onto the eye with cotton wool twice a day sometimes removes the film.

Chlorine damage
It is inevitable that the majority of pool owners have to fill their pools initially, or after cleaning out, directly from a tap. This water contains chlorine as a disinfectant for killing bacteria, but it can also be harmful to young fish and fry. In large volumes of water it takes some time to disperse and occasionally fish will suffer from its toxicity. Damaged fish have very pale gills with edges that are bleached white and an overall appearance of lethargy.

To prevent this occurring never introduce fish to a freshly filled pool; always leave the water standing for several days to allow the chlorine to evaporate.

Constipation
This is a most unpleasant disorder, usually associated with fish that live in small volumes of water and with a restricted diet. Affected fish trail a stream of excrement from the vent interspersed with tiny bubbles. This usually results from an unbalanced diet and any starchy foods must be immediately withdrawn and the fish placed in an aquarium where it can be fed a diet of boiled chopped cabbage or spinach along with regular introductions of live food.

If the condition persists the fish can be immersed in a solution of magnesium sulphate, but this is a last resort for if the change of diet has no effect within a few days it is likely that the fish will succumb.

Loss of balance
This is a physiological disorder in which fish swim in a drunken manner or suspend themselves upside down in the water. Sometimes constipation can bring about this condition, but it is more usually associated with a derangement of the swim bladder, the balancing mechanism of the fish.

A number of dubious remedies have been tried from time to time, including purging and altering the water temperature or the diet, but most are of little use. It is better to put such fish out of their misery from the beginning, as they become increasingly distressed with each day that passes.

Spawn binding
This disorder is more frequently encountered in an aquarium, but is not uncommon in small garden pools. Under normal circumstances a female fish can spawn when her body dictates. In an aquarium or small pool this is not always possible, especially when confined in an unpleasant crowded environment. In such circumstances the fish attempts to dissolve and reabsorb the eggs that were being developed. If this is unsuccessful, which can be the case when the female is undernourished, the eggs become hard and incapable of being expelled. They then decay within the fish and an accumulation of gas occurs which leads ultimately to the death of the fish.

Stripping the fish as described on p. 111 is occasionally successful and is well worth trying, although care must be taken to ensure that the internal organs are not damaged. Rather than trying to cure the condition it is better to try to prevent it from occuring. Fish with plenty of room and a varied diet seldom suffer from spawn binding.

Tumours
Any hard or raised lump that appears on the body of a fish should be treated with suspicion. Sometimes it is the beginning of an anchor-worm infestation, but where it clearly is not, then the fish should be destroyed, for treating tumours on small fish is a hazardous and painful business. Some aquarists are prepared to use a razor blade to investigate and sometimes operate, but the success rate is very low.

Wasting
Some fish which look emaciated and have arched backs and pinched bodies are merely suffering from the passage of time, but more likely they have become infected with

Carex pendula is one of the most graceful sedges. A most useful plant for shaded wet spots.

Iris laevigata grows in the water all the year round. One of the finest and toughest marginal plants for the garden pool.

Iris kaempferi, although associated with the water garden, is really a bog-garden plant. It will not tolerate standing in water during winter.

Iris pseudacorus
'Variegatus' is the
only yellow flag that
can be recommended
for the small pool.
Very fine foliage
during early spring.

Myosotis scorpioides is an aquatic and perennial version of our popular forget-me-not. Provides long lasting colour at the water's edge.

Discoloured water

Apart from the plants and fish, the greatest joy of a garden pool is the water itself, and it should be clear. Most water gardeners measure their success by the clarity of the water. Opaque water iş a pond owner's nightmare.

Dirty water

Dirty water is considered to be that which is brown, black or dark blue and often has a foul smell. Brown water is the result of fish stirring up the compost in plant containers while foraging for food. When a pool is planted as suggested earlier, with each container having a generous covering of pea gravel, there is rarely a problem.

Sometimes if the soil is rather light it drifts out through the lattice-work sides of the container. This can be prevented by lining the container initially with a square of hessian, thus retaining the soil but allowing water to percolate through and roots to escape.

If plants have been put into containers without a generous topdressing of gravel, then the only course of action is to clean out the pool and replant.

Water that is blue-black or has a thick whitish scum or oily film around the edges is usually polluted by decaying organic matter, usually the build-up of decomposing leaves from nearby trees. It almost inevitably has a foul smell, is very low in oxygen and regular deaths of fish and snails occur.

A thorough clean out is the only answer. The walls of the pool must be thoroughly scrubbed and it is advantageous if the pool can then be left to dry out in the open air for a day or two. Any plants that look in good health can be returned to the pool, but not without being thoroughly washed and replanted in good clean compost in containers that have received a vigorous scrubbing.

Algae-laden water

Aquatic algae are probably the greatest problem that the pool keeper encounters. They occur in a wide range of forms from the free floating dust-like kinds to the clinging mermaid's hair and the long filamentous spirogyra. The tiniest kinds are suspended in the water and if a hand is passed through, a greenish smear is deposited. Filamentous algae or blanket weed are more substantial and can be pulled out of the water by the handful, while the kind known as mermaid's hair clings to baskets and the poolside and can be removed in tufts if pulled sharply.

Control of the free-floating kinds is not difficult with an algaecide based on potassium permanganate, but its effect is short lived and if not carefully administered during warm weather will turn the water yellow.

Filamentous algae can be controlled with algaecides based on copper sulphate, but it is important that all dead algae is removed after treatment to prevent the deoxygenation of the water. Proprietary algaecides should always be used. Straight chemicals must never be used by the uninitiated.

Some gardeners believe that the use of copper-sulphate crystals in a muslin bag dragged through the water will assist in algae control. While it is true that this can be effective, a lot depends on the chemistry of the water. If the water is hard the copper sulphate will unite with the carbonate of the calcium carbonate to form a precipitate of copper carbonate, thus reducing its effect. Water temperature is also critical: for example, it is likely that the unstable calcium bicarbonate normally found in tap water will leave a higher concentration of calcium carbonate during warmer weather. Fish can be harmed by copper sulphate, for when applied too liberally it combines with their body slime and causes asphyxiation.

The foregoing algae controls are not permanent cures for the problem, nor do they replace the natural balance which produces healthy conditions. They are essentially temporary aids for a new pool until the submerged plants have become established and can compete on an equal footing with the algae. They can also be used in difficult periods in an established pool, particularly during the spring when an algal bloom develops before the higher plants have really got growing. Clear water at this time is not only visually desirable, but permits the submerged plants to make more rapid growth.

the virulent fish tuberculosis. This cannot be contracted by humans. It causes extensive wasting and eventual death with no prospect of relief or cure.

Other problems

There are few other problems which regularly present themselves to the pool owner. Birds bathing in the margins sometimes bring herbicides in on their feathers and cause losses among the fish. Planting marginal areas generously overcomes this problem. Cats sometimes make themselves a nuisance when they fish for goldfish, but this is not a serious problem and decisions have to be taken as to priorities — cat or pool! The only other serious nuisance is the heron.

Coping with the heron

Most pools will be visited from time to time by a heron, but few people will realize it, for the heron visits early in the morning. It fishes by standing in or beside the water, making a stab for its unfortunate victim. Large goldfish are regularly taken and young fish are equally vulnerable.

Some garden centres sell special anti-heron netting for covering pools, but this is unsightly and creates all kinds of difficulties when surrounding vegetation grows through.

The simplest and most effective method of control is by erecting a series of short canes around the perimeter of the pool about 15 cm (6 in) high from which black garden cotton or fishing line is fastened to give the effect of a low fence. When the heron goes fishing it naturally walks towards the water, but its legs come into contact with the line which it cannot see. After making several attempts to reach the pool, and being met with the same hazard each time, it generally flies off.

PART 3

ENCYCLOPAEDIA OF PLANTS

WATER LILIES
Hardy Water Lilies ● *Tropical Water Lilies*

DEEP-WATER AQUATICS
Pond Lilies ● *Sacred Lotus*

MARGINAL PLANTS
Hardy Marginal Plants ● *Tender Marginal Plants*

SUBMERGED AQUATICS
Hardy Submerged Plants ● *Tender Submerged Plants*

FLOATING PLANTS
Hardy Floating Plants ● *Tender Floating Plants*

BOG GARDEN PLANTS
Bog Garden Perennials ● *Bog Garden Ferns* ● *Shrubby Bog Plants*

CHAPTER 10
Water Lilies

The true water lilies or *Nymphaea* are among the loveliest aquatic plants, providing elegance and colour throughout the summer. They mostly live in the deeper parts of pools, although some of the smaller pygmy kinds enjoy shallow margins or a tub or sink garden. Although in larger stretches of water they are planted directly into mud on the pool floor, they are most easily cultivated in containers.

The figures following the description of each plant indicate the depths of water in which it will grow successfully. The surface spread of each plant can be judged as being between one and one and a half times the depth at which the plant is growing. Therefore, a plant suited to growing in 60 cm (2 ft) of water and living in that depth will have a spread of between 60 and 90 cm (2 and 3 ft).

Hardy water lilies

'Albatross'
Medium-growing water lily with white blossoms up to 15 cm (6 in) across. Leaves purplish when young but passing to deep green with age. 30–60 cm (1–2 ft).

'Amabilis'
Large star like salmon-pink flowers up to 25 cm (10 in) across. These deepen to soft rose with age. The bright yellow stamens turn to fiery orange before the blossoms fade. Large deep green leaves. 45–60 cm (1½–2½ ft).

'American Star'
A new introduction with bold star-like pink flowers up to 15 cm (6 in) across held just above the water. Bold green leaves. 45–90 cm (1½–3 ft).

'Andreana'
Cup-shaped blossoms up to 20 cm (8 in) across, of deep brick red streaked and shaded with cream and yellow. These are held above the glossy green, maroon-blotched leaves which have characteristic overlapping lobes. 60–90 cm (2–3 ft).

'Arc-en-ciel'
Until recently this bizarre variegated-foliage cultivar was believed to be extinct. It was rediscovered in Japan, taken to the United States where it has been redistributed and can now be found in Europe as well. An old cultivar, but one with a great future. Small, papery, scented, blush-pink flowers with sepals that are splashed and stained with rose. Leaves boldly splashed with purple rose, white and bronze. 45–60 cm (1½–2 ft).

'Arethusa'
Rounded deep rose-pink flowers up to 15 cm (6 in) across. The centre intensifies to crimson and the rose-pink outer petals are tipped with light red., 45–60 cm (1½–2 ft).

'Atropurpurea'
Deep crimson blossoms up to 15 cm (6 in) across and of a satiny texture. Pale yellow stamens and distinct incurving petals. The foliage is deep red when young, but passes to green with maturity. 30–45 cm (1–1½ ft).

'Attraction'
This is a splendid cultivar for larger pools. Unfortunately there are a number of different plants masquerading as 'Attraction' but most commercially available stock is fairly close to the following description. Large garnet-red flowers, up to 23 cm (9 in) across, attractively flecked with white. Rich mahogany stamens tipped with

yellow. Sepals off-white suffused with rose-pink. Leaves large, plain green. 30 cm–1.2 m (2–4 ft).

'Aurora'

A small-growing water lily well suited to tub culture. Cream flower buds which open to yellow and then pass through orange to blood red with each succeeding day. Small olive-green leaves heavily mottled with purple. 30–45 cm (1–1½ ft).

N. candida

A very hardy species native to northern Europe and parts of Asia. Small scentless white cup-shaped blossoms with golden stamens and crimson stigmas. Rarely as much as 10 cm (4 in) across and sporting ovate sepals strongly tinged with green. The leaves have basal lobes which overlap and prominent veins beneath. 30–45 cm (1–1½ ft).

N. caroliniana

A North American plant believed to be a natural hybrid rather than a species. Very fragrant soft pink blossoms with slender petals and striking yellow stamens. The leaves are pale green. There are three named cultivars of this plant, each very different and extremely beautiful. 'Nivea' has large pure white fragrant flowers, 'Perfecta' is salmon pink and 'Rosea' bold blossoms of rose pink. The named sorts are very free-flowering. 30–45 cm (1–1½ ft).

'Charles de Meurville'

A vigorous hardy water lily with large plum-coloured blossoms, the petals of which are tipped and streaked with white. The flowers darken to deep wine with age. Leaves large, deep olive green. 60 cm–1.2 m (2–4 ft).

'Col. A.J. Welch'

A large and rather coarse water lily well suited to large expanses of water. Not a good plant for small garden pools but widely offered in garden centres. Soft yellow flowers among abundant green foliage. Sometimes reproduces viviparously. 60 cm–1.2 m (2–4 ft).

'Collosea'

Probably the most vigorous pink water lily. Requires a large expanse of water to do it justice. Flowers flesh pink, fragrant and up to 23 cm (9 in) across. Foliage dark olive-green. 60 cm–1.8 m (2–6 ft).

'Comanche'

Like 'Aurora', another of the 'changeable' water lilies. Small deep orange blooms change to bronze with age. These are held just above the foliage, which is purplish when young, turning quickly to green when fully expanded. 30–45 cm (1–1½ ft).

'Conqueror'

Large crimson cup-shaped flowers flecked with white and up to 15 cm (6 in) across. Broad incurving petals, sepals with white interiors and bright yellow stamens. Juvenile foliage purple, turning to green. 45–60 cm (1½–2 ft).

'Ellisiana'

Small wine-red flowers with bright orange stamens. Green foliage. Most reliable and free flowering. One of the best reds. 30–60 cm (1–2 ft).

'Escarboucle'

One of the best-known reds, but only suitable for large expanses of water. Large crimson flowers up to 30 cm (1 ft) across, richly fragrant and with a central boss of bright yellow stamens. Bright green foliage. Although frequently offered by garden centres, this should be regarded with caution as it is too vigorous for most garden pools. 60 cm–1.8 m (2–6 ft).

'Formosa'

Fragrant blossoms of bright shocking pink up to 15 cm (6 in) across which fade to pale mauve with age. Leaves pale green. 45–60 cm (1½–2½ ft).

'Froebeli'

Deep blood-red flowers with orange stamens. Dull purplish-green leaves. A very popular and free-flowering cultivar. Leaves medium sized, plain green. 45–60 cm (1½–2 ft).

'Gladstoniana'

Very large flowers, up to 30 cm (1 ft) across. Pure white, waxy, and with a bold cluster of golden stamens. Leaves large, circular and dark green with leaf stalks distinctively marked with brown. One of the largest hardy water lilies and best suited to very large ponds and lakes, although frequently offered at garden centres to home gardeners. 60 cm—2.4 m (2—8 ft).

'Gloire de Temple sur Lot'

One of the finest but most expensive water lilies. Fragrant, fully double rosy-pink blossoms. Petals numerous and incurved giving each flower something of the appearance of a show chrysanthemum. The petals tend to pale with age. Stamens bright yellow. This cultivar usually takes at least a season before settling into a regular flowering pattern. Leaves large, green. 45—90 cm (1½—3 ft).

'Gloriosa'

Very fragrant, deep current-red flowers up to 15 cm (6 in) across with five conspicuous sepals and a cluster of reddish-orange stamens. Leaves rounded and dull bronze green. 45—90 cm (1½—3 ft).

'Gonnere'

This is sometimes refered to as 'Crystal White', a fully double pure white cultivar in which each blossom has conspicuous bright green sepals. Foliage medium or large and a fresh pea green colour. One of the finest hardy water lilies. The flowers look just like snowballs bobbing about on the water. 45—75 cm (1½—2½ ft).

'Graziella'

Orange-red blossoms, rarely more than 5 cm (2 in) across, each with a cluster of deep orange stamens. Very free flowering. Small olive-green leaves blotched with purple and brown. An excellent sink or tub plant. 30—60 cm (1—2 ft).

'Hermine'

Pure white tulip-shaped flowers held slightly above the water. Leaves dark green, medium-sized and more or less oval. A good tough character for the average pool. 45—75 cm (1½—2½ ft).

'Indiana'

Small orange-red flowers which darken to deep red with age. Green foliage heavily blotched and splashed with purple. 45—75 cm (1½—2½ ft).

'James Brydon'

A very distinctive water lily with large crimson paeony-shaped flowers and dark purplish-green leaves often flecked with maroon. 45—90 cm (1½—3 ft).

N. × laydekeri 'Alba'

A small-growing plant well suited to the modern water garden. Pure white blossoms with bright yellow stamens and an unusual fragrance rather akin to that of a freshly opened packet of tea. Small to medium plain green leaves. 30—60 cm (1—2 ft).

N. × laydekeri 'Fulgens'

Fragrant bright crimson flowers with reddish stamens and dark green sepals with rose-blush interiors. Foliage dark green with purplish undersides and brown speckling around the leaf stalks. 30—60 cm (1—2 ft).

N. × laydekeri 'Lilacea'

Fragrant soft pink flowers which turn to deep rosy-crimson with age. Bright yellow stamens and dark green sepals edged with rose. Glossy green leaves sparingly blotched with brown. 30—60 cm (1—2 ft).

N. × laydekeri 'Purpurata'

Rich vinous-red blossoms with acutely pointed petals and bright orange stamens. Small green leaves, purplish beneath, with black or maroon splashes on the upper surfaces. 30—60 cm (1—2 ft).

N. × laydekeri 'Rosea'

Small, deep rose, fragrant, cup-shaped flowers which turn to crimson with age. Petals somewhat incurved and surrounding clusters of orange-red stamens. Leaves green above, reddish beneath. 30—60 cm (1—2 ft).

'Louise'
Fully double, deep red, cup-shaped blossoms up to 15 cm (6 in) across. Stamens yellow, sepals brownish green. 60−90 cm (2−3 ft).

'Madame Wilfron Gonnere'
Large cup-shaped almost fully double white blossoms spotted with deep rose and intensifying to soft pink in the centre. 45−75 cm (1½−2½ ft).

N. × marliacea 'Albida'
A very popular large-flowered white cultivar. Fragrant blossoms up to 15 cm (6 in) across held just above the water. Sepals and reverses of petals often flushed with pink. Leaves deep green with purplish undersides. 45−90 cm (1½−3 ft).

N. × marliacea 'Carnea'
A vigorous and widely grown cultivar, too large for most garden pools. The flesh-pink blossoms with bright golden stamens are often 20 cm (8 in) or more across and have a distinct vanilla fragrance. Leaves large and plain green, but purplish when young. Newly planted specimens often produce white blossoms for the first season. 45 cm− 1.5 m (1½−5 ft).

N. × marliacea 'Chromatella'
Flowers rich canary yellow up to 15 cm (6 in) across. Petals broad and incurved. Sepals pale yellow flushed with pink. Large olive-green leaves boldly splashed with maroon and bronze. 45−75 cm (1½−2½ ft).

N. × marliacea 'Flammea'
Fiery-red flowers flecked with white. Outer petals deep pink. Stamens rich orange. Large olive-green leaves heavily mottled with chocolate and maroon. 45−75 cm (1½−2½ ft).

N. × marliacea 'Ignea'
Deep crimson tulip-like flowers up to 15 cm (6 in) across. Sepals pale green edged with rose. Leaves rich coppery bronze, passing to dark green with age. There is often a sprinkling of chocolate-brown mottling on adult foliage. 45−75 cm (1½−2½ ft).

N. × marliacea 'Rosea'
Very similar to *N*. × *marliacea* 'Carnea', but of a much more intense pink. Fragrant blossoms. Purplish-green immature foliage, older leaves dark green. 45 cm−1.2 m (1½−4 ft).

'Masaniello'
Fragrant cup shaped rose-pink flowers flecked with crimson and ageing to deep carmine. Sepals white, stamens deep orange. 45−90 cm (1½−3 ft).

'Meteor'
Crimson blossoms streaked with white, but darkening with age. Sepals striped with red, stamens bright yellow. Deep green leaves with purplish undersides. 45−75 cm (1½−2½ ft).

'Moorei'
Soft yellow blossoms that are very similar to those of *N*. × *marliacea* 'Chromatella'. Green leaves irregularly sprinkled with purple spots. 45−75 cm (1½−2½ ft).

'Mrs. Richmond'
Pale rose-pink blossoms which pass to crimson as they mature. The bases of the petals are bright red and the stamens golden yellow. Sepals are tipped with white. 45− 75 cm (1½−2½ ft).

'Norma Gedye'
An Australian cultivar with semi-double deep rose-pink blossoms among olive-green foliage. 30−45 cm (1−1½ ft).

'Odalisque'
Attractive rose-pink star-like flowers which pale to shell-pink. Bright golden stamens. Foliage light green. Very free-flowering, but often a short-lived inhabitant of pools. 45−75 cm (1½−2½ ft).

N. odorata (Sweet-scented water lily).
A first-class species for the average modern pool. Sweet-smelling white blossoms up to 15 cm (6 in) in diameter. Petals numerous,

elliptical, mostly pointed and grading through intermediate stages to stamens. Sepals green, but often purplish within. Bright green leaves, usually purplish beneath and often entirely this colour when young. 45–75 cm (1½–2½ ft).

N. odorata var. minor (Millpond water lily)
A much smaller-growing plant with fragrant, white star-shaped blossoms some 8 cm (3 in) in diameter. Sepals pale green or olive. Flower stalks mahogany coloured. Soft green leaves with dark red undersides. A good water lily for tubs or shallow pools. 30 cm (1 ft).

N. odorata var. rosea (Cape Cod water lily).
A soft pink variety of the white species. Flowers fragrant, 10 cm (4 in) or more across. Stamens yellow. Leaves bronze at first, but turning green with maturity. 45–60 cm (1½–2 ft).

N. odorata 'Eugene de Land'
Star-shaped blossoms of deep apricot pink held above the water. Petals long and incurved. Stamens deep yellow. Sweetly scented. 45–75 cm (1½–2½ ft).

N. odorata 'Firecrest'
Deep pink blossoms with distinctive red-tipped stamens. Dark green leaves with a strong purplish caste. 45–90 cm (1½–3 ft).

N. odorata 'Helen Fowler'
Heavily scented deep rose flowers up to 25 cm (10 in) across above large soft green leaves. 45–90 cm (1½–3 ft).

N. odorata 'Sulphurea'
Small star shaped moderately fragrant canary-yellow blossoms above dark green heavily mottled foliage. 30 cm (1 ft).

N. odorata 'Sulphurea Grandiflora'
This is similar in almost all respects, but more substantial and generally freer flowering. 45–60 cm (1½–2 ft).

N. odorata 'Turicensis'
Heavily fragrant soft rose blossoms. Similar to *N. odorata* var. *rosea*, but with slightly smaller flowers. 45–75 cm (1½–2½ ft).

N. odorata 'William B. Shaw'
Probably the finest *odorata* cultivar. Large, fragrant, open, creamy-pink flowers with deep red internal zoning. Petals narrow and pointed. Leaves rounded and plain green. 45–60 cm (1½–2 ft).

'Pearl of the Pool'
Fully double bright pink flowers with bright yellow stamens. Rounded plain green foliage, coppery beneath. 45–75 cm (1½–2½ ft).

'Picciola'
Large, open, star-shaped flowers up to 20 cm (8 in) across of deep crimson are held just above the water. Leaves reddish green, splashed and daubed with maroon. 45 cm–1.5 m (1½–3½ ft).

'Pink Opal'
Delicate cup-shaped blossoms of coral pink. Unopened buds are always spherical, like small marbles. Foliage green flushed with bronze. 45–75 cm (1½–2½ ft).

'Pink Sensation'
Very free flowering fragrant pink water lily with starry blossoms. Deep green rounded leaves with reddish undersides. 45–75 cm (1½–2½ ft).

N. × pygmaea 'Alba'
The tiniest water lily of all. Each white blossom is no more than 2.5 cm (1 in) across. The leaves are small, oval, dark green with purple reverses. Up to 30 cm (1 ft).

N. pygmaea 'Helvola'
Canary-yellow flowers with orange stamens produced in abundance. Leaves olive green, heavily mottled with purple and brown. Up to 30 cm (1 ft).

N. pygmaea 'Rubra'
Tiny blood-red blossoms with bright

orange stamens. Small rounded purplish-green leaves with reddish undersides. Up to 30 cm (1 ft).

'René Gérard'
Medium-sized open blossoms of rose-pink splashed with crimson towards the centres. Leaves rounded, plain green. 45–75 cm (1½–2½ ft).

'Rose Arey'
Large star shaped rose-pink flowers with a distinctive aniseed fragrance. Stamens bright yellow. Juvenile foliage crimson, adult leaves green tinged with red. 45–75 cm (1½–2½ ft).

'Sioux'
Pale yellow blossoms which pass through orange to crimson with each succeeding day. Petals acutely pointed and delicately spotted with red. Leaves dark green mottled purple. 30–45 cm (1–1½ ft).

'Somptuosa'
An early flowering water lily with large, fragrant, double pink flowers. Stamens vivid orange. Leaves rounded, plain green. 45–60 cm (1½–2 ft).

'Sultan'
Bright cherry-red flowers irregularly streaked with white. Leaves rounded, dark green. 45–75 cm (1½–2½ ft).

'Sunrise'
Large, fragrant, canary-yellow blossoms up to 20 cm (8 in) across. Dull green rounded-elliptical leaves, occasionally blotched with brown, reddish beneath. 45–90 cm (1½–3 ft).

N. tuberosa var. rosea
The pink-flowered variety of the North American magnolia water lily. Pink blossoms with bright red stamens. Leaves pale green. Only suitable for large pools. 60 cm–1.2 m (2–4 ft).

N. tuberosa 'Richardsonii'
A very fine large-flowered white water lily only useful for large expanses of water.

Immense globular blossoms with golden stamens and conspicuous pea-green sepals. 75 cm–1 m (2½–3½ ft).

'Virginalis'
Semi-double flowers of pure white. Sepals rose tinged towards their base. Stamens bright yellow. Leaves green flushed with purple. 45–75 cm (1½–2½ ft).

'Virginia'
Broad white starry blossoms 15 cm (6 in) across with green sepals infused with brown. Rounded leaves green above, reddish beneath. 60 cm–1.2 m (2–4 ft).

'William Falconer'
Medium sized blood-red flowers with yellows stamens. Leaves purplish when young, but turn deep olive green as they mature. 45–75 cm (1½–2½ ft).

Tropical water lilies

Day blooming
'Aviator Pring'
Rich yellow star-like blossoms held well above the water. Large green toothed leaves with wavy margins. 45–75 cm (1½–2½ ft).

'Blue Beauty'
Fragrant deep blue flowers with a central golden disc from which the yellow stamens with golden anthers are produced. Sepals lined and spotted with black. Leaves large, dark green with brown freckling above, purplish green beneath. 45–90 cm (1½–3 ft).

'Daubeniana'
Small blue blossoms rarely more than 5 cm (2 in) across with a sweet spicy aroma. Petals narrow with a greenish caste, sepals whitish, stamens yellow. Leaves oval or roughly arrow-like, brownish green splashed with chocolate. A first-class plant for a tub. 15 cm (6 in).

'General Pershing'
Large, deep pink, sweetly scented blossoms held well above the water. Sepals green

with light pink interiors, stamens yellow tipped with pink. Large purplish-green leaves splashed with red beneath. 45–75 cm (1½–2½ ft).

'Panama Pacific'
The flower buds on opening are a purplish blue but turn rich reddish purple when the blossoms are expanded. Golden stamens with violet anthers. Leaves bronze green with reddish veins. One of the hardiest of the tropical water lilies. 45–75 cm (1½–2½ ft).

'St. Louis'
Large star shaped canary-yellow flowers with yellow stamens. Pea-green leaves that are spotted with brown when young. 45–75 cm (1½–2½ ft).

Night blooming
'Emily Grant Hutchings'
Large cup shaped pinkish-red flowers with deep amaranth stamens which turn a rich mahogany colour with age. 45–75 cm (1½–2½ ft).

'Maroon Beauty'
Very free-flowering cultivar with maroon star-like blossoms. 45–75 cm (1½–2½ ft).

'Missouri'
Pure white blossoms up to 38 cm (15 in) across held high above the water. The dark green leaves with indented margins are strikingly mottled with purple and brown. 75 cm–1 m (2½–3½ ft).

'Red Flame'
Intense red, fragrant, star-like blossoms held above deep mahogany foliage. 45–75 cm (1½–2½ ft).

The foregoing water lilies are among those most widely cultivated by gardeners and nurserymen. In the past a vast array of both hardy and tropical cultivars have been grown. In recent years the International Water Lily Society, the international registration authority for *Nymphaea*, has been sorting out the tremendous confusion which exists among these plants. Anyone with a serious interest in water lilies should write to the Society for the latest checklist. This gives information about cultivars both past and present.

CHAPTER 11
Deep-water Aquatics

While it is true that water lilies, pond lilies and lotus could be considered to be deep-water aquatics, this term is popularly ascribed to other aquatics which demand deep water. The interpretation of deep water is wide, but most water gardeners regard plants that demand 30 cm (1 ft) of water or more in which to grow successfully as coming into this category.

Although they are few in number they are most important inhabitants of garden pools, especially the smaller surface areas where water lilies tend to swamp the glassy stillness of the water. The figures quoted indicate the range of depths tolerated by each plant.

Aponogeton distachyos (Water hawthorn)

A South African plant that is completely hardy and in temperate areas often evergreen. Flowers from spring until late autumn during favourable years. White blossoms, forked and bearing a double row of bract-like organs at the base of which are jet-black stamens. A sweetly scented plant with floating flowers among more or less oblong leaves which are often splashed with maroon. Propagation by seed or division of clumps during the growing season. It is impractical to divide the tubers. 30–90 cm (1–3 ft).

Nymphoides peltata (Water fringe)

A bold plant rather like a pygmy water lily in appearance and for that reason sometimes called the poor man's water lily. Small rounded green leaves often spotted or mottled with brown. Flowers bright yellow, fringed and produced freely from midsummer until early autumn, just above water level. Easily increased by division of the scrambling rootstock. 30–75 cm (1–2½ ft).

Orontium aquaticum (Golden club)

This relative of the arum is among the most bizarre aquatic plants the gardener can grow. Exceptionally fine pencil-like flowers of yellow and white are held above the surface of the water and surrounded by glaucous lance-shaped foliage. Propagation by seed sown in trays of mud immediately after it has been gathered. Only fresh seed germinates freely. Up to 45 cm (1½ ft).

Pond lilies

Pond lilies are related to water lilies, being members of the same family, the *Nymphaeaceae*. However, they are not so decorative, having smaller bottle-shaped or button-like flowers and much larger, more vigorous, green leathery floating foliage. While for the most part undesirable in the well-ordered garden pool, they are useful in shaded situations, or where moving water precludes the successful cultivation of nymphaeas. Most have beautiful membraneous, transluscent underwater foliage and are often used as temporary inhabitants of cold water aquaria. Cultivation is identical to that recommended for hardy water lilies.

Nuphar advena (American spatterdock)

A common vigorous species with large, thick, fresh green floating leaves and globular yellow blossoms about 8 cm (3 in) across. These are tinged with purple or green and have bright coppery-red stamens. 45 cm–1.5 m (1½–5 ft).

N. japonica (Japanese pond lily)

Large, slender, arrow-shaped floating leaves and small yellow flowers no more than 8 cm (3 in) across. Unlike most other nuphars, this only prospers in relatively still water. 45–75 cm (1–2½ ft).

N. lutea (Yellow pond lily, brandy bottle)

Leathery green, more or less oval, floating leaves are produced in abundance. Flowers bottle shaped, yellow and with a distinctive alcoholic odour. A very vigorous plant which is only suited to extensive areas of water. 30 cm–2.4 m (1–8 ft).

N. minimum (Dwarf pond lily)
A small-growing pond lily which can be accommodated successfully in the average pool, although where water lilies can be grown they should take preference. Tiny yellow blossoms among small almost heart-shaped foliage. 30–45 cm (1–1½ ft).

N. polysepala (Indian pond lily)
A large vigorous plant but one which will grow in shallow water. Deep green broadly lance-shaped leaves up to 30 cm (1 ft) in length and as much across. The golden blossoms are sometimes tinged with red and may be as much as 15 cm (6 in) across. 30 cm–1.5 m (1–5 ft).

N. sagittifolia (Cape Fear spatterdock)
Most of the foliage of this unusual plant remains submerged. This is narrow, lance-shaped and translucent. The few floating leaves are lance-shaped and it is among these that the small soft yellow blossoms are produced. A much better cold-water aquarium plant than pond plant, although it is sold for both purposes. 30 cm–1.5 m (1–5 ft).

Sacred lotus

Popular plants in the tropical regions of the world, the nelumbos or lotus are also widely cultivated in southern Europe and much of the United States and Canada where the summers are bright and hot. In northern Europe they are not so popular, being almost exclusively the perogative of the greenhouse gardener.

Nelumbos are half-hardy plants with plate-like leaves, for the most part held above the surface of the water on strong centrally placed leaf stalks. The upper surfaces are very waxy so that when droplets of water fall on them they run about like quick silver. The water-lily-like blossoms are carried on long slender stems and are followed by strange seed heads which look rather like small watering-can roses. All grow from long, creeping, banana-like rootstocks. All except the pygmy kinds will grow in water depths between 30 and 90 cm (1–3 ft).

Nelumbo nucifera (East Indian lotus)
Huge blossoms up to 30 cm (1 ft) across which change from vivid rose to flesh pink as they age. Large rounded blue-green leaves on tall stalks up to 1.8 m (6 ft) high.

N. pentapetala (American lotus)
Pale sulphur-yellow flowers up to 20 cm (8 in) across on stems about 90 cm (3 ft) high. A tougher but less attractive plant than *N. nucifera*.

Nurseries in the United States and Australia offer a wide range of cultivars. Few of these are ever grown in northern Europe as light levels are too poor to ensure reliable results. Of the modern cultivars the following are considered to be the best.

'Kermesina'
Double red Japanese cultivar.

'Lily Pons'
American cultivar with salmon pink cup-shaped flowers.

'Mrs Perry D. Slocum'
Large fully double rose-pink blossoms which age to creamy yellow. The best American cultivar.

'Momo Botan'
Small-growing cultivar for a tub. Fully double carmine blossoms.

'Pygmaea Alba'
A miniature cultivar with small pure white blossoms 10 cm (4 in) across. The foliage is no more than 30 cm (1 ft) high.

CHAPTER 12

Marginal Plants

This group of plants comprises those that grow happily around pools in mud or several centimetres of water. In modern preformed pools they are usually grown on the marginal shelves in individual containers. It is best to use container cultivation as many of these plants have strong vigorous root systems which readily swamp their neighbours if planted in close proximity. This system also permits the water level under which the plant is growing to be easily adjusted if necessary without affecting any other plants.

The measurement following the description of each plant indicates the approximate height of that plant. Most will grow in conditions of mud and up to 15 cm (6 in) of water.

Hardy marginal plants
Acorus calamus (Sweet flag)
Although a relative of the arum lily this has much more in common visually with the iris, except that the flowers are much less significant. The leaves are fresh green, long, sword like and arise from a fat fleshy rootstock. They smell of tangerines when bruised and support strange yellowish green horn-like flower spikes. Easily increased by division during the growing season. 90 cm (3 ft).

A. c. 'Variegatus' Bold sword-shaped leaves with a strong tangerine fragrance when bruised. Handsomely variegated with cream, green and rose, the latter colour being particularly evident during the spring. Rarely flowers. One of the finest foliage plants for pool margins. Propagation by division during the growing season. 60–90 cm (2–3 ft).

A. gramineus
A dwarf grassy-leaved species with very dark green foliage. Flowers insignificant. Often treated as a half-hardy plant and sometimes as a subject for cold-water aquaria. Easily increased by division during the growing season. 15 cm (6 in).

A. g. 'Variegatus' A cream and dark green foliage variety of the common species. Often not regarded as completely frost hardy. Increase by division during the growing season. 15 cm (6 in).

Alisma plantago-aquatica (Water plantain)
A bold marginal aquatic with attractive ovate bright green foliage and loose pyramidal panicles of pink and white flowers. These flower heads become hard and woody after flowering and are first class for winter decoration indoors. They produce very viable seed which, if allowed to disperse unchecked, will rapidly yield choking masses of seedlings. Propagation by seeds sown as soon as they have ripened. 60–90 cm (2–3 ft).

A. parviflora
This is very similar to the foregoing, but with rounded leaf blades on strong leaf stalks and shorter, neater heads of white, or sometimes pink, blossoms. The dried heads of this species are not as spectacular as those of *A. plantago-aquatica*, but are worth preserving. Propagation by seeds sown immediately they ripen. 30–75 cm (1–2½ ft).

A. ranunculoides
This is the plant which scientists now refer to as *Baldellia ranunculoides*, but most nurserymen still leave it among the water plantains. A creeping fellow of dwarf stature with delicate arching stems which bend down and root wherever they touch moist soil. Rapidly forms a spreading colony of bright green lance-shaped foliage, sprinkled with crowded umbels of rose or blush flowers during late summer and early autumn. 15 cm (6 in).

Butomus umbellatus (Flowering rush)
A lovely rush-like marginal plant with handsome bright green foliage. Beautiful showy pink blossoms produced on spreading umbels during late summer. A perfect companion for *Pontederia cordata*. Grows from a creeping root that is often host to masses of small bulbils, each capable of producing a new plant if removed and transplanted independently. Propagation by the removal of bulbils in the spring or by division of established plants during the spring or early summer. 60—90 cm (2—3 ft).

Calla palustris (Bog arum)
A wonderful plant for hiding the unsightly edge of a pool. It has strong creeping roots which are clothed in handsome glossy heart-shaped foliage. The white blossoms are rather like small sails, or flattened versions of the common florist's arum lily. These are followed by dense spikes of succulent orange-red fruits which persist into autumn. Propagation is by cutting the creeping roots into short sections in early spring. Each section should have a bud. These are planted in trays of mud. Seed can be sown immediately after ripening and will usually produce young plants the following spring. 15—30 cm (6 in—1 ft).

Caltha leptosepala (Mountain marigold)
A most attractive, but as yet not widely available, white-flowered marsh marigold. Broad white saucer-shaped blossoms with a distinctive silvery tinge are produced above handsome dark green foliage during late spring. Easily increased by division, or seed when this is produced, sown immediately after ripening. 15—45 cm (6 in—1½ ft).

C. palustris (Marsh marigold)
One of the loveliest marginal aquatics for early spring, growing in damp soil or as much as 30 cm (1 ft) of water without wavering. Dark green mounds of glossy, scalloped, dark green foliage smothered in bright golden yellow, waxy, saucer-shaped blossoms. Propagation by seed sown immediately after ripening, or division during the growing season. 30—60 cm (1—2 ft).

C. p. alba (White marsh marigold). A widely commercialised, but generally smaller version of the white-flowered marsh marigold. Unfortunately this is rather prone to mildew and is not such a good plant as its cousin *C. leptosepala*. Flowers white with golden centres and borne above glossy green leaves during late spring. Propagation by division of the plants during the growing season. 30—45 cm (1—1½ ft).

C. p. 'Flore Pleno'. (Double marsh marigold) One of the loveliest pool plants for spring and early summer flowering. Fully double, bright golden-yellow blossoms like small pom-pon chrysanthemums. Neat tight mounds of bright green glossy foliage. As this does not set seed it can only be increased by division during the growing period. 15—30 cm (6 in—1 ft).

C. polypetala (Himalayan marsh marigold)
A very large species suited only to the larger pool or streamside. Big bold hummocks of foliage, the individual dark green leaves being as much as 25 cm (10 in) across. Large trusses of bright golden-yellow blossoms during late spring. Propagation by division during the growing season or by seed sown immediately after ripening.

Carex pendula (Pendulous sedge)
This is one of the few sedges worth considering for modern pools; even then it does not enjoy growing in water any deeper than a few centimetres. It is much happier as an inhabitant of wet soil. A tall dignified plant with broad green strap-like leaves and long drooping spikes of brownish green catkin-like flowers which appear during the summer and persist into early autumn. Can be increased by careful division during early spring, but much better results are obtained from sowing seeds immediately after ripening. Even seed that is kept through the winter and then sown during the spring germinates adequately. 90 cm—1.2 m (3—4 ft).

C. riparia (Great pond sedge)
Only the uninformed would plant this

vigorous marginal in their water garden, but the cultivars derived from it are well behaved and appealing.

C. r. 'Aurea' A charming tufted grassy perennial with bright golden foliage which illuminates the poolside throughout the summer. Insignificant brownish flower spikes are sprinkled among the foliage. Although usually offered as a marginal subject, it much prefers boggy soil at the waterside. Propagation by careful division of established clumps during early spring. 30−75 cm (1−2½ ft).

C. r. 'Variegata' Very similar in habit and cultural requirements to the golden-leaved form. Foliage variegated green and white. Propagation by careful division of established clumps during early spring. 30−75 cm (1−2½ ft).

Cotula coronopifolia (Brass buttons)
Most gardeners are familiar with cotulas as alpine or trough plants, but this one is truly aquatic and extremely useful as a component of plantings in shallow water. It produces masses of bright yellow rounded heads of flowers all summer long above a solid mass of strongly scented light green foliage.

Unfortunately *C. coronopifolia* is mono-carpic and therefore dies after flowering. However, there is usually sufficient seed scattered around to ensure continuity. The prudent gardener clips off the seed heads before the seeds ripen and thereby exercises some control over their distribution, at the same time preserving a small group of plants so that seed can be gathered for sowing under controlled conditions the following spring. Cotula seed remains viable until the spring and should be sown in trays of damp compost rather like annual bedding plants. For the most part early cultivation should follow that advocated for bedding plants, except that cotula can be grown much cooler in a garden frame or a sheltered corner outside. The plants are transplanted to containers on the marginal shelves during late spring or early summer. 15 cm (6 in).

Cyperus longus (Sweet galingale)
A grassy plant somewhat reminiscent of the popular house plant called umbrella grass (*Cyperus alternifolius*), but perhaps a little less mathematical in arrangement. It has fresh green stiff spiky leaves which radiate from the stem like the ribs of an umbrella. Small insignificant brownish flower spikes are sprinkled among the leaves of the umbrella-like heads. A good creeping foliage plant which is ideal for stabilizing streamside banks and eroded soil areas at the waterside. The strong scrambling rhizomes can be cut into small lengths during early spring to serve as a ready means of propagation. Large clumps can also be divided and seed germinates freely, especially that which has been freshly gathered. 90 cm−1.2 m (3−4 ft).

C. vegetus
This plant looks even more like the indoor umbrella plant, but is much more compact with spreading umbels of bright green foliage and dense tufted spikelets of reddish mahogany flowers during late summer. Easily increased from seed sown immediately after ripening or during the following spring. Established plants can be divided at any time during the growing period. 30−60 cm (1−2 ft).

Damasonium alisma (Starfruit)
This is not the most significant of marginal aquatics but one that is loved by many, especially those who have a small water garden. Green strap-shaped leaves arise from a hard corm-like root. Spikes of milky-white flowers during summer are followed by curious star-shaped fruits. Large clumps can be divided during the growing season, but most gardeners increase this plant from seeds sown either immediately they ripen, or the following spring. 15−20 cm (6−10 in).

Decodon verticillatus (Water willow)
A tall vulgar plant that is not well suited to the formal water garden, but which is ideal for the modern wildlife water garden. For large pools or stream sides it is invaluable, naturalizing freely and providing a haven for all manner of wildlife. A native of North America, it has tall willowy stems and

sprays of rose-pink tubular flowers. However, it is for its autumn colour that it is best loved. The green leaves turn pinkish as summer fades and then pass through rose and vermilion to an intense fiery crimson. The first sharp frost of winter then defoliates the plants. Propagation is by soft stem cuttings taken during summer. Propagate by division of established plants during spring, or by detaching fallen stems that often root along their length when in contact with mud or water. 90 cm−1.5 m (3−5 ft).

Eriophorum angustifolium (Cotton grass)
This is the most frequently encountered and most easily cultivated of the popular cotton grasses. Like all eriophorums this must have acid conditions in order to thrive. Plant in a container with acid soil liberally laced with course peat or bark. Fine grassy foliage among which cotton-wool-like flower heads are produced during early summer. Propagation by division of established plants during spring. 30−45 cm (1−1½ ft).

E. latifolium (Broad-leaved cotton grass)
A species of similar habit to the popular cotton grass, but with broader dark green foliage. Liberal quantities of cotton-wool-like flower heads are produced throughout the summer. Requires an acid soil. Propagation by division of established plants during spring. 30−45 cm (1−1½ ft).

Glyceria aquatica 'Variegata' (Variegated water grass)
A most handsome and vigorous perennial grass that grows in damp soil or several centimetres of water. An excellent plant for stabilizing stream-side banks. Elegant green and cream foliage which, during spring, has a strong red infusion. Spires of rather dull grassy flower heads. These are best removed when they appear as they detract from the beauty of the plant and cause deterioration in the quality of its foliage. Easily increased by division of established clumps during spring. 60 cm−1.2 m (2−4 ft).

Houttuynia cordata
An easily grown creeping plant for the shallow margins of the pool. This is so adaptable that it can be grown even in a damp spot in a herbaceous border. Bluish green heart-shaped leaves with a maroon or purplish caste produce a somewhat acrid smell when crushed. The flowers are creamy white, four petalled and have a hard white central cone. Ideal for carpeting bare soil among taller-growing rushes. Propagation by division of established plants during early spring. 15−30 cm (6 in−1 ft).
  H. c. 'Plena' This equally amenable plant is exactly the same as the common single-flowered species, but has flowers with a dense central ruff of petals. A much more showy form. Propagation by division of established plants during spring. 15−30 cm (6 in−1 ft).
  H. c. 'Variegata' A very popular variegated foliage form with darker purplish-green leaves splashed with yellow and cream. Flowers sparsely. This plant needs very careful placing in a garden on account of its brightly coloured foliage. Propagation by division of established plants during spring. 15−30 cm (6 in−1 ft).

Hypericum elodes (Marsh hypericum)
Although a relative of the popular garden rose of sharon, this little fellow tolerates really wet conditions or several centimetres of water without difficulty. A first-class carpeting plant for disguising the edge of a pool. Small green leaves studded with small bright yellow saucer-shaped flowers. Propagation by seed sown during spring, division during early spring or stem cuttings during summer. 8−15 cm (3−6 in).

Iris laevigata
This is the true blue-flowered aquatic iris. An easy plant to establish, forming clumps of sword shaped smooth green leaves and blossoming during early summer. There is a number of variations in commerce and it is the best of these that should be increased by division immediately after flowering. Seed can be sown during spring or early

summer, but the flower colour of the resulting plants is likely to be variable, although almost inevitably blue. 60–90 cm (2–3 ft).

I. l. 'Alba' A pure white cultivar. Must be propagated by division. 60–90 cm (2–3 ft).

I. l. 'Atropurpurea' A vivid purple-blue cultivar. Free flowering. Must be propagated by division. 60–75 cm (2–2½ ft).

I. l. 'Colchesteri' This is a handsome large-flowered iris with violet-purple and white blossoms. Often available under the name 'Monstrosum'. Must be propagated by division. 60–90 cm (2–3 ft).

I. l. 'Mottled Beauty' White blossom liberally mottled with blue. Must be increased by division. 60–90 cm (2–3 ft).

I. l. 'Muragumo' A beautiful free flowering cultivar with six prominent petals rather than three. Otherwise rather like the common blue *I. laevigata*, but with the petals sporting gold reticulations. Must be increased by division. 60 cm (2 ft).

I. l. 'Regal' Lovely magenta-red flowered iris. Must be increased by division. 60–75 cm (2–2½ ft).

I. l. 'Rose Queen' Allegedly a cross between cultivars of *I. laevigata* and *I. kaempferi*, but usually listed by growers as a cultivar of *I. laevigata* owing to its ability to tolerate standing water. However, it is not as amenable to any significant depth of water as the other *I. laevigata* cultivars. Soft pink flowers and pale green leaves. Must be increased by division. 60–75 cm (2–2½ ft).

I. l. 'Semperflorens' A free-flowering blue cultivar not far removed from the species, but generally producing many more blossoms. Must be increased by division. 60–90 cm (2–3 ft).

I. l. 'Snowdrift' Large-flowered cultivar with pure white blossoms of quality and substance. Bold green sword-like leaves. Must be increased by division. 60–90 cm (2–3 ft).

I. l. 'Variegata' A lovely variegated variety often listed in catalogues as 'Elegantissima'. This has small blue flowers and the most startling gold and green variegated foliage. Rarely attains a height of 75 cm (2½ ft). Must be increased by division.

I. l. 'Violet Parasol' Large flowered violet-blue cultivar with bold sword-shaped leaves. Must be increased by division. 60–90 cm (2–3 ft).

I. pseudacorus (Yellow flag)
A very vigorous and easily grown iris for large expanses of water. Rapidly swamps small garden pools, forming large clumps and seeding freely. It has yielded a number of interesting and useful cultivars. This species is frequently used for wildlife ponds. Tall mid green strap-like leaves and bright yellow blossoms with small black markings during summer. Easily increased by seed sown during spring or early summer, or division immediately after flowering. 75–90 cm (2½–3 ft). In situations to its liking, unrestricted by a container, the iris can attain a height of 1.2 m (4 ft).

I. p. var. **bastardii** Not such a vigorous plant as the species, but equally bulky. Has creamy yellow flowers among bold sword-shaped foliage. Must be increased by division. 75–90 cm (2½–3 ft).

I. p. 'Beuron' A recently introduced yellow tetraploid cultivar. Must be increased by division. 75–90 cm (2½–3 ft).

I. p. 'E. Turnipseed' A strangely named cultivar with creamy white blossoms. Must be increased by division. 75–90 cm (2½–3 ft).

I. p. 'Flore-plena' A double-flowered form of the common yellow flag. A slightly more restrained and generally more colourful plant than the species. Must be increased by division. 75–90 cm (2½–3 ft).

I. p. 'Golden Queen' Of more modest proportions than the common species. A selection with more refined golden blossoms in greater numbers. Bold sword shaped green leaves. Must be increased by division. 75–90 cm (2½–3 ft).

I. p. 'Sulphur Queen' Beautiful sulphurous-yellow flowers freely produced among bold sword-shaped green foliage. Must be increased by division. 75–90 cm (2½–3 ft).

I. p. 'Variegata' Unquestionably the loveliest form of the yellow flag. Handsome cream and green sword-shaped leaves which are startlingly effective during late spring and early summer. These gradually fade to pale green, during which time the yellow flowers are produced. A much slower-growing plant of more modest habit. Must be increased by division. 60—75 cm (2—2½ ft).

I. versicolor

This is the North American version of the European *I. pseudacorus* in distribution, but not in stature. It is an altogether better plant for the average pool, being of modest stature and free flowering. The blossoms are produced during early summer and are violet-blue veined purple with a conspicuous patch of yellow on the falls. Leaves mid green and sword shaped. Easily increased from seed sown during spring or early summer, or division after flowering. Seed-raised plants will produce flowers of variable colour and quality. 60—75 cm (2—2½ ft).

I. v. 'Alba' A white-flowered selection. Should be increased by division. 60—75 cm (2—2½ ft).

I. v. 'Claret Cup' An attractive deep claret-purple cultivar. Must be increased by division. 60—75 cm (2—2½ ft).

I. v. 'Kermesina' The most popular and widely grown cultivar. Beautifully marked and veined blossoms of deep plum with petals of a satin-like quality. One of the loveliest and most reliable aquatic irises. Bold green sword-like leaves. Must be increased by division. 60—75 cm (2—2½ ft).

I. v. 'Rosea' A rose-purple selection. Should be increased by division. 60—75 cm (2—2½ ft).

I. v. 'Stella Main' A recent blue-flowered introduction not yet widely available commercially. Must be increased by division. 60—75 cm (2—2½ ft).

Juncus effusus 'Spiralis' (Corkscrew rush)

One of the few *Juncus* worthy of cultivation. Similar in appearance to the common soft rush, but the dark green needle-like leaves are twisted and contorted like a corkscrew. A bizarre addition to a pool which serves as a talking point rather than as a plant of great beauty. Must be propagated by division during spring. Selection of suitable material for propagation is most important. Any portions of the plant showing straight 'needles' should be discarded. Only increase the contorted portions. Straight-needled parts of the plant will revert to the wild type. 30—45 cm (1—1½ ft).

J. e. 'Vittatus' An old and well-loved rush sometimes listed under the name 'Aureo-striatus'. Not frequently encountered, probably because it is very slow to reproduce. A handsome gold and green variegated rush with straight needle-like leaves. Not a terribly stable plant, often reverting to green if not carefully watched. Remove any green shoots immediately they are seen. Propagation is by division of the variegated portions during early spring. 30—45 cm (1—1½ ft).

Ludwigia palustris (False loosestrife)

A relative of the popular leafy submerged ludwigias of tropical and cold-water aquaria. Not infrequently offered for planting in wildlife ponds. Handsome spiky green foliage and strange petal-less flowers. Increase from seed sown during early spring, summer stem cuttings or division during the growing season. Not a plant for the decorative garden pool. 30 cm (1 ft).

Mentha aquatica (Water mint)

An easy going and occasionally rampant plant for shallow water at a poolside. When used sensibly the water mint can tie a pool and the surrounding ground together, completely disguising the harsh pool edge. It will grow in several centimetres of water or just damp soil, scrambling about and rooting at almost every leaf joint. Like all mints it is heavily aromatic with dense, rounded, hairy green foliage on slender reddish stems and soft lilac-pink blossoms like miniature powder puffs in mid- and late summer. There are many hybrids between water mint and other species, so this is a plant that should be purchased by sight. Plants with a good cover of foliage and bold outstanding blossoms are desirable. Increased easily by early spring division or by taking soft stem cuttings during summer. 30−45 cm (1−1½ ft).

Menyanthes trifoliata (Bog bean)
A very distinctive plant for shallow water. It produces showy white fringed flowers during spring above dark green foliage somewhat reminiscent of a broad bean. Both the leaves and flowers are protected by a short scaly sheath towards the end of each sprawling olive-green stem. If this is chopped into sections, each with a root attached, the plant is very easily propagated. 20−30 cm (8 in−1 ft).

Mimulus luteus (Yellow musk)
It is difficult to decide whether to include the various mimulus as true marginal aquatics or bog-garden plants. Most can be very colourful inhabitants of pools during summer but few survive winter in the water. *Mimulus luteus*, often one of the parents of the modern hybrids and itself a worth-while garden plant, usually does. This has soft green rounded foliage and spikes of bright yellow blossoms not unlike those of an antirrhinum. It flowers for much of the summer and is very easily increased from seed sown during spring or early summer, or by division of the over-wintered rosettes in spring. 20−30 cm (8 in−1 ft).

M. ringens
This is a truly aquatic mimulus from North America. A delicate-looking plant with much branched slender stems and handsome narrow green leaflets. Flowers somewhat tubular, lavender to blue and produced freely along the spiky stems in summer. Although it seldom seeds itself in a pool it is a plant that is easily raised from seed sown during early spring under glass in pans of mud. Soft stem cuttings taken during summer root readily. 45 cm (1½ ft).

Myosotis scorpioides (Water forget-me-not)
This is a perennial aquatic version of the popular bedding forget-me-not. Unlike that species, the water forget-me-not has smooth leaves and less-compact heads of light blue flowers which are produced for much of the summer. An ideal plant for helping to disguise where pool meets land and absolutely reliable in almost every situation. Easily increased from seed sown during the spring, the plants ideally being raised in small pots in a garden frame where they can be stood in a tray of water. Old plants can sometimes be divided successfully, but the older woody central portion should be discarded. Only use lively young pieces from around the edge. Division only in spring. 20 cm (8 in).

M. s. var. **alba** A white variety that often occurs in seed-raised plants. Seed saved from this rarely comes true. White-flowered plants should be perpetuated by division. 20 cm (8 in).

M. s. 'Mermaid' This is said to be an improved form of the species; frequently perpetuated by division. It appears to differ little except in being more floriferous. 20 cm (8 in).

M. s. 'Semperflorens' When purchasing water forget-me-not the chances are this is what the gardener will receive. A free flowering seed-raised selection of the species of less rank habit. A relatively neat compact plant that is ideal for the nurseryman and excellent for the home gardener with limited space. Seed is also available from some seedsmen and is easily raised in trays of ordinary seed compost in a garden frame if sown during spring or early summer. 20 cm (8 in).

Narthecium ossifragum (Bog asphodel)
This is not a spectacular plant, but one that is well suited to the smaller water garden. A diminutive plant with wiry creeping roots and small fans of reddish green iris-like foliage among which are produced heads of bright yellow flowers. Although it will tolerate standing water it does not appreciate having much more than a centimetre, especially during winter. Easily increased by division of the clumps during early spring or seed sown in very damp compost at about the same time. 20−30 cm (8 in−1 ft).

Peltandra alba (Arrow arum)
An interesting member of the arum family

with dark green, glossy, arrow like foliage and narrow whitish-green spathes in summer, sometimes followed by reddish fruits. Easily increased by division during early spring. 45 cm (1½ ft).

P. virginica

A very similar plant to the fore-going, but less showy and with narrower greenish spathes during summer. Easily increased by division in early spring. 45–60 cm (1½–2 ft).

Phragmites australis (Spire reed)

A fast growing and very common reed which needs introducing with great care into the smaller waterscape. It produces a very vigorous root system, so if considered for an average pool it needs restricting in a container. Of bamboo-like appearance, it has handsome silvery white or purplish silky flower heads. Although it is possible to cultivate it in a restricted area, it is essentially a plant of wide-open spaces, looking best around the perimeter of lakes. It can be readily increased by division, the woody runners, each with a shoot, being detached and planted where required. 1.2–1.5 m (4–5 ft).

P. a. 'Variegatus' A much slower growing, shorter and more decorative marginal plant than the preceeding. Handsome cream and green striped foliage. Propagated by lifting and dividing established clumps during early spring. Only select material for replanting that is wholly variegated. 90 cm–1.2 m (3–4 ft).

Polygonum amphibium (Amphibious bistort)

A rather rank native of ponds and slow-moving streams. Not particularly useful in garden pools but frequently included in a wildlife pond. Dense rosy-red spikes of blossom are produced during late summer above green or purplish rounded floating foliage. Easily increased by division during spring.

Pontederia cordata (Pickerel weed) A

plant of noble proportions producing numerous stems each consisting of an oval

or lance-shaped shiny green leaf and a leafy bract from which the spike of soft blue flowers appears during late summer. There are variable colour forms about including one that is pinkish and another almost white. These seem to have been discovered in the United States in wild populations and are now being propagated commercially. Small stocks are being established in Europe, but to date nobody seems to have formally named these colour variants. Propagation by seed sown immediately it can be detached from the fruiting spike and while still green can be very effective, but most gardeners opt for early spring division of the crowns of established plants. Do not divide the plants until they are seen to be actively growing. Dormant pontederias rot quickly if divided before awakened by spring sunshine. 60–90 cm (2–3 ft).

P. lanceolata

This is one of the more unusual marginal plants seldom offered by the horticultural trade, but a plant that should be promoted. Very similar to the pickerel weed, *P. cordata*, but larger in every part and with bold lance-shaped foliage. When encountered in nurseries it has almost invariably been increased by division rather than seed which is generally of erratic germination. Flowers blue and in neat spikes. 90 cm–1.2 m (3–4 ft).

Preslia cervina

A most desirable aquatic plant forming spreading clumps of slender erect stems densely clothed in small lance-shaped leaves and crowned during late summer with stiff whorled spikes of dainty ultramarine or lilac flowers. The whole plant is aromatic and happiest when growing in very shallow water. Easily increased by short stem cuttings taken during spring and inserted in pots of mud. 30 cm (1 ft).

Ranunculus flammula (Lesser spearwort)

A very fine early summer flowering buttercup-like plant with glistening golden flowers above dark green roughly oval leaves and slender reddish scrambling stems. An ideal plant for masking the harsh edge of a pool where it meets up with the garden. Propagation is by separating the emerging shoots during early spring and planting them seperately. 25–30 cm (10 in–1 ft).

R. lingua (Greater spearwort)
A lovely tall-growing buttercup with strong, reddish flushed, erect hollow stems well clothed with dark green leaves. Easily increased by early spring division. 60–90 cm (2–3 ft).
    R. l. 'Grandiflora' This is the plant that is sold by most aquatic specialists for garden pools. A much-improved natural octoploid variant. Increased by early spring division. 60–90 cm (2–3 ft).

Rumex hydrolapathum (Water dock)
A tall-growing plant for the wildlife pond or lake. It looks very much like an enlarged version of the common garden dock, but with bold dark green foliage that changes from green to bronze and crimson at the approach of autumn. Easily increased from seed sown during the spring or division just as the plant starts to break ito growth. Up to 3 m (10 ft).
    R. h. var. **maximus** This form is slightly smaller but with much larger individual leaves which have the same autumnal hues. Up to 2 m (6½ ft).

Sagittaria japonica (Japanese arrowhead)
Botanists are still at loggerheads over this plant, most assigning it to *S. sagittifolia*, although within the nursery trade each is a very distinct plant. European botanists have even refered to it as *S. sagittifolia* var. *leucopetala*, so this plant may sometimes be offered under that name too. Like many sagittarias, this grows from a winter bud or turion which sprouts when conditions warm up during early spring. It is at this time that ducks come foraging for them. They seem to find sagittaria turions a delicacy and can play havoc if not carefully watched. Thus leading to the turions being popularly refered to as duck potatoes. *Sagittaria japonica* has broad, light-green, arrow-shaped foliage and bold spikes of papery white single flowers with conspicuous

yellow centres. These are produced from mid- to late summer. Propagation is by dividing clumps of growing plants during the summer and seperating out the turions in winter or early spring. 45–60 cm (1½–2 ft).
    S. j. 'Flore Pleno' (Double Japanese arrowhead) This is the same in every respect as the foregoing, except that it has fully double blossoms, rather like small white powder puffs. 45–60 cm (1½–2 ft).

S. latifolia
An imposing arrowhead from North America, rather taller than the others popularly in cultivation but not so frequently encountered. Foliage bold, impressive, clearly arrow shaped, from among which pure white blossoms are produced. Prefers a slightly acid mud. Easily increased by summer division or the re-distribution of turions during the dormant period. 90 cm–1.2 m (3–4 ft).
    S. l. 'Flore Pleno' As the ordinary species, but with fully double white flowers. Propagation by the redistribution of winter turions. 90 cm–1.2 m (3–4 ft).
    S. l. var. **pubescens** A very hairy leaved form, similar in most respects to the species. This is often encountered as *S. latifolia* in gardens. White flowers during late summer. Propagation by the re-distribution of winter turions. 90 cm–1.2 m (3–4 ft).

S. sagittifolia (Arrowhead)
A very popular marginal aquatic with sharply cut arrow-shaped foliage. The flower spike is stiff and supports white papery-petalled blossoms with black centres during late summer. Propagation by division of growing plants and the redistribution of winter turions. 45–60 cm (1½–2 ft).

Saururus cernuus (Lizard's tail)
A bizarre but nevertheless attractive aquatic plant for shallow water. It produces strong-growing clumps of heart-shaped foliage which often takes on autumnal tints. The flowers are creamy white and produced in quaint nodding terminal sprays during summer. Easily increased by division during early spring. 30 cm (1 ft).

S. loureri

A scarce Chinese species which is sometimes seen in cultivation. It has much paler foliage than *S. cernuus*, but otherwise is very similar. Erect rather than nodding heads of white flowers. Increased by division during early spring. 30 cm (1 ft).

Scirpus lacustris (Bulrush)

This is the true bulrush: the plant that allegedly cradled the infant Moses. The popular conception of a bulrush, the brown poker-headed reedmace or *Typha* is incorrect. *Scirpus lacustris* is an extremely useful plant for shallow water, producing stiff, dark green needle-like leaves from short creeping roots. During late summer the foliage is bedecked with pendant tassels of crowded reddish-brown flowers. Propagation by seed sown during spring in pans of mud, or more usually by division of the creeping root system during spring as soon as the plants start sprouting. 60−90 cm (2−3 ft).

S. tabernaemontani (Glaucous bulrush)

A much nicer plant than the common bulrush, much more refined in all respects. Not only is it taller, but it has slender foliage of steely grey with a conspicuous mealy bloom. Propagation by division of the creeping roots during spring as soon as the plants start sprouting. 90 cm−1.5 m (3−5 ft).

  S. t. 'Albescens' A plant of uncertain origin, but one with stout upright stems of glowing sulphurous white conspicuously marked with thin longitudinal stripes. These are produced from thick creeping roots that are allegedly not fully hardy in very cold districts. Propagation by division in spring just as the plants start to sprout. 90 cm−1.2 m (3−4 ft).

  S. t. 'Zebrinus' (Zebra rush) A very popular mutant of *S. tabernaemontani* with stems that are alternately barred white and green. When occasional plain green stems are produced these should be removed before they outgrow the more desirable variegated portion. The shortest of the bulrushes, this prefers to grow in really shallow water. Propagation by division during spring just as the plants are starting to sprout. 90 cm (3 ft).

Sparganium erectum (Branched bur-reed)

A very resilient rush-like marginal plant which needs introducing with great caution as it can be very invasive. It has sharp pointed roots that are capable of puncturing a polythene pool liner. Nevertheless an excellent aquatic for a wildlife pool. It has branching stems with greenish bur-like heads and handsome, narrow, bright green strap-like foliage. There is also a variety called *S. e.* var. *neglectum* but this differs mainly in its stem which is red towards the base. Propagation by seed or division during early spring. 45−90 cm (1½−3 ft).

S. emersum (Unbranched bur-reed)

This is similar in every respect to the foregoing, except that the stem is unbranched. This gives a narrower, spire-like appearance to the inflourescence. Increases readily from seed or division during early spring. 45−90 cm (1½−3 ft).

S. minimum (Small bur-reed)

As the name suggests, a diminutive plant, but one which can spread rather quickly. Very similar in many respects to the previously described species, but instead of being an erect marginal aquatic it tends to have foliage which floats. It has thin green leaves and conspicuous oval bur-like fruits. Increases readily from seed or division during early spring. Another plant for the wildlife pool rather than the decorative water garden.

Triglochin palustris (Marsh arrowgrass)

A plant of doubtful merit for a decorative garden pool, but ideal for a wildlife pond. It produces crowded tufts of slender succulent foliage and terminal spikes of greenish-white flowers. Increases readily from seed or by careful division during spring. 30 cm (12 in).

Typha angustifolia (Narrow-leaved reedmace)

A tall growing elegant reedmace or 'bulrush' with slender grey-green foliage and bold brown poker-like seed heads. A most elegant plant for a larger pool, but too vigorous for an ordinary suburban water garden. The fruiting heads are mature during early autumn and often cut for indoor dry floral arrangements. Increased by division of the creeping roots in spring just as they start to sprout. Seed raising is a possibility but rarely worth while as germination is erratic. 90 cm−1.8 m (3−6 ft).

T. latifolia (Great reedmace)
One of the most strikingly handsome hardy marginal aquatic plants, but also one of the most difficult to grow satisfactorily in a modern water garden. A very vigorous plant which in a soil-bottomed pool is rampant, yet when in a container is difficult to manage owing to its height and the weight of foliage which doom it to constantly turning over into the water. This is best enjoyed in the wild or when planted in a large expanse of water. Although a difficult plant to manage, most water-garden nurseries offer this plant. A distinguished looking reed with broad, grey green, strap-like foliage and fat chocolate-coloured fruiting heads during late summer and early autumn. Increased by division during spring as soon as growth commences. Seed raising is a possibility but germination is very erratic. 90 cm−1.8 m (3−6 ft).

T. l. 'Variegata' A lovely creamy and green variegated variety which can be safely introduced to the average pool. Not a vigorous grower. Increase by division during spring just as growth commences. 90 cm−1.2 m (3−4 ft).

T. laxmannii
This is a well-proportioned reed with slender, willowy greyish-green leaves and handsome brown fruiting heads. Not as invasive as those previously described, but nevertheless needs carefully monitoring. If a reedmace is essential for a pool this is likely to be the one that is easiest to deal with. Increases readily by division during early spring. 90 cm−1.2 m (3−4 ft).

T. minima
The tiniest reedmace of all. A little fellow with dark green grassy foliage and chunky, rounded, brown fruiting heads. Not at all invasive, but easy to grow and ideal even for a sink garden. Although it does not possess the dignity of its more robust relatives, it does mean that the gardener with limited water resources can enjoy at least one member of this fascinating group of aquatics. Easily increased by division during early spring as the plants start into growth. 45 cm (1½ ft).

Veronica beccabunga (Brooklime)
An aquatic member of a very familiar family of herbaceous plants. Dark blue flowers with a white eye are produced in profusion in the axils of the leaves. The foliage is dark green, rounded and liberally clothes rapidly growing procumbent stems which provide an excellent disguise for a pool edge where the structure meets the soil. Flowers throughout the summer and although not strictly speaking evergreen, retains its foliage for much of the year. Easily increased by short stem cuttings rooted in pans of mud, or by cutting of pieces of stem with roots attached. It naturally roots freely along the length of its stems. Gardeners with a small pool generally find that they get a better effect if this plant is replaced annually from cuttings. 15−20 cm (6−8 in).

Zizania aquatica (Canadian wild rice)
An annual plant that is frequently offered, but not for decorative pools. It is a prime attractant of wild fowl and therefore more commonly used in wildlife or game ponds. A handsome grass with slender arching reed-like foliage. Increase from seed sown during early spring in trays of mud. Transplant the seedlings in much the same way as rice is transplanted into a paddy field. 1.8−2.4 m (6−8 ft).

Z. latifolia
A perennial species of more modest stature. Another inhabitant of wildlife pools. Bold green grassy foliage. Rarely ever flowers in northern Europe. Increased from imported seed or more usually by division during early spring. 1.2−1.5 m (4−5 ft).

Tender marginal plants

The following is a selection of tender marginal aquatics for indoor culture, or outside planting in frost-free locations. One or two have an element of frost-hardiness about them, but are better cultivated in a frost-free environment. The figures following the description of each plant indicate the approximate height of that plant. Most will grow in conditions of mud and up to 15 cm (6 in) of water.

Acorus gramineus

An aquatic plant for the edge of a pool, bog garden or submerged in an aquarium. It does not prosper well outdoors in areas where prolonged cold is likely, and is always seen at its best in warmer climates or with protection. Semi-evergreen, with stiff, grassy, dark green foliage. Rarely produces its insignificant flowers. Easily increased by division, preferably during spring, but at almost any time during the growing season. 25 cm (10 in).

A. g. 'Variegatus' A slower growing variety of *A. gramineus* with green and creamy white striped foliage. 25 cm (10 in).

Colocasia esculenta (Taro)

A bold foliage plant with large heart shaped mid-green leaves. Relatively insignificant arum-type flowers. A strongly architectural plant that grows freely from a tuberous root. It is these tubers which are lifted and divided during their dormancy in the winter that provide a ready means of propagation. In a warm climate taro can be encouraged to continue growing all the year round. 90 cm–1 m (3–3½ ft).

C. e. 'Fontanesii' Handsome heart-shaped plain green leaves with dark green leaf margins and veins. Increased by division of the tubers during winter. 90 cm–1 m (3–3½ ft).

C. e. 'Illustris' A bold architectural plant with large dark green heart-shaped leaves spotted with purple. Vivid violet leaf stems. Increased by division of the tubers during winter. 90 cm–1 m (3–3½ ft).

Cyperus 'Haspan'

A dwarf version of the large and ungainly papyrus, *C. papyrus*. A lovely elegant plant for the water's edge. Strong green stems support finely-divided umbrella-like heads of foliage. Grows actively all the year round and is easily increased by division. 60–90 cm (2–3 ft).

Thalia dealbata

A handsome foliage plant with rather odd-looking flowers. The leaves have a long stalk and oval green blades with a white mealy covering. Violet flowers in summer. Easily increased by division during early spring or seed sown immediately it becomes available. 1.5 m (5 ft).

T. geniculata

This is not so tolerant of cool conditions as *T. dealbata*. The leaves have long stalks with a green oval blade. The flowers are violet and produced in lax spikes during summer. A plant sold under the name *T. g. rubra* is the same in every respect, but has reddish stems and a reddish infusion in the leaf blades. This is popularly known as red-stemmed canna, but should not be confused with *Canna indica* and its cultivars, the brightly coloured cannas of greenhouse and bedding displays. Easily increased by division during early spring or seed sown immediately it becomes available. 1.8 m (6 ft).

Zantedeschia aethiopica (White arum lily)

This is the arum lily of the florist. A handsome plant for damp compost or up to 30 cm (1 ft) of water. Almost hardy, it sometimes survives in frosty areas when it has become established in deeper water. A handsome plant with bold heart-shaped bright green leaves and beautiful white spathes each with a central yellow spadix. These are produced during spring and summer. Easily increased by lifting and dividing the tuberous roots during the dormant period or dividing growing plants early in the season. 60–90 cm (2–3 ft).

Z. a. 'Crowborough' A slightly smaller version of the common species, but allegedly much hardier and therefore well suited to cool conditions. Leaves heart shaped, bright green. Spathes white with yellow spadix. 60–75 cm (2–2½ ft).

CHAPTER 13
Submerged Aquatics

Hardy submerged plants

These are the plants that are popularly refered to as 'water weeds'. Largely unattractive grassy aquatics, they are essential for creating a balance in garden pools, using up all the available mineral salts in the water and starving out the troublesome free-floating algae. They also benefit various aquatic creatures by regularly releasing oxygen into the water. In some pools they are planted directly into soil on the floor, but most are easiest to manage when they have been planted in containers, even in larger expanses of water. Most are sold as bunches of cuttings fastened together at the base with a strip of lead.

In the following list those that are naturally clump forming and never bunched will be indicated as such in the description. All the remainder will be what are popularly termed 'bunched plants'. There is no indication as to size of plant as this is totally dependent on the depth and temperature of the water. All the plants require being totally submerged, but few will tolerate a depth of more than 90 cm (3 ft) of water. Despite being capable of absorbing mineral salts in the water, all submerged aquatics, bunched or clump forming, must be planted properly in a growing medium if they are to prosper.

Apium inundatum (Water celery)

This is a charming if uninspiring aquatic with delicate fern-like foliage and crowded heads of small white flowers held above water level. It has a distinctive celery aroma. Not to be confused with the coarser *A. nodiflorum*, a weedy, invasive plant with much coarser celery-like leaves. This is known as the procumbent marshwort, although some nurseries offer it as water celery. These are both clump forming and easily increased by division.

Callitriche hermaphroditica (Autumnal starwort)

This is the plant sometimes still offered by nurserymen as *C. autumnalis*. A totally submerged species with lovely evergreen cress-like foliage beloved of goldfish. A very beautiful underwater plant that only prospers in water that is well balanced. Its success indicates that the water chemistry is about right. Increased by cuttings.

C. platycarpa

Often listed in catalogues as *C. verna*. A very useful species for a shallow pool where it will produce handsome whorls of star-like foliage on the surface of the water. Much loved by goldfish as a food plant. In a situation to its liking it produces dense forests of underwater cress like bright green leaves. The foliage dies back completely during winter. Increased by cuttings.

C. stagnalis

A luxuriant underwater foliage plant of fairly short summer duration, often dying back after fruiting. Another excellent plant for fish with masses of small, oval, bright green leaves. Increased by cuttings.

Ceratophyllum demersum (Hornwort)

This and the closely related *C. submersum* behave in an almost identical fashion (Fig. 138). From the point of view of the gardener they may as well be one and the same thing. Indeed, nurseries offer both species under the name *C. demersum*, sometimes as cuttings in the same bunch. Invaluable for difficult pools, preferring cool deep water and not objecting unduly to shade. For the gardener with a badly sited pool they are a Godsend. They produce dense whorls of dark green bristly foliage on slender brittle stems. In early spring these root strongly in accumulated debris on the pool floor or in the surface of aquatic planting baskets. As

Fig. 138 The hornwort or coontail, *Ceratophyllum demersum*, is ideal for cool or deep water and will tolerate some shade.

Fig. 138

the summer progresses they break free and float to the surface, where they remain free floating until forming turions or winter buds in which they remain for the winter. Increased by cuttings during spring and summer.

Chara aspera (Stonewort)

Although not frequently introduced into garden pools deliberately, the stoneworts will often find their own way in. They can be likened to an intermediate between higher submerged plants and filamentous algae. *Chara aspera* is of a thick hairy appearance, light green to bluish green in colour, and roots strongly to the pool floor. Apart from its virtue as a submerged oxygenating plant, it is capable of extracting lime from the water. When a piece of chara is removed from a pond and allowed to dry out in the sun, it will be grey or white with the accumulated chalky deposit. Easily increased by tearing apart established clumps and bunching the pieces with strips of lead weight and then replanting. Many different stoneworts could appear naturally in a pool and all behave similarly *Chara aspera* is the only species likely to be offered as a bunched plant by the horticultural trade.

Eleocharis acicularis (Hair grass)

A very fine submerged plant that spreads across the top of a basket or the floor of a pool in a dignified fashion. A carpeting plant that looks rather like seedling grass. It is always purchased as small clumps with roots attached, but rapidly knits together in a solid carpet. As it is related to the sedges it is impossible to propagate from cuttings. Division is the only method of reproduction.

Elodea canadensis (Canadian pondweed)

This is a first-class submerged oxygenating plant but one which often causes concern among gardeners. This has arisen through the story of its introduction into Europe at the end of the last century, a story which has influenced many gardeners and caused them to fear its presence pools. In fact, if managed properly it is one of the finest submerged aquatics and makes a major contribution to the balance of a pool, in most instances almost guaranting clear water. The reason that many gardeners fear it is the story of its rapid spread through canals and waterways making them virtually unnavigable. After several years of spread and attendant havoc it died out naturally and was replaced by a less-vigorous form. It is believed by some botanists that the plant originally introduced was the male form, separated at that time as *E. planchonii*, a plant now very rare in cultivation, and the *E. canadensis* now commonly encountered is the female form. The plant now raised in cultivation has small, dark green, curved, lance-like leaves borne in whorls around long branching stems and tiny floating lilac flowers with trailing thread-like stalks. Generally speaking, it is an easy plant that is easily managed in all but the largest expanses of water.

Fontinalis antipyretica (Willow moss)

A striking evergreen plant with dark green moss-like foliage (Fig. 139). Thrives equally well in sun or shade, but enjoys moving water, in the wild often clinging merely to stones but in a pool best planted properly. Divide established clumps and bunch them with lead weights when increasing stock. A first-class plant for fish, providing a perfect repository for spawn.

F. gracilis

A much smaller and generally more elegant version of *F. antipyretica*. Dark green mossy foliage of smaller stature. A first–class plant for fish spawning. Increase by carefully pulling apart an established plant and bunching the pieces separated with small strips of lead.

Hottonia inflata

A curious North American plant of great beauty which is sometimes offered for pools. It has whorls of lovely pale green divided foliage and strangely inflated branching flower stems. Flowers above the surface of the water with attractive white or pale lilac blossoms during summer. Hottonia will only flourish in pools with good water chemistry; it is therefore unwise to choose such plants in the initial stages of planting. Allow the pool to settle down and become balanced before introducing this plant. Increase from cuttings taken during summer.

H. palustris (Water violet)

The most beautiful of this group of aquatics (Fig. 140). Lovely whorled bright green foliage and fine upstanding spikes of whitish or lilac blossoms. This should not be introduced during the early stages of the establishment of a pool as the water is unlikely to be clear enough or of suitable chemistry. Essentially a plant for introduction to a pool that is in its second season. In common with other hottonias, the water violet produces turions as autumn approaches and therefore cannot be restricted to specific areas in a pool. Its turions will start into growth wherever they fall and this may be nowhere near a container. If newly emerging water violet looks in a yellow and sickly condition it is probably free floating and just needs pushing back into a basket. Increase from cuttings taken during summer.

Isoetes lacustris (Quillwort)

These are surprisingly members of the fern family, even though they look not unlike small rushes. There are various species but it is only *I. lacustris* that is likely to be

Fig. 139 Willow moss, *Fontinalis antipyretica*, is a useful submerged plant, especially in moving water.

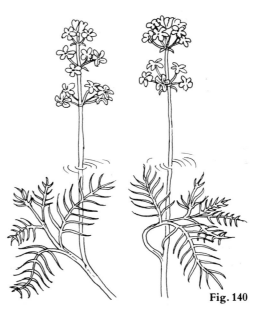

Fig. 140 The water violet, *Hottonia palustris*, is the most beautiful submerged aquatic, but is not always easy to get established.

encountered. It is a sturdy little plant with dark olive green quill-like leaves which arise from a circular brown root which is rather like a corm. Although growing up to 25 cm (10 in) in the wild, when cultivated it rarely achieves more than 10 cm (4 in). Must be increased by division. It is not possible to root stem cuttings of isoetes. 10–25 cm (4–10 in).

Lagarosiphon major

This is a submerged plant that is known to almost everyone who has kept a goldfish, for it is the common dark green 'weed' that is sold widely through the pet trade as goldfish weed (Fig. 141). Older gardeners and aquarists still call it *Elodea crispa*, although botanists have proved conclusively that even though it looks rather like an elodea there are very many differences. It

Fig. 141
Lagarosiphon major is the most popular submerged aquatic. It is commonly referred to as 'fish weed'.

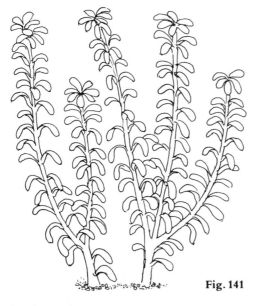

Fig. 141

has long, dark green, succulent stems densely clothed in whorls of dark green crispy foliage. One of the finest of all oxygenating subjects. Easily increased from cuttings. Old plants which become stringy should be Every two or three years, replace old stringy plants with cuttings.

Fig. 142 *Lobelia dortmanna*, a choice and lovely submerged aquatic for the tub or small pool.

Fig. 142

Lobelia dortmanna

An extraordinary relative of our common bedding lobelia. Forms dense carpets of erect, blunt, dark green foliage from which arise wiry stems producing terminal clusters of lavender blossoms (Fig. 142). A plant for shallow water rather than the central depths of the pool. Can only be increased by division.

Myriophyllum proserpinacoides
(Parrot's feather)

A totally submerged or sometimes partially submerged feathery foliage plant. Blue-green finely cut leaves on scrambling stems which, if emerging above the water at the pool-side, turn reddish with the approach of autumn. A plant of many parts, but one which does not greatly enjoy growing in deep water. Although frost tolerant this plant is not reliably hardy in all districts. Increase from cuttings taken either during spring as young shoots emerge or in late summer and over-winter in trays of mud in a frost-free garden frame or greenhouse.

M. spicatum (Spiked milfoil)

A very popular and extremely useful plant for both the water gardener and fish fancier. A first-class plant for assisting in maintaining a balance and excellent for the pool owner who breeds fish, the fine foliage providing a perfect place for the deposition of spawn. The whorls of tiny leaflets are produced in abundance and are of a bronze-green colour. The terminal of each stem on reaching the water surface produces small crimson or yellowish flower spikes. Increased by cuttings of non-flowered shoots at any time during the growing season.

M. verticillatum (Whorled milfoil)

Long trailing stems which produce dense whorls of narrow, bright green needle-like foliage. An excellent plant for fish to spawn in and a valuable submerged aquatic for providing a balance in a pool. The small flowers which are produced in short spikes just above the surface of the water are yellowish or greenish and of little significance. Increase from cuttings of non-flowering shoots at any time during the growing season.

Oenanthe fluviatilis (Water dropwort)
An interesting aquatic for the wildlife pool or more extensive water garden. Dense carrot-like foliage is followed by umbels of rather indifferent white flowers. A plant for shallower water. Increase by division during the growing season, or seed when this is available.

Potamogeton crispus (Curled pondweed)
A lovely aquatic with foliage reminiscent of a high class bronze-coloured sea weed (Fig. 143). Handsome serrated and undulating bronze-green translucent foliage and small striking crimson and creamy white flowers which peep just above the water. Easily increased from cuttings taken during spring or early summer. The foliage becomes very brittle from mid-summer onwards and cuttings are more difficult to take and establish.

P. pectinatus (Fennel-leaved pondweed)
Delicate, finely divided, bronze-green grassy foliage. Good in deeper cool water. Easily increased from cuttings taken during spring or early summer. From mid-summer onwards the stems become very brittle and the cuttings are much more difficult to get established.

P. nodosus (Loddon pondweed)
This is a more unusual potamogeton for the garden pool with both submerged and floating foliage of green with a bronze flush and distinctive etching of black lines. The fine upstanding fruits are particularly interesting. Can be increased by division or from cuttings of submerged foliage taken during early spring.

Ranunculus aquatilis (Water crowfoot)
One of the finest of all hardy submerged aquatics, producing beautiful blossoms, a sprinkling of good-looking floating leaves and some beautiful underwater foliage (Fig. 144). The deeply dissected submerged foliage gives the plant its common name, for it resembles an out-stretched bird's foot. Just

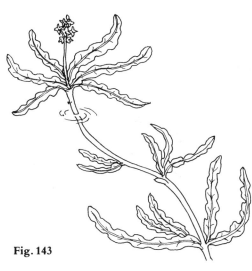

Fig. 143

before flowering time groups of dark green, deeply lobed, floating leaves, rather like those of a clover, appear, followed by glistening white and gold papery chalice-like blossoms during mid-summer. A truly lovely aquatic which should be in every water garden. Increased from cuttings of submerged foliage taken in the spring before any floating leaves are produced.

Tillaea recurva
A very fine submerged plant, especially for a new pool. A generous planting of this bright green small-leaved aquatic will rapidly starve out free-floating algae. Surprisingly it is related to the crassulas, to which it should apparently now be assigned. It has hard cress-like foliage and tiny white axillary flowers. Although it roots very easily from cuttings taken during the summer it gets away much quicker and is more effective when grown from small divisions. One of the best submerged aquatics.

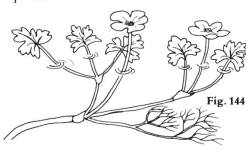

Fig. 144

Fig. 143
Potamogeton crispus has handsome crisped and crimped underwater foliage of a lovely bronze-green hue.

Fig. 144 The water crowfoot, *Ranunculus aquatilis*, is unquestionably the most useful dual purpose submerged aquatic. Handsome blossoms and very fine foliage.

157

Tender submerged plants

A selection of the more popular and easily managed submerged plants for an indoor or frost-free pool. There are many more very fine submerged aquatics, but the majority demand more specialised management in an aquarium. In most instances those described here will prosper better in the carefully maintained environment of an aquarium, but are equally amenable to the rough and tumble of a pool.

Anubias lanceolata (Water aspidistra)
The common name of this plant is very indicative of its appearance. Thick shiny leaves on short stout stems which appear from a fleshy rhizome. Propagation by division of established plants. Each small piece of plant with a root attached will grow independently.

Bacopa caroliniana
Scrambling, somewhat hairy and fleshy leaves on stems which root readily at their leaf joints. Mid- to pale green, deciduous plants of vigorous growth. Easily increased from stem cuttings taken at any time during the active growing period.

Cabomba caroliniana
A deciduous or semi-evergreen submerged aquatic with bright green, coarsely cut, fan-shaped leaves, which scrambles around and forms dense hummocks of foliage. Increased from stem cuttings taken at any time during the active growing period.

Cryptocoryne ciliata
Semi-evergreen aquatic commonly encountered in tropical aquaria. Leaves deep green, lance shaped and with a distinctive pale mid-rib. Flowers small, purplish and fringed, not unlike a small arum and produced at the base of the plant. Increased by division.

C. spiralis
Semi-evergreen aquatic often seen in tropical aquaria. Leaves lance shaped, green with a pronounced purplish caste. Flowers small, purplish and arum like, at the base of the plant. Increased by division.

Echinodorus intermedius (Amazon sword plant)
A bold and handsome aquatic that needs care if it is to give of its best. Lovely green sword-like clumps of foliage. Can be increased by careful division of the crown, or seeds sown in trays of mud on the rare occasions that they are available.

E. radicans
A not so inspiring but easily grown sword plant. Short lance-shaped leaves produced at right-angels from the stem. Can be increased by very careful division.

Egeria densa
Very similar to the popular hardy *Lagarosiphon major* but not so curled and crinkled. Dark green crispy leaflets borne in dense whorls around strong green stems. Easily increased by short stem cuttings taken at any time during the growing period. A plant that is much loved by fish fanciers.

Heranthera graminea (Water stargrass)
A small-growing submerged aquatic rather akin in general appearance to *Egeria densa* but unlike that plant has its leaves arranged alternately on either side of the stem rather than in whorls. Produces tiny pale yellow floating blossoms. Increased by careful division during the growing season.

H. zosteraefolia
Very similar in every respect to *H. graminea*, but with soft blue flowers. Can be increased by careful division.

Hygrophila polysperma
A broad-leaved submerged plant, pale green with lance-shaped leaflets on strong reddish or purplish stems. Can be increased by short stem cuttings during the growing season. Often stems produce roots at their leaf joints and these pieces of growth can be removed to start new plants.

Ludwigia natans (*L. mulertii*)
Handsome lance-shaped leaves of bronze green with crimson-purple undersides. Can be readily propagated from short stem cuttings taken at any time during the growing season.

Marsilea quadrifolia (Water clover)
An interesting relative of the ferns which can be grown either partially or completely submerged in water. Its common name is very descriptive, the plant looking rather like a four-leaved clover. A creeping, scrambling plant that can be easily divided. Short pieces of scrambling roots can also be cut for propagation purposes.

Myriophyllum hippuroides (Western milfoil)
Bright green feathery foliage that is ideal for accommodating fish spawn. Like most milfoils this produces underwater forests of foliage. Can be increased by short stem cuttings taken at any time during the active growing season.

M. scabratum *(M. pinnatum)*
Reddish bronze feathery foliage and occasional spikes of small purple flowers. Easily increased from stem cuttings taken during the growing season. Another good plant for the fish fancier.

Riccia fluitans (Crystalwort)
This can best be described as a free-floating submerged aquatic. It forms thick mats of starry foliage just beneath the surface of the water. An excellent plant for fish spawning purposes and easily increased by division and re-distribution of the foliage. It is always purchased by the portion, never as a bunched plant.

Sagittaria lorata
A relative of the hardy arrowhead, distinguished marginal subjects. Dense underwater foliage that looks rather like spring onions in dense clumps. During the summer floating oval or arrow-shaped leaves are produced together with tiny white papery flowers. Readily increased by division.

S. subulata
A similar species to *Sagittaria lorata*, but with much shorter grassy foliage. The plant can easily be increased by division.

Vallisneria gigantea
A very vigorous plant with long, unbranched, tape-like bright green leaves. The flowers, although regularly produced, are insignificant. A very handsome plant that is easily increased by division.

V. spiralis (Tape grass)
Tape like but grassy foliage of the brightest green. One of the most popular of all tender submerged aquatics. Can be increased by separation of the innumerable plant lets which grow in dense clusters from the creeping root system. Occasional tiny white flowers of very little significance are produced.
   V. c. 'Torta' A much shorter-growing plant than *V. spiralis* with generally darker foliage and tape-like leaves which are twisted like a corkscrew.

CHAPTER 14
Floating Plants

Hardy floating plants

Floating plants are crucial in assisting in the maintenance of a happy balance in garden pools by cutting down the amount of light that falls directly into the water, thereby making life difficult for water discolouring algae. Floating plants exist on the mineral salts present in the water and are completely free floating. They should never be planted — merely tossed on to the surface of the water. Most floating plants reproduce freely so it is very difficult to give any indication of spread. All floating aquatics are kept within bounds by pulling off runners when they start getting out of hand or netting off areas of the plant.

Azolla caroliniana (Fairy moss)

A tiny elegant floating 'fern' which congregates in large patches (Fig. 145). It provides a thick lacy carpet of floating bluish green or sometimes purplish red congested foliage. Although generally thought to be hardy, it is desirable to over-winter a portion of the plant in a frost-free porch or greenhouse for the winter. This not only ensures survival if the weather becomes really severe, but it gives the gardener a head start in the spring when the pool water has warmed up sufficiently to encourage the development of green free-floating algae, yet not enough to encourage the light-excluding floating plants to appear. A

generous portion of fairy moss being available for placing out on the pool in spring is a godsend. It is easily increased by redistributing portions of the plant. Likewise it is easy to control if it starts to get out of hand, netting being an easy and reliable method of disposal.

Hydrocharis morsus-ranae (Frogbit)

This charming little floating plant looks rather like a tiny water lily. The small leaves are kidney shaped and produced in neat rosettes. The flowers are fairly simple, three-petalled, papery and white with a yellow centre. The frogbit forms turions which over-winter on the bottom of pools. They disappear during autumn and then reappear during late spring. It is a wise precaution to remove a few plants in the autumn before they disappear completely. Place them in a jar of water with a little soil in the bottom. This will enable them to sprout earlier than in a pool and provide a head start when the algae is first noticed as the water warms up. The little leafy plants can be tossed on to the water as soon as the danger of sharp frost has passed. Increased by separating out the plantlets during the growing season. These form sizeable groups, plantlets being carried on short creeping stems.

Lemna trisulca (Ivy-leaved duckweed)

This is the only species of duckweed that the water gardener should consider. All other lemna species are invasive and a constant source of irritation. They spread rapidly across the surface of the water, reducing light and devastating the submerged aquatics trying to grow in the water beneath. The ivy-leaved duckweed, however, is moderately well behaved. It is a pretty little plant with dark green crispy foliage which floats just beneath the surface of the water. Although it apparently pro-

Fig. 145 Fairy moss, *Azolla caroliniana*, is a charming floating fern that quickly becomes established.

Fig. 145

Scirpus tabernaemontani 'Zebrinus' is popularly known as the zebra rush on account of its green and white banded foliage.

Typha minima is the only member of the reedmace family that can be allowed unrestricted access to the pool. A wonderful plant for the flower arranger.

Zantedeschia aethiopica is better known as the arum lily. Although not reliably hardy, it will often survive the winter when growing right in the water.

Eichhornia crassipes is not hardy and should be replaced annually. A beautiful floating plant from the tropics.

duces small greenish flowers these are not readily observed — it is a plant grown solely for its foliage. Increased by dividing the plant into portions and re-distributing it.

Stratiotes aloides (Water soldier)

A remarkable floating plant that has the appearance of a pineapple top floating on the surface of the water. It produces creamy white papery flowers in the leaf axils. The solitary flowers are female while the male ones are produced in clusters in a pinkish spathe. When in a situation to its liking stratiotes reproduces freely, producing generous quantities of young plants from wiry stolons. These can be detached as a means of propagation. Like most other floating aquatics, the water soldier over-winters as a dormant bud or small plantlet.

Trapa natans (Water chestnut)

An annual floating aquatic. A handsome plant (Fig. 146) with rosettes of dark green rhomboidal floating foliage and pretty white axillary flowers. Towards the end of the summer it produces hard black spiny seeds or 'nuts' and these fall to the bottom of pools. In the spring they germinate and yield a fresh crop of young plants. Some gardeners like to collect a few 'nuts' during the autumn so that they can be certain of perpetuating their plants in a controlled environment in a bowl in a garden frame or greenhouse. If 'nuts' are collected during the autumn they must be kept in water or wet sphagnum moss. If they dry out they perish.

Utricularia minor (Lesser bladderwort)

A small growing but nonetheless attractive little carnivorous plant. It has wand-like spikes of soft primrose pouched flowers which arise from a tangled mass of delicate lacy olive-green foliage interspersed with tiny almost translucent bladders which capture all manner of minute aquatic insect life. Increased by re-distributing the mass of tangled foliage.

U. vulgaris (Greater bladderwort)

Very showy bright yellow antirrhinum-

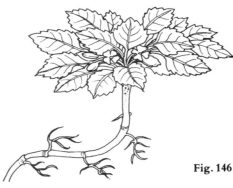

Fig. 146

Fig. 146 The water chestnut, *Trapa natans* has lovely white flowers and handsome rosettes of rhomboidal leaves.

like flowers are produced on strong stems which emerge from a mass of bright green filigree foliage (Fig. 147). Bladders are distributed widely throughout the foliage, providing an additional source of nutrients from captured aquatic insect life. Plants are increased by re-distributing the tangled mass of foliage. Long stringy pieces can be broken into sections of reasonable length and these will regenerate.

Wolffia arrhiza

A plant of little horticultural merit, but not infrequently cultivated as a novelty as it is thought to be one of the smallest flowering plants. It grows in dense green floating masses, each plant consisting of a globular or more or less oval thallus no more than

Fig. 147

Fig. 147 The greater bladderwort, *Utricularia vulgaris*, not only produces attractive yellow flowers, but captures aquatic insects in its small bladders.

1 mm across. It is almost evergreen and easily re-distributed using a net and removing portions to a different location.

Tender floating plants

There are many tender floating plants, but very few that have been made commercially available. Those that are described here are representative of what is commonly available from specialist aquatic-plant suppliers. These represent the most attractive floating plants for pools.

Ceratopteris pteridoides (Floating fern)

Attractive soft green heart shaped or lance-like foliage with wavy margins. The crimpled edges are barren; the fertile fronds are more upright and give each plant a rosette-like appearance. Propagation by removing plantlets which appear on the edges of mature leaves.

C. thalictroides

Almost identical to *C. pteridoides* except that this species will often root and grow submerged as well as float around on the surface of the water. Can be increased by division of plantlets.

Eichhornia crassipes (Water hyacinth)

One of the loveliest of all cultivated aquatics. A plant that will flower for long periods in a frost-free environment, but can equally be used as a temporary inhabitant of outdoor water gardens, the young plantlets that cluster around the parent being removed and brought into the sanctuary of a greenhouse before the first frost. A most attractive plant with dark green shiny leaves with inflated bases which are honey-combed inside, but resemble small green balloons. It is these that give the plant its buoyancy. From the midst of this bizarre foliage strong flower spikes are produced yielding orchid-like blossoms of blue and lilac with a bright peacock eye. When growing outside the plants are squat and compact, but within the confines of a greenhouse they tend to be much taller and rather leggy.

Propagation is by the removal of young plants that have been produced on runners during the summer. When plants are being over-wintered inside following a season in an outdoor pool, it is wise to select the smaller individuals and place these in pans of mud rather than allowing them to float freely in a bowl. There is a better chance of them surviving when rooted into mud than when floating, especially where there is a low temperature regime.

Pistia stratiotes (Water lettuce)

An interesting member of the arum family with small greenish spathes. These are of little significance. It is the bold rosettes of lettuce-like foliage that is the attraction of this plant. Indeed, the plant looks like a gorgeous green downy lettuce when in a situation to its liking. An easily grown aquatic that can be readily increased by separating the profusion of plantlets from the parent.

Salvinia auriculata

A popular flowerless floating plant beloved of fish that delight in its dark fibrous roots which trail in the water. Its leaves are small, green, oval or heart shaped and borne in opposite pairs on branching stems. Separate plants and break up congested groups of stems and re-distribute when necessary.

S. natans

Almost identical to *S. auriculata* from the gardener's point of view, with oval or elongated green leaves in opposite pairs on branching stems. To increase, separate plants and break up congested groups of branching stems and re-distribute as desired. This species will tolerate much cooler conditions than *S. auriculata*.

Utricularia exoleta

A free-floating aquatic with dense green filigree foliage rather like that of a submerged aquatic. A carnivorous plant with small bladders scattered among the feathery foliage. These capture minute aquatic insect life. Flowers like small yellow antirrhinums are produced on a short stout spike well above the water. Increase by redistributing the tangled mass of floating foliage.

CHAPTER 15
Bog Garden Plants

Bog-garden perennials

There is no clear definition of what a bog plant is, for there are so many variables in the interpretation of the bog garden as a feature. The plants that are described here reflect the diversity that is available for growing in really wet soil. While a few, such as aconitum and hemerocallis, are often found in herbaceous borders, it is in the constant dampness of a bog garden that they flourish. The measurement following the description of each plant indicates the height of that plant.

Aconitum napellus (Monkshood)

An old-fashioned cottage-garden plant of delphinium-like habit. Erect spikes of hooded navy-blue flowers above mounds of glossy green, deeply cut foliage during summer. Much better in the wet conditions of a bog, rather than an ordinary herbaceous border. Can be easily increased from a summer sowing of seed, although it divides readily during winter or early spring. 1.2–1.5 m (4–5 ft).

A. n. 'Bicolor' A bicoloured form with blue and white hooded flowers. Foliage glossy green, deeply cut. Increased by division during winter or early spring. 90 cm–1.2 m (3–4 ft).

A. n. 'Bressingham Spire' A delightful stocky plant with violet-blue blossoms in dense spikes. Increased by division during winter or early spring. 90 cm (3 ft).

A. n. 'Carneum' A shell-pink cultivar with glossy green deeply cut foliage. Increased by division during winter or early spring. 90 cm (3 ft).

A. n. 'Grandiflorum Album' This is the white form. An interesting plant, but not as effective as its conpanions; nevertheless worth considering. Increased by division during winter or early spring. 90 cm (3 ft).

A. n. 'Spark's Variety' A very popular violet-blue monkshood with beautiful large blossoms in bold spikes. Handsome green foliage. Increased by division during winter or early spring. 90 cm (3 ft).

A. wilsonii

This is sometimes refered to as *A. carmichaelii* var. *wilsonii*, although the nursery trade tend to stick with the name with which it is familiar. It produces tall spires of bright blue hooded flowers above dark green three-lobed leaves. A most useful bog plant as it flowers during autumn. Increased by division during winter or early spring. 1.2–1.8 m (4–6 ft).

A. vulparia (Wolfsbane)

An interesting scrambling aconitum often still listed in catalogues as *A. lycoctonum*. Produces an untidy scrambling mound of finely cut dark green foliage. Throughout summer it's alight with short spikes of soft-yellow blossoms. Increased by seed or division during winter or early summer. 90 cm–1.2 m (3–4 ft).

Ajuga pyramidalis

A scrambling plant that is excellent for pool or streamside, flourishing in wet soil, but also capable of existing in moderately damp soil. It has plain green leaves and during summer is smothered with short spikes of bright gentian-blue flowers. Easily increased by division during spring. 15–30 cm (6 in–1 ft).

A. p. 'Metallica' A very fine foliage plant with leaves of deep metallic bronze. Flowers intense blue. Sometimes offered by nurserymen under the name 'Crispa'. Easily increased by division during spring. 15–30 cm (6 in–1 ft).

A. reptans 'Burgundy Glow'

A glowing rosy leaved cultivar of the rather drab and sometimes invasive common bugle, *A. reptans*. Short spikes of blue flowers during summer. A rapidly spreading plant which is ideal for masking the edge where bog garden and pool meet. Increased by division during spring. 15 cm (6 in).

A. r. 'Jungle Beauty' The tallest and most vigorous of this group of bugles. Plain green leaves and spikes of intense blue flowers. Needs plenty of space to develop to its full potential. Readily increased by division in early spring. 15–30 cm (6 in – 1 ft).

A. r. 'Purpurea' Deep purple-bronze foliage and short spikes of blue flowers. Increased by division during early spring. 15 cm (6 in)

A. r. 'Rainbow' A multicoloured foliage form with pink, green and cream leaves. Blue flowers in short spikes during summer. Increased by division during early spring. 15 cm (6 in).

Anemone rivularis

A splendid spring or early-summer-flowering plant producing loose umbels of snow-white flowers with bright violet anthers. Handsome, somewhat downy toothed foliage which arises from a swollen root. Increased by seed. 30–60 cm (1–2 ft).

A. virginiana

The best anemone for really wet conditions, even being tolerant of periodic flooding. Soon forms clumps of toothed green leaves from among which emerge clusters of greenish white or greenish purple flowers during early summer. Best propagated from seed. 45–90 cm (1½–3 ft).

Anemopsis californica (Apache beads)

A plant of anemone-like appearance with flowers that consist of a hard cone surrounded by a single whorl of pearly white petal-like bracts. Prefers mud or even shallow water and this must be alkaline if the plant is to prosper. The roots are strongly aromatic and have been used for medicinal purposes in the past. Propagate by division of established clumps during spring, or seed when this is available. 30–45 cm (1–1½ ft).

Anthericum liliago (St. Bernard's lily)

A beautiful summer-flowering perennial with tufts of narrow grassy foliage from among which are produced slender spikes of elegant white more or less tubular flowers. Increase by division during early spring or seed sown immediately it ripens. 60 cm (2 ft).

Aruncus dioicus (Goat's beard)

This plant is still offered by nurserymen as *A. sylvester*. It is a tall handsome fellow of astilbe-like appearance bearing bold plumes of creamy white flowers during late summer. The leaves are pale green, deeply cut and lobed and produced on stems reminiscent of bamboo canes. Easily increased by division during the dormant period. Provided each piece of root has a shoot or bud, it should grow. Large roots can even be sliced up with a knife into small cube-like pieces and these will grow away quickly. 90 cm–1.5 m (3–5 ft).

A. d. 'Kneiffii' A much smaller plant, well suited to modern gardens. It has the charm of the large *A. dioicus* but none of the disadvantages of bulk. Associates well with the popular cultivars of astilbe. Creamy white plumes of blossom arise from among deeply divided green foliage. Increased by division during the dormant period. 90 cm (3 ft).

Asclepias incarnata (Swamp milkweed)

A much neglected water-side plant that prospers in really damp situations. Stout leafy stems are crowned during summer with crowded umbels of rose-pink flowers. Can be increased by division during early spring. 60–90 cm (2–3 ft).

A. incarnata var. **alba** This has white blossoms but is otherwise similar to *A. incarnata*, with lance-shaped green leaves and typical crowded flower heads, similar to those of the popular house plant *A. curassavica*. 60–90 cm (2–3 ft).

Aster puniceus (Swamp aster)

A rather unruly but lovely plant with reddish stems and rough hairy foliage. Very showy flowers of lilac or pale violet-purple, rather like those of a Michaelmas daisy, during late summer and early autumn. Can be increased from seed, but more readily by division in early spring as it starts to shoot. 90 cm−1.5 m (3−5 ft).

Astilbe × arendsii 'Fanal'

One of the most striking and popular astilbes. Plumes of deep crimson flowers during mid- and late summer above neat mounds of deeply cut dark green foliage. This, along with the other cultivars of *A. × arendsii*, are first-class bog garden plants and should find a place in every planting. Increased by division during dormant period. 30−45 cm (1−1½ ft).

A. × a. 'Irrlicht' A lovely cool icy white cultivar with dark green foliage. Increase by division during dormant period. 60−75 cm (2−2½ ft).

A. × a. 'Ostrich Plume' Rich pink flowers in lean feathery spikes. Green divided foliage. Increased by division during dormant period. 75−90 cm (2½−3 ft).

A. × a. 'Peach Blossom' Salmon-pink flowers in feathery plumes above deeply divided green leaves. Increased by division during dormant period. 60−90 cm (2−3 ft).

A. × a. 'White Gloria' A pure white cultivar of compact habit. Green divided foliage. Increased by division during dormant period. 60−75 cm (2−2½ ft).

A. chinensis 'Pumila' This is a charming short-growing cultivar with low spreading mats of dark green somewhat ferny foliage which, during late summer, is a mass of bright pinkish-mauve flowers in short stiff spikes. Increased by division during dormant period. 30−45 cm (1−1½ ft).

A. crispa 'Lilliput'

A charming small-growing plant that enables the gardener with the tiniest bog garden to enjoy astilbes. Congested tufts of dark green crinkled foliage and tightly packed spires of salmon-pink flowers during late summer. Increased by division during winter. 15 cm (6 in).

A. c. 'Perkeo' Very similar to *A. c.* 'Lilliput' but with tightly packed spikes of intense deep pink flowers. Dark green con-

gested foliage. Increased by division during winter. 15 cm (6 in).

Buphthalmum salicifolium

A fairly frequently encountered herbaceous plant which flourishes in damp soil. Slightly unruly with hairy, green, lance-shaped leaves and heads of yellow daisy flowers during summer. Propagated by seed sown during spring or division during dormant period. 45−60 cm (½−2 ft).

B. speciosum

A strange daisy-like plant with large drooping yellow flowers during summer. Hairy, green, somewhat aromatic foliage. Easily raised from spring-sown seed, or division during dormant period. 90 cm−1.2 m (3−4 ft).

Cardamine pratensis (Cuckoo flower)

A charming spring-flowering perennial for a wet spot at the waterside. Single rosy-lilac flowers are produced in abundance above tufts of pale green ferny foliage. Easily increased by seed or, when necessary, division during dormant period. 30−45 cm (1−1½ ft).

C. p. flore pleno A fully double form of more compact growth. This has to be increased by division during the dormant period. 30 cm (1 ft).

Eupatorium ageratoides

A coarse branching perennial with coarsely toothed leaves and numerous pure white blossoms in compound heads during summer. Easily increased by division during early spring. 60 cm−1.2 m (2−4 ft).

E. cannabinum (Hemp agrimony)

A plant for the wildlife garden rather than the manicured feature. Downy, toothed foliage of rather vulgar aspect gives rise during the summer to terminal clusters of reddish-purple flowers. Propagated by division in early spring. 60 cm−1.2 m (2−4 ft).

E. purpureum (Joe-pye-weed)

This is a plant for gardens only where there is plenty of room. A coarse-leafed perennial with crowded heads of small purple flowers during late summer and early autumn. Increased by division during early spring. 1.2 m (4 ft).

Euphorbia palustris

This is a moisture-loving member of the spurge family and is very typical in general appearance of the popular herbaceous euphorbias. It produces lush green mounds of foliage smothered in yellow-green flower heads. Best increased from division in spring, just as young shoots are emerging. 45–90 cm (1½–3 ft).

Filipendula hexapetala (Dropwort)

A relative of the popular meadow-sweet, *F. ulmaria*, with most attractive fern-like foliage and stems of tiny creamy-white flowers during summer. Its foliage is an attractive feature throughout the growing period and good account should be taken of this when planning the positioning of the plant. Increased readily by division in early spring. 60–90 cm (2–3 ft).

F. h. flore pleno A fully double form of great merit. Increase by division during early spring. 60 cm (2 ft).

F. palmata

Large lobed dark green leaves from among which tall slender plumes of tiny pale pink blossoms are produced. These tend to fade to white or off-pink with age. Increased by division during dormant period. 90 cm (3 ft).

F. purpurea

Large feathery spikes of carmine or deep pink blossoms on crimson flower stems during mid- to late summer. Leaves lobed, dark to mid-green in tidy mounds. Increased by division during dormant period. 60 cm–1.2 m (2–4 ft).

F. rubra (Queen of the prairie)

An enormous plant with big, bold feathery plumes of deep peach pink blossoms during mid- to late summer. Leaves green, very large and both lobed and toothed. The form of this usually seen in the nursery trade is called 'Magnifica'. Increased by

division during dormant period. 90 cm–1.8 m (3–6 ft).

F. ulmaria (Meadow-sweet)

Frothy spires of sweetly scented, creamy-white blossoms during mid-summer above handsome deeply cut mid-green foliage. Easily increased from a spring sowing of seed or division during dormant period. 90 cm–1.2 m (3–4 ft).

F. u. 'Aurea' This plant is not usually allowed to flower, for the meagre flower spikes detract from its wonderful rich golden divided foliage. The most startling golden-leaved plant for the bog garden. Increased by division during dormant period. 60–90 cm (2–3 ft).

F. u. flore pleno The double-flowered form of the common species. Dense feathery spires of sweetly scented, creamy-white blossoms during mid-summer. Increased by division during dormant period. 90 cm (3 ft).

Gratiola officinalis (Hedge hyssop)

A useful plant for the wildlife bog garden. It is related to mimulus and has fresh green lance-shaped leaves and small white flowers striped with purple. Will grow successfully in standing water as well as wet soil. Easily propagated by division in spring. 30 cm (1 ft).

Gunnera magellanica A strange little creeping plant with scalloped green kidney-shaped leaves and odd reddish-green flower spikes. This is rarely grown for its horticultural value, but rather as a contrast to the magnificent *G. manicata*, thus making an interesting conversation piece! Increased by division during early spring. Height 7.5 cm (3 in).

G. manicata

Often referred to as giant Brazilian prickly rhubarb, this is probably the herbaceous plant with the greatest leaf span, individual leaves being capable of attaining a diameter of 1.5 m (5 ft) on stems as much as 1.8 m (6 ft) tall. A huge plant in every respect and unfortunately not well suited to the smaller garden. Essentially a plant of the larger landscape, it has the general appearance of an enormous rhubarb, but with leaf stems that are liberally sprinkled with unpleasant bristly hairs. During mid-summer an enormous branched flower spike, rather like a huge red-green bottle brush and up to 90 cm (3 ft) tall, is produced from a thick procumbent rhizome that is densely clothed in brown papery scales. This massive rhizome looks like a reclining bear during the leafless winter months.

As it is a South American plant and starts into growth early, gardeners in cold frosty locations usually provide some kind of winter protection. This consists of the frosted leaves being placed over the crowns and secured with pegs and string. The leaves turn crisp and papery, but provide excellent protection from the weather. Propagation is from seed sown immediately it ripens. Packeted seed is unlikely to be viable. The crowns can be divided during early spring, each 'nose' with a vestige of root attached being likely to grow on successfully. 1.8–2.4 m (6–8 ft).

Hemerocallis fulva (Day lily)

A vigorous plant more often associated with old herbaceous borders and cottage gardens than bog gardens. However, it is a lover of very wet conditions and flourishes well in a bog garden or at the waterside. It has glossy, pale green grassy foliage and strong flower stems with blossoms of orange or brown. These last a single day, but as there are many buds following a display can be expected for much of the summer. Increased by division during dormant period. 90 cm–1.2 m (3–4 ft). Many hybrids have been derived from the use of this species with *H. lilio-asphodelus*, *H. minor* and *H. aurantiaca*. There are now literally thousands of cultivars. Those described here are among the most popular and readily obtainable. All are increased by division during dormant period.

H. 'Black Prince' Deep velvety mauve. Slender green foliage. 60–90 cm (2–3 ft).

H. 'Bonanza' Flowers of light orange and maroon-brown. 60–90 cm (2–3 ft).

H. 'Burning Daylight' Rich deep orange blossoms. 60–90 cm (2–3 ft).

H. 'Buzz Bomb' Rich velvety red flowers. 60–90 cm (2–3 ft).

H. 'Chartreuse Magic' Flowers with an unusual combination of canary yellow with an infusion of green. 60–90 cm (2–3 ft).

H. 'Esther Walker' Beautiful rich golden-yellow blooms. 60–90 cm (2–3 ft).

H. 'Golden Orchid' Flowers of deep rich gold. 60–90 cm (2–3 ft).

H. 'Hornby Castle' A very fine cultivar with blossoms of deep brick red and yellow. 60–90 cm (2–3 ft).

H. 'Hyperion' An old favourite with beautiful large lemon-yellow blossoms. 90 cm–1.5 m (3–5 ft).

H. 'Margaret Perry' A widely cultivated variety with Jaffa-orange flowers borne in profusion. Essential for the bog garden! Well tried and reliable. 60–90 cm (2–3 ft).

H. 'Marion Vaughan' Bright canary yellow. 60–90 cm (2–3 ft).

H. 'Mikado' An old but reliable cultivar with orange blossoms each with a brown throat. 60–90 cm (2–3 ft).

H. 'Pink Charm' A well-tried small pink day lily with slender strap-like leaves. 60–75 cm (2–2½ ft).

H. 'Pink Damask' Said to be the best pink currently available. Rose pink and very free flowering. 60–90 cm (2–3 ft).

H. 'Salmon Sheen' Very free flowering salmon pink. 60–90 cm (2–3 ft).

H. 'Spectacular' Golden blossoms with striking bright red centres. 60–90 cm (2–3 ft).

H. 'Stafford' One of the most outstanding reds. Almost iridescent. Needs placing very carefully for the best effect. 60–90 cm (2–3 ft).

H. 'Tejas' Smaller flowers than most, but produced in profusion. Deep reddish orange. 60–90 cm (2–3 ft).

H. 'Whichford' An outstanding introduction having lemon-yellow blossoms with a greenish throat. 60–90 cm (2–3 ft).

Hosta crispula

Splendid foliage plant having oval or lance-shaped green leaves banded with white. Lavender tubular blossoms on slender stems during late summer. Increase by division as soon as growth is observed during early spring. 60−75 cm (2−2½ ft).

H. fortunei

Oval leaves of greyish green or green. Flowers tubular, lilac to violet, during summer. Can be raised from seed, but more usually propagated by division during early spring. 75−90 cm (2½−3 ft).

H. f. 'Albo-picta' Similar in most respects to the species, but with a distinctive golden centre to each leaf in spring. The leaves turn completely green by late summer. Propagate by division during early spring. 75−90 cm (2½−3 ft).

H. f. 'Aurea' A very fine cultivar that has bright yellow leaves during spring and early summer. These eventually return to green. Increase by division during early spring. 60−75 cm (2−2½ ft).

H. f. 'Aureo-marginata' Dark green foliage with persistent gold margins. Increase by division during early spring. 75−90 cm (2½−3 ft).

H. lancifolia

Broadly lance-shaped leaves, glossy green, arching. Tubular flowers of deep purple borne on stout flower stems during late summer. Increase by seed sown immediately it ripens or division during early spring. 60 cm (2 ft).

H. l. 'Kabitan' A very fine dwarf cultivar with bright golden leaves with a green rippled edge. Increase by division during early spring. 30−60 cm (1−2 ft).

H. plantaginea

Rounded green leaves and bold spikes of fragrant pure white trumpet-shaped flowers in late summer. Increase from seed sown immediately after ripening or division during early spring. 60−75 cm (2−2½ ft).

H. p. 'Grandiflora' A plant with larger leaves and bigger flowers than the ordinary species. Increase by division during early spring. 60−75 cm (2−2½ ft).

H. p. 'Royal Standard' This is the finest of this group. Large white fragrant blossoms and handsome glossy green leaves. Increase by division during early spring. 60−75 cm (2−2½ ft).

H. sieboldiana

Beautiful oval glaucous leaves of substance and quality. One of the finest plain-leaved hostas. Pale lilac tubular flowers on strong flower stalks throughout summer. Seed sown shortly after ripening is a successful method of propagation, but most gardeners prefer division during early spring. 60−75 cm (2−2½ ft).

H. s. 'Elegans' Leaves large, much bluer than the species and with a more corrugated surface. Flowers off-white to pale lilac in summer. Increase by division during early spring. 60−75 cm (2−2½ ft).

H. s. 'Mira' Very much like *H. s.* 'Elegans' but larger in every respect. Increase by division during early spring. 75−90 cm (1½−3 ft).

H. tardiflora

A species of similar appearance to *H. lancifolia*, but flowering later. Lance-shaped glossy green leaves and sprays of purple blossoms in the autumn. Increase from seed or division during early spring. 60 cm (2 ft).

H. undulata

Small lance-shaped wavy green leaves marked with white. Lilac tubular blossoms on slender stems during late summer. Propagate by division in early spring. 60 cm (2 ft).

H. u. 'Albo-marginata' Green foliage with distinctive white margins. Increase by division during early spring. 60 cm (2 ft).

H. u. 'Erromena' Strong plain green leaves and lovely lavender blossoms. Increase by division during early spring. 60 cm (2 ft).

H. u. 'Univittata' Plain green leaves, each with a prominent white splash in the centre. Must be increased by division in early spring. 60 cm (2 ft).

H. ventricosa Large oval to more or less heart-shaped leaves of deep glossy green. Flowers deep violet and carried on strong stems during summer. Increase from seed sown immediately it ripens or lift and divide during early spring. 90 cm (3 ft).

H. v. 'Aureomaculata' Strong broadly oval green leaves with yellow centres. Increase by division during early spring. 90 cm (3 ft).

H. v. 'Variegata' Large green leaves with a bold creamy-yellow margin. Increase by division during early spring. 90 cm (3 ft).

Iris aurea

A tall-growing iris with beautifully formed blossoms of intense golden-yellow during summer. A very resilient and adaptable plant with bold sword-like green leaves. Easily increased by division immediately after flowering, or seed sown as soon as ripe or in early spring. 1.2 m (4 ft).

I. bulleyana

A lovely little Chinese iris with blue flowers produced during early and mid-summer. Bold tufts of grassy foliage. Can be propagated by division immediately after flowering or from seed sown immediately it ripens or during early spring. 60–75 cm (2–2½ ft).

I. chrysographes

An excellent small iris for a sunny damp position. Narrow sword-shaped green foliage among which arise strong short stems with blossoms of rich velvety purple. Can be raised from seed, but the results are variable. Best lifted and divided after flowering. 60 cm (2 ft).

I. kaempferi (Japanese clematis-flowered iris)

A beautiful swamp iris with tufts of broad grassy foliage and rich broad blossoms of deep purple during mid-summer. The species itself has an elegance and charm of its own, but it is more often the named cultivars that are offered to gardeners. Propagation is from seed sown during spring or division of established clumps immediately after flowering. Must have acid soil. 60–75 cm (2–2½ ft).

I. k. 'Blue Heaven' Rich purple-blue velvety petals marked with yellow. Propagate by division immediately after flowering. 60–75 cm (2–2½ ft).

I. k. 'Landscape at Dawn' Fully double, pale rose lavender. The blossoms look

rather like tropical butterflies at rest among the foliage. Propagation by division immediately after flowering. 60–75 cm (2–2½ ft).

I. k. 'Mandarin' A lovely deep violet cultivar with blossoms that look rather like those of a clematis. Increase by division immediately after flowering. 60–75 cm (2–2½ ft).

I. k. 'Tokyo' This is not a 'straight' cultivar but a mixed strain which is raised from seed. Many different colours and colour combinations. Easily raised from a spring sowing of seed. Good colours can be selected and reproduced by division immediately after flowering. 60–75 cm (2–2½ ft).

I. k. 'Variegata' Of neat habit, this iris has lovely cream and green striped foliage and rather small violet-blue flowers during summer. Increased by division immediately after flowering. 60 cm (2 ft).

I. ochroleuca

A big bold yellow and white species for almost any wet spot. Flowers during summer among tall glaucous sword-like leaves. These are particularly attractive during spring as they emerge through the soil covered with a lovely 'bloom', rather like that encountered on grapes. Can be increased from seed sown immediately it ripens or in the early spring. Division of established clumps immediately after flowering. 1.5 m (5 ft).

I. sibirica (Siberian iris)

This is a versatile blue iris that is now rarely grown as a species because of the wealth of cultivars that are available. *Iris sibirica* has strong tufts of grassy foliage and erect stems of elegant pale blue flowers. Easily raised from seed, but flower colour will be variable. Good selections can be lifted and divided immediately after flowering or in early spring as the young spears of growth appear. 90 cm (3 ft).

I. s. 'Emperor' Deep violet-purple. An outstanding cultivar with flowers of a lovely velvety texture. Increase by division immediately after flowering on in early spring as the plants start into growth. 90 cm (3 ft).

I. s. 'Ottawa' Another deep violet cultivar which is widely grown. Increase by division immediately after flowering or in the early spring when the plants start to grow. 90 cm (3 ft).

I. s. 'Perry's Blue' This is the sky-blue cultivar that has largely replaced the ordinary species. Very consistent blossoms of high quality. Increase by division immediately after flowering or in early spring as growth commences. 90 cm (3 ft).

I. s. 'Perry's Pygmy' One of the finest small-growing irises for the waterside. Deep violet blossoms. Increase by division immediately after flowering or during early spring when the first signs of growth are observed. 45 cm (1½ ft).

Ligularia clivorum

A most attractive member of the daisy family with large violet green heart-shaped leaves and huge mop heads of droopy orange flowers. A first-class plant producing a late-summer display. Although easily raised from seed the results are variable. Best propagated by division during dormant period. 90 cm–1.2 m (3–4 ft).

L. c. 'Golden Queen' Golden-yellow mop heads of flowers in late summer. Green heart-shaped leaves. Increase by division in winter. 90 cm–1.2 m (3–4 ft).

L. c. 'Orange Princess' A superb orange cultivar. The leaves are green with a purplish infusion. Increase by division when dormant. 90 cm–1.2 m (3–4 ft).

L. stenocephala 'The Rocket'

Soaring wands of bright yellow daisy-like flowers during late summer. Big bold clumps of green, more or less triangular, coarsely toothed foliage. Increase by division when dormant. 1.5–2 m (5–6½ ft).

L. veitchiana

A most accommodating plant for a wet and partially shaded spot. Coarse green, almost triangular leaves and tall spires of yellow daisy-like flowers. These are produced in profusion during late summer and early autumn. It is prudent to propagate by division during the dormant period. 90 cm–2 m (3–6½ ft).

Lobelia cardinalis (Cardinal flower)

This is a perennial lobelia but one which does appreciate a little winter protection. The prudent gardener lifts one or two over-wintering rosettes and places them in a garden frame or unheated greenhouse for safe-keeping. In very cold areas a protective layer of straw or bracken during winter is beneficial. An upright plant with bright green foliage and spires of vivid red flowers. This is often confused with the purple-leaved *L. fulgens* which in nurseries is often sold as *L. cardinalis*. Increase by dividing the rosettes of over-wintered foliage, from stem cuttings in spring or seed sown at the same period. 60–90 cm (2–3 ft).

L. fulgens

Beetroot-coloured stems and leaves and spikes of bright red blossoms during summer. Can be increased by division during spring, stem cuttings at the same time or seed sown before early summer. 60–90 cm (2–3 ft).

L. 'Huntsman'

Brilliant scarlet flowers in late summer and green foliage. Increased by division of over-wintered rosettes in spring. 60–90 cm (2–3 ft).

L. 'Queen Victoria'

Maroon foliage and bright red flowers during late summer. Increased by division of over-wintered rosettes in spring. 60–90 cm (2–3 ft).

L. syphilitica

Green foliage and spires of blue, or occasionally white, flowers during late summer. Enjoys a little shade, often flagging in full sun, even when growing in really boggy soil. Easily raised from seed sown during spring under glass. 60–90 cm (2–3 ft).

L. × vedrariensis

Mid-green foliage flushed and infused with purple. Flowers intense violet and produced during late summer and early autumn. Easily raised from a spring sowing of seed under glass or division of over-wintered rosettes in early spring. 75–90 cm (2½–3 ft).

Lysichiton americanum (Skunk cabbage)
A member of the arum family with bright yellow spathes which appear during early spring well ahead of the large green cabbagy foliage. Should be increased from seed sown in a tray of mud immediately it is harvested. Stored seed is unlikely to be viable. It is very difficult to divide skunk cabbages even though they are clump-forming plants. When this is attempted it should be done in spring before they come into flower. 60–90 cm (2–3 ft).

L. camtschatcense
The white-flowered skunk cabbage. Rather smaller-flowered than its American cousin and much less impressive. Increase from seed sown immediately it ripens. 60–90 cm (2–3 ft).

Lysimachia nummularia (Creeping Jenny)
This is a more or less evergreen carpeting plant that is ideal for disguising the union of bog garden with pool. It also provides attractive ground cover between taller-growing plants in marshy areas, although its spread does need to be carefully monitored. During summer the fresh green foliage becomes studded with starry butter-cup-like blossoms. Easily increased from short stem cuttings taken at any time during the growing season. 5 cm (2 in).

L. n. 'Aurea' The most wonderful golden-leaved creeping plant. Has all the virtues of the common species but the added bonus of brightly coloured foliage. Easily increased from short stem cuttings taken during the growing period. 5 cm (2 in).

L. punctata
An upright-growing plant with rugged downy foliage and spikes of bright yellow flowers almost the same in general appearance as those of the creeping Jenny. Increased by division during dormant period. 60–90 cm (2–3 ft).

Lythrum salicaria (Purple loosestrife)
For mid- to late-summer flowering few bog-garden plants can surpass the lythrum for colour and reliability. The common species has a bushy upright habit and produces myriad slender spires of deep rose-purple blossoms. Easily increased by division during dormancy. 1.2 m (4 ft).

L. s. 'Brilliant' A very fine pink-flowered sort. Increase by division during dormant period. 90 cm–1.2 m (3–4 ft).

L. s. 'Lady Sackville' Strong rose-pink selection. A plant of excellent habit. Increase by division during dormant period. 90 cm–1.2 m (3–4 ft).

L. s. 'Robert' Another soft-pink cultivar of exceptional merit. Divide during dormant period. 90 cm–1.2 m (3–4 ft).

L. virgatum
A much more restrained loosestrife; not so impressive as *L. salicaria* but better suited to the small garden. Shorter spires of purple blossom and dark green foliage. Increase by division during dormant period. 45 cm (1½ ft).

L. v. 'Dropmore Purple' A deep purple cultivar of consistent performance. Flowers during mid- to late summer. Increase by division during dormancy. 45 cm (1½ ft).

Mimulus cardinalis (Cardinal monkey flower)
A plant for damp rather than really wet conditions. It has attractive hoary foliage and brilliant scarlet-orange flowers during late summer. Not always reliably hardy. In wet conditions in cold areas it is easily over-wintered in a cold greenhouse or frame as rooted cuttings taken during late summer. Seed sown during early spring in a propagator provides an alternative method of propagation. 45–60 cm (1½–2 ft).

M. 'Highland Red'
A fairly short growing hybrid with obviously some *M. luteus* and probably *M. cupreus* in its background. Soft green foliage and bright red blossoms throughout summer. Increase by spring division of over-wintered rosettes. 15 cm (6 in).

M. 'Highland Pink'
This is a pink-flowered version of *M.* 'Highland Red'. 15 cm (6 in).

M. 'Hose-in-hose'

Bright yellow-flowered cultivar probably derived directly from *M. luteus*, in which each blossom has another inside, almost like a double. Increase by spring division of over-wintered rosettes. 20–30 cm (8 in–1 ft).

M. lewisii

Closely allied to *M. cardinalis* and requiring the same method of over-wintering as short, rooted stem cuttings. Somewhat hoary foliage and lovely rose-lilac blossoms throughout summer. A little gem for the smaller bog garden. 30–45 cm (1–1½ ft).

M. 'Monarch Strain'

One of the very free flowering, mixed coloured, seed-raised strains of the monkey flower. Gorgeous exotic-looking blossoms throughout summer. Not reliably perennial and best raised from seed sown under glass early in the spring. 20–30 cm (8 in–1 ft).

M. 'Whitecroft Scarlet'

One of the tiniest bog-garden plants. Dense carpets of fresh green foliage and masses of brilliant scarlet blossoms. Often does not survive winter intact in cold areas, patches of foliage dying out. Easily raised from seed sown under glass during early spring. Flowers all summer, even from a sowing during the current year. 10 cm (4 in).

Parnassia palustris (Grass of Parnassus)

A real challenge for any gardener is this little gem from mountain streams and wet places. It grows best near moving water and is perfectly happy in the splash of a stream or cascade. A lime hater, it bears its charming snow-white flowers, occasionally blotched with green, on slender wiry stems among neat clumps of heart-shaped leaves. It is easily raised from seed but the seedlings must be pot grown if they are to stand any chance of being successfully transplanted. 15–30 cm (6 in–1 ft).

Peltiphyllum peltatum (Umbrella plant)

Stout stems bear immense leaves of bronze green, often 30cm (1 ft) in diameter. They are handsomely lobed and toothed and preceded in spring by globular heads of rose-coloured blossoms on sturdy stems 45 cm (1½ ft) high. It is possible to raise it from seed, but it is quicker to divide the fleshy rhizome during early spring. 45–90 cm (1½–3 ft).

Petasites japonicus (Butterbur)

This is suitable only where plenty of space is available, for it produces large unwieldy cabbage-like foliage during summer. It is a welcome harbinger of spring, producing crowded heads of white flowers on neat short stems scarcely after winter has passed. 1.5 m (5 ft).

Phormium tenax (New Zealand flax)

Not usually associated with bog gardens, the phormiums are plants of wet places, although most modern kinds do not visually rest easily among other bog-garden plants. The common species is sometimes used as a pool-side or water-side plant, especially in a formal situation where its bold sword-like leaves add an architectural quality. The foliage is a metallic bronze green and from among it is sometimes produced an odd-looking flower stem with curious reddish and ochre flowers. It is readily raised from seed, the young plants being grown on in pots. Old plants can sometimes be divided successfully in spring. 90 cm–1.5 m (3–5 ft).

P. t. 'Atropurpurea' Attractive reddish-purple foliage. Variable when reproduced from seed. Careful division of good-coloured plants is best. 90 cm–1.2 m (3–4 ft).

P. t. 'Variegata' Strongly variegated foliage of green, yellow and white. Less vigorous than the preceding. 75–90 cm (2½–3 ft).

P. 'Cream Delight'

Foliage vivid creamy yellow banded with green. Increased by careful division in spring. 75–90 cm (2½–3 ft).

P. 'Dark Delight'

Leaves of deep maroon. Increased by careful division in spring. Height 75–90 cm (2½–3 ft).

P. 'Emerald Green'
A plain green cultivar. Increased by careful division in spring. 75 cm (2½ ft).

P. 'Maori Maiden'
Extraordinary foliage of red, pink and brown. Increased by careful division. 45–60 cm (1½–2 ft).

Primula alpicola (Moonlight primula)
Early summer flowering hardy perennial with pendant bell-shaped flowers varying in colour from yellow to white and purple carried on slender flower stems. Leaves small, rounded and bright green. A plant for a cool moist position in the less water-logged part of the bog garden. Propagation by early spring division or seed, preferably sown shortly after harvesting. 15–60 cm (6 in–2 ft).

  P. a. alba A pure white form that comes almost 100% true from seed. 15–60 cm (6 in–2 ft).

  P. a. luna A beautiful sulphurous-yellow form. Like its white counterpart this comes almost completely true from seed. 15–60 cm (6 in–2 ft).

  P. a. violacea A purple to violet selection which is fairly erratic from seed. To ensure plants of even stature and colour propagate by division in early spring, just as the young shoots are emerging. 15–60 cm (6 in–2 ft).

P. anisodora
A strongly aromatic plant, both flowers and foliage. Flowers brownish purple with a green eye and borne in small tiered whorls around a strong flower stalk during summer. Leaves large, green, more or less oval and rather coarse. A reliable perennial well suited to a moist position in either sun or shade. Easily increased from seed, especially if sown immediately after harvesting. Plants can be carefully divided during early spring or immediately after flowering. 30–60 cm (1–2 ft).

P. aurantiaca
Early summer flowering hardy perennial primula with bright reddish-orange blossoms arranged in neat tiered whorls. Leaves green, long, broad and rather coarse, slightly aromatic. A reliable plant for bog garden or water-side. Revels in a richly organic damp medium. Increase from seed, preferably sown immediately after harvesting. Packeted seed sown the following year usually germinates in an erratic fashion. Established plants can be divided as they emerge through the soil during early spring, or immediately they finish flowering. 60–90 cm (2–3 ft).

P. beesiana
A vigorous early summer flowering hardy perennial. Flowers rosy carmine with a yellow eye, borne in dense tiered whorls on stout flower stalks. Leaves large, green, cabbagy, up to 30 cm (1 ft) long. An excellent strong-growing plant for bog garden or pool-side. Enjoys a cool deep root run in a richly organic damp soil. Grows well in either sun or partial shade. Increase by division of the emerging crowns in spring, or from seed sown immediately after harvesting. Packeted seed sown during spring usually germinates, but somewhat erratically. 60–75 cm (2–2½ ft).

P. bulleyana
A hardy perennial primula that flowers during early summer. Large deep orange flowers arranged in tiered whorls on strong flower stalks. Leaves large, green and cabbagy. An excellent companion for *P. beesiana* and *P. burmanica* at the water-side. Must have a cool damp root run in a deep richly organic soil. Grows well in sun or partial shade. Can be propagated by careful division in early spring just as the shoots are emerging, or immediately after flowering. Freshly gathered seed germinates freely. Packeted seed sown the following spring germinates in an erratic manner. 60–90 cm (2–3 ft).

P. burmanica
Vigorous hardy perennial primula flowering during early summer. Large reddish-purple blossoms with conspicuous yellow eyes are borne in tiered whorls on strong flower stems. Leaves green, large and cabbagy. Must have a damp, deep, cool soil rich in organic matter. Will grow well in

sun or shade. Propagate by careful division of the crowns during early spring just as they are coming into growth, or immediately after flowering. Seed that has been freshly gathered germinates freely if sown immediately. Older seed usually germinates, but in an erratic fashion. 60 cm (2 ft).

P. capitata
Mid- to late-summer flowering hardy perennial with small deep violet bell-shaped flowers arranged in rounded flattened heads on short stout flower stems. The small rosettes of lance-shaped green leaves are covered generously in white meal, especially beneath, as are the flower stems. A lovely plant for a damp but not water-logged corner. Does not divide easily, plants tending to be individuals which grow larger without producing young. Easily raised from seed, especially when freshly gathered and sown immediately. 15−30 cm (6 in−1 ft).

P. c. mooreana Very similar to the species and flowering over a slightly later period. Flowers open in a more flattened head; leaves green above with a dense white meal beneath. This is a plant often sold as *P. mooreana*. A robust and easily grown form. 15−30 cm (6 in−1 ft).

P. c. sphaerocephala Another variation of the species. Funnel-shaped deep violet flowers in tight rounded heads during mid- and late summer. Leaves lance shaped, green above and beneath. 15−30 cm (6 in−1 ft).

P. chungensis A lovely hardy perennial primula with handsome tiered whorls of pale orange blossoms during early summer. Leaves green, coarse and rather cabbagy in large clumps. Revels in a moist richly organic soil in full sun or partial shade. Readily increased from seed sown as soon as possible after harvesting. Older seed will germinate but maybe somewhat erratically. 60−75 cm (2−2½ ft).

P. cortusoides
Spring flowering hardy but often short-lived perennial. Flowers small, purplish rose in many-flowered umbels. Leaves rounded, soft green and downy. A very easily grown plant for a damp shady spot. Plants grow well for two or three years but then start to deteriorate and often die out. Replace regularly from seed which germinates reasonably freely at any time. 15−30 cm (6 in−1 ft).

P. denticulata (Drumstick primula)
Very popular, vigorous, spring-flowering perennials for the bog garden. Large heads of lilac, pink or purplish blossoms crowded into globular heads on strong flower stalks during early spring. Leaves long, broad and coarse, often dusted with a white or yellowish meal. Flower stems often coated as well. Completely hardy and easily increased from seed sown during spring or early summer, seedlings flowering during their second year. Good forms can be reproduced from root cuttings taken during dormant period. 30−60 cm (1−2 ft).

P. d. var. **alba** (White drumstick primula). Similar in almost every respect to *P. denticulata* but producing heads of pure white flowers. Extremely variable when raised from seed, some occasional purplish or lilac-flowered forms appearing. The vigour of the plants and density of the globular flower heads are very variable among seed-raised plants. The most reliable method of reproduction of the drumstick primula is root cuttings of selected forms. 30−60 cm (1−2 ft).

P. d. var. **cachemiriana** A vigorous variety of *P. denticulata* with fairly consistent purple blossoms. This is generally more robust than the species with flower heads that are slightly larger and bold cabbagy foliage coated beneath with yellow meal. Most plants are grown from seed but any particularly fine forms can be propagated from root cuttings during dormant period. 30−60 cm (1−2 ft).

P. d. 'Rosea' A rich crimson form identical to *P. denticulata*, except in colour. Best increased from root cuttings during dormant period. 30−60 cm (1−2 ft).

P. florindae (Himalayan cowslip)
A giant primula which flowers from mid-summer into early autumn. Large heads of

pendant sulphur-yellow blossoms above broad, coarse, green leaves. The whole plant has a musky aroma. Perfectly hardy and reliably perennial. A big bold bog plant that will grow in damp soil as well as standing water. A lovely stream-side plant fully tolerant of the rising and falling of the water. Enjoys a deep cool soil with plenty of organic matter incorporated. Propagates freely from seed sown at any time during spring or summer. Plants can be divided during early autumn when flowering is over. 60–90 cm (2–3 ft).

P. f. 'Art Shades' This is a seed-raised selection in which the flowers vary from palest primrose and apricot to burnt orange. Handsome plants for adding colour variation during late summer. Although popularly seed raised, exceptionally fine colour forms can be reliably increased by division immediately after flowering. 60–90 cm (2–3 ft).

P. 'Harlow Car Hybrids'

This is probably the best-known strain of candelabra primulas ever developed. Flowering from early spring into summer they embrace almost every colour. A complex group of hybrids, they have large blossoms, mostly with conspicuous yellow 'eyes', arranged in crowded tiered whorls on strong flower stems. The leaves are varying shades of green and rather coarse and cabbagy. This strain was developed over many years at the famous gardens of the Northern Horticultural Society at Harlow Car, Harrogate, North Yorkshire. Their origins are unclear, but the strain is constantly being up-graded and improved by re-selection. Plants for a wide range of situations provided they have a cool moist root-run. The extensive plantings at Harlow Car embrace sun, partial shade and full shade, the hybrids doing tolerably well under all conditions. Propagation is by seed sown immediately after harvesting or in spring. This yields a good mixture of colours. Especially fine colours that appear can be reproduced by careful division in early spring as the shoots start to appear or immediately after flowering. 60–75 cm (2–2½ ft).

P. helodoxa

Hardy summer-flowering perennial primula with vivid yellow, open, bell-shaped flowers in tiered whorls. Leaves bright green, long and tapering. An excellent subject for bog gardens. While enjoying dampness, it will not tolerate standing with its roots in water. Easily increased from freshly gathered seed sown immediately. Packeted seed retains little viability and relatively few seedlings are produced from its erratic germination. Divide clumps in early spring just as they are coming into growth. Or lift and divide immediately after flowering. 60–90 cm (2–3 ft).

P. heucherifolia

Spring-flowering hardy perennial with small mauve-pink to deep purple blossoms in many-flowered umbels. Leaves rounded and lobed, coarse and sparsely hairy. An easy plant for a damp spot. Benefits from a little shade. Readily increased from seed, the old plants periodically being replaced as they deteriorate rather quickly with age. 15–30 cm (6–12 in).

P. 'Inverewe'

The most spectacular candelabra primula. An early summer flowering perennial with bright orange flowers in dense tiered whorls. The flower stems are heavily coated with white meal and contrast beautifully with the vivid blossoms. Leaves plain green, rather coarse, more or less elliptical and rather cabbagy. An excellent plant for bog gardens. Demands a good richly organic soil and constant moisture. It will grow happily in sun or partial shade. As it does not set seed it must be divided either in early spring as shoots are just starting to push through the soil, or immediately flowering is over. 45–75 cm (1½–2½ ft).

P. japonica

A strong-growing hardy perennial primula with bold flowers of deep red produced in tiered whorls on extremely stout flower stalks during late spring and early summer. Large cabbage-like leaves, coarse, green with a slight bluish tint. One of the most reliable moisture-loving primulas. Needs a damp, richly organic soil. Will grow in either full sun or partial shade. Easily increased from seed, even packeted seed producing tolerable results. Plants can also be divided during early spring, just as new shoots are emerging, or immediately flowering is over. 45–75 cm (1½–2½ ft).

P. j. 'Miller's Crimson' The finest form of *P. japonica*, the colour being particularly intense and uniform. In every other respect identical to the species. Although a named cultivar, this comes true from seed. Seed sown immediately after harvesting is best, but packeted seed also yields creditable results. Plants can be divided in early spring or immediately after flowering. 45–75 cm (1½–2½ ft).

P. j. 'Postford White' This has flowers of a cool icy white with a conspicuous orange-yellow central ring. Sometimes the flowers show a hint of pink. A vigorous plant, the same in most respects to *P. japonica*, but with somewhat paler foliage. Another primula that comes almost 100% true from seed. Freshly gathered seed produces the best results, but reasonable germination can be expected from packeted seed. Plants can be lifted and divided during early spring or immediately after flowering. 45–75 cm (1½–2½ ft).

P. muscarioides

Mid-summer flowering hardy perennial with many-flowered heads of similar appearance to that spring-flowering bulb, the grape hyacinth. The individual flowers are very different, though, being tubular, pendant and deep purplish blue. The leaves are rounded, dull green and slightly downy. Best grown in a damp spot with a little dappled shade. Easily raised from seeds sown as soon after harvesting as possible. Well-established plants can be divided during early spring, as soon as signs of growth are detected. 30–45 cm (1–1½ ft).

P. poissonii

An interesting early summer flowering hardy perennial primula with tiered whorls of deep purplish-crimson flowers with yellow eyes. Leaves oblong or obovate, coarse, glaucous, in neat clumps. Requires a moist richly organic soil in sun or partial shade. Will not tolerate standing in water. Easily raised from seed, especially if it is sown directly after harvesting. Plants can be divided during early spring as shoots start to appear, or immediately following flowering. 30–45 cm (1–1½ ft).

P. polyneura

Spring-flowering hardy perennial with pale rose, rich rose or purple blossoms on slender flower stalks. Leaves more or less triangular, green and downy. A good subject for richly organic soil at the water-side. Easily increased from seed and best replaced every few years. 15–30 cm (6 in–1 ft).

P. pulverulenta

A great favourite among gardeners. Spring and early summer flowering, with deep red blossoms with conspicuous purple eyes. Bold tiered flower stems densely covered in white meal. Green cabbagy leaves. One of the finest moisture-loving primulas. A hardy plant of great versatility and reliability growing in any moist, richly organic soil in either sun or shade. Easily increased from seed. Readily divisible in spring when its shoots are just peeping through the soil, or during mid-summer when flowering is over. 60–90 cm (2–3 ft).

P. p. 'Bartley Strain' A fine pink-flowered strain that is the same in every other respect as ordinary *P. pulverulenta*. Easily raised from seed, although established plants can be divided in spring as evidence of growth is seen. They can also be divided after flowering. 60–90 cm (2–3 ft).

P. rosea

An early spring flowering perennial for a wet place at the water-side. Beautiful glowing pink primrose-like blossoms appear among green leaves that are attractively flushed with copper or bronze. These spring tints are short lived, the broadly lance-shaped leaves reverting to plain green. A marvellous plant for stream or pool-side. Flourishes anywhere, in sun or partial shade, provided the soil contains a liberal quantity of organic matter and is constantly moist. Easily increased from seed, ideally sown directly it ripens. The plants produced in this manner are sometimes variable in both colour and stature so selection of the best forms for propagation by division is desirable. Division should be undertaken immediately after flowering. 10–15 cm (4–6 in).

P. r. 'Delight' A lovely cultivar with brilliant rose-pink blossoms superior in both quality and size. Must be increased by division. 10–15 cm (4–6 in).

P. r. 'Grandiflora' A larger-flowered form with similar rose-pink blossoms and plain green leaves that have a hint of bronze in the spring. Not as consistent as 'Delight' because the plants commonly offered in garden centres are usually seed raised. The true 'Grandiflora' is increased by division to maintain consistency. When a group of 'Grandiflora' is in flower it is prudent to mark the best ones and reproduce those by division. 10–15 cm (4–6 in).

P. saxatilis

Spring and early summer flowering short-lived perennial with many-flowered umbels of rosy-violet or pinkish-mauve blossoms. Leaves rounded, toothed and lobed with long leaf stalks, green, soft and downy. An easy plant for a shady spot in a richly damp organic soil. Plants start to deteriorate after a couple of years and need replacing. Easily raised from seed sown during spring or summer. 10–30 cm (4 in–1 ft).

P. secundiflora

A charming hardy summer-flowering perennial with reddish purple, pendant, funnel-shaped blossoms borne in groups on slender flower stems. Leaves lance shaped, green, often with a yellowish meal beneath in the spring. Enjoys a little dappled shade and a cool, moist root run. Well suited to a bog garden but will not enjoy sitting in water during winter. Easily increased from seed sown directly after harvesting, or by division of established plants in early spring. 30–45 cm (1–1½ ft).

P. sieboldii

Early summer flowering perennial primula with umbels of rounded, white, pink or purple blossoms with conspicuous eyes. Leaves rounded and toothed, soft green and finely downy. Gorgeous plant for a shady spot in moist soil. Easily increased from seed, or in the case of named cultivars by careful division in early spring or directly after flowering. In years gone by there were many cultivars available. These have gone into decline and only a few old favourites like 'Wine Lady' are popularly available. 15–20 cm (6–8 in).

P. sikkimensis

Hardy summer-flowering perennial with soft yellow, pendant, funnel-shaped flowers on slender stems. Leaves coarse, green, rounded and shiny. A bog plant that revels in wet soils with a high organic-matter content, preferably in partial shade. Easily increased from division of established plants after flowering. Seed sown during spring or early summer is usually successful, even if it has been packeted the previous year. 45–75 cm (1½–2½ ft).

P. sinoplantaginea

Late spring flowering, short-lived hardy perennial. Deep purple, fragrant, tubular blossoms in small umbels. Leaves narrow, lance-shaped, smooth green with yellowish farina beneath. There are distinctive reddish scales at the base of the plant. There is always some question as to whether the plants offered by nurserymen under this name really are the true species as it hybridizes so freely. Established plants do not divide well, but seed is set freely and young plants are easily raised, especially if the seed can be sown fresh. A plant for a damp but not wet spot at the water-side. 15–20 cm (6–8 in).

P. sinopurpurea

A delightful hardy perennial late spring flowering primula. Gorgeous violet-purple tubular blossoms in six- to twelve-flowered umbels. Broadly lance shaped plain green leaves with serrated edges, sparingly covered with meal beneath. A more reliable and vigorous plant than *P. sinoplantaginea*, but of the same general aspect. Excellent

177

for water-side planting. Readily raised from seed, especially if sown shortly after harvesting. Spring division is possible, but needs great care to ensure a reasonable percentage re-establishment. 30−45 cm (1−1½ ft).

P. viali (Orchid primula)

Late spring or early summer flowering hardy perennial, although some gardeners suggest that it is monocarpic and dies after flowering. This does happen, but it is usually the result of poor cultivation rather than the plant's inevitable behaviour. One of the most bizarre primulas sporting short spikes of blossom that look rather like miniature red-hot pokers. Dense heads of small tubular flowers of red and bluish purple. Small, lance shaped, soft, downy green leaves. Suitable for a damp but not waterlogged spot in a bog garden. Easily raised from seed, preferably sown shortly after collection. Lifting and dividing plants is largely futile as almost half of them are likely to be lost during the operation. A regular supply of young seed-raised plants should always be maintained to counter the plants' habit of fading out after flowering. 30−45 cm (1−1½ ft).

P. waltoni

Late spring or early summer flowering hardy perennial with deep wine purple occasionally pink flowers in neat heads on strong wiry stems. Leaves lance shaped, but rounded, bright green. A good plant for a damp but not waterlogged spot. Appreciates dappled shade. Does not always divide freely but is very easily raised from seed, especially that which has been freshly gathered. 30−45 cm (1−1½ ft).

P. yargongensis

Late spring flowering hardy perennial primula for a damp but not waterlogged spot at the pool-side. Flowers tubular, bell-shaped, mauve, pink or purple with a white or cream eye, in small umbels. Leaves rounded or elliptical, plain green. A native of wet stream-sides in north-western Yunnan and south-eastern Tibet, this is an ideal plant for the pool-side. Benefits from a very damp, richly organic soil, but will rot off if forced to sit in permanent moisture. Easily raised from seed sown immediately it ripens. Plants set seed freely provided they receive constant moisture. 10−30 cm (4 in−1 ft).

Rheum palmatum (Ornamental rhubarb)

Although a number of rheums are grown in gardens this is the most reliable for the bog garden. It has broad spreading foliage and spikes of small decorative creamy white blossoms. It is best propagated by division of the crowns during spring just as they are breaking into growth. Seed-raised plants are very variable. 1.5−1.8 m (5−6 ft).

R. p. var. **tanguticum** The foliage of this form usually has a purplish cast and is always deeply cut. The flowers should be pink or rose purple but sometimes plants yield white blossoms. The best forms should be propagated by division during early spring. Seed raising cannot be recommended. 1.5−1.8 m (5−6 ft).

R. p. 'Bowles' Crimson' This is almost identical to the species but has foliage with a strong purplish-red infusion and crimson flower spikes. Propagation from spring division of the crowns. Seed-raised plants are totally unreliable from the point of view of colour or form. 1.5−1.8 m (5−6 ft).

Rodgesia tabularis

One of the most suitable rodgersias for bog gardens. Pale green circular leaves and dense panicles of creamy white flowers during summer. Easily increased by division of established crowns during early spring, or by seed sown under glass at the same period. 90 cm−1.2 m (3−4 ft).

Schizostylis coccinea (Kaffir lily)

An attractive stream-side plant that flowers during autumn with bright red flowers among grassy foliage rather like a small day lily or hemerocallis. Easily propagated by division during early spring. 30−60 cm (1−2 ft).

S. c. 'Grandiflora' The same as the ordinary Kaffir lily, but with much larger flowers. Increased by division during early spring. 30−60 cm (1−2 ft).

S. c. 'Mrs Hegarty' A rose-pink cultivar with elegant slender stems of blossoms. Propagate by division during early spring. 30–60 cm (1–2 ft).

Symplocarpus foetidus (Skunk cabbage) A curious bog plant with quaintly hooded arum-like flowers of purple and green. These appear before its large, bright green cabbagy foliage. Propagation by division during early spring before the flowers appear. 75–90 cm (2½–3 ft).

Trollius asiaticus
Deep yellow butter-cup-like flowers on strong wiry stems above compact mounds of finely toothed, bronze-green leaves. Spring and early summer flowering. Propagate by seed sown in spring, or division of established crowns during dormant period. 30–45 cm (1–1½ ft).

T. chinensis
Beautiful yellow globular flowers are produced above hummocks of round or kidney-shaped leaves during spring and early summer. Propagate by seed sown in spring, or division of established crowns during dormancy. 30–45 cm (1–1½ ft).

T. × cultorum 'Earliest of All'
The most popular of all the trollius or globe flowers. Rich canary yellow, almost globular flowers on strong wiry stems during spring and early summer. Handsome mounds of rounded toothed foliage. Increase by division during dormant period. 30–45 cm (1–1½ ft).

    T. × c. 'Fireglobe' A reddish-orange cultivar of exceptional merit. Increase only by division during dormant period. 30–45 cm (1–1½ ft).

    T. × c. 'Golden Queen' A well-tried cultivar with golden-yellow blossoms during spring and early summer. Bright green toothed foliage. Increase by division during dormant period. 30–45 cm (1–1½ ft).

    T. × c. 'Orange Globe' The finest orange-flowered trollius. Blooms during spring and early summer. Leaves dark green and toothed. Increase by division during dormant period. 30–45 cm (1–1½ ft).

T. europaeus (Common globe flower) A lovely lemon-yellow species with globular blossoms that appear during spring and early summer. Compact mounds of bright green lobed foliage. Propagate from seed sown during spring, or division in dormant period. 30–60 cm (1–2 ft).

T. yunnanensis
Bright yellow cup-shaped or almost flat flowers during late spring on strong wiry stems. Basal clusters of rather irregular or oval leaves. Propagate by seed sown during spring or division of established plants during dormant period. 60 cm (2 ft).

Bog-garden ferns
There are a few ferns that live happily in bog-garden conditions. Those described enjoy it really wet and will often tolerate standing water.

Dryopteris palustris (Marsh buckler fern) An elegant creeping fern that enjoys spreading from moist soil into water at the poolside. Upright, pale green, much-divided fronds that persist well into winter in their brown dried state. Propagate by division during spring. 30 cm (1 ft).

Matteuccia struthiopteris (Ostrich feather fern)
Handsome bright green lacy fronds arranged in a shuttlecock fashion around a stout woody crown. The fertile fronds are half the length of the barren ones and produced from the centre of the shuttlecock during mid-summer. A tough but beautiful species which spreads by wiry underground rhizomes. Propagate by division in spring. 90 cm (3 ft).

Onoclea sensibilis (Sensitive fern)
A lovely fern for a stream-side with erect flattened fronds which grow from thick black creeping roots. In spring they emerge with a rose-pink flush, but pass to pale green as summer progresses. This species will grow in standing water or wet ground. Increase by division during spring. 45–60 cm (1½–2 ft).

Osmunda regalis (Royal fern)
A tall and stately fern with large leathery fronds which change colour from pale green in spring, through darker greens to rich burnished bronze in autumn. Although completely hardy, most gardeners protect the emerging fronds in spring with a generous covering of straw or dead bracken. It can be propagated from spores sown immediately after gathering, but more usually by division of established crowns in spring. 1.2–1.8 m (4–6 ft).

O. r. 'Cristata' A smaller version of the common royal fern, but with attractively tasseled and twisted fronds. Propagate by division only. Spore-raised plants are variable. 90 cm–1.2 m (3–4 ft).

O. r. 'Purpurescens' Very similar to *O. regalis*, but with fronds that have a permanent purplish flush. Propagate by division in spring. 1.2–1.8 m (4–6 ft).

O. r. 'Undulata' Attractive crimped and crested mid-green fronds. Propagate by division of the crowns in spring. Spore-raised plants are unreliable and generally yield inferior progeny. 90 cm–1.2 m (3–4 ft).

Woodwardia virginica (Virginian chain fern)
Broad olive-green fronds of a soft felty texture arise from a stout creeping rhizome. A difficult fern to establish, but a lovely plant for pool-side or bog garden when in a situation to its liking. Readily propagated by division during spring. 60 cm (2 ft).

Shrubby bog plants

Apart from the many plants of an herbaceous nature that flourish in a bog garden there are a few woody plants that can make a major contribution to this garden feature.

Cornus alba (Red-barked dogwood)
A thicket-forming shrub with red stems and green leaves that change to copper and gold in autumn. If pruned to the ground each spring it is unlikely to flower. Grown predominently for its coloured stems. Increase by hardwood cuttings taken during winter. 1.2 m (4 ft) if pruned back each spring.

C. a. 'Sibirica' A less-vigorous cultivar with brilliant red stems during winter if regularly pruned down each spring. Propagate from hardwood cuttings during winter. 90 cm–1.2 m (3–4 ft) if pruned back annually.

C. a. 'Spaethii' This cultivar has almost as good winter stems as *C. a.* 'Sibirica' and the added bonus of handsome gold and green variegated foliage in summer. Propagate from hardwood cuttings taken during winter. 90 cm–1.2 m (3–4 ft), if pruned back annually.

C. stolonifera 'Flaviramea'
A handsome shrub that also needs regularly pruning down to give of its best. Bright yellow to olive-green stems during winter. 90 cm–1.2 m (3–4 ft) if pruned back annually.

Salix alba 'Chermesina' (Scarlet willow)
If pruned back as recommended for cornus this becomes a most useful shrub for winter colour. Brilliant orange-scarlet stems are produced if they are cut hard back each spring. This also maintains a manageable shrubby plant. Propagate from hardwood cuttings during winter. 1.2–1.5 m (4–5 ft) if pruned back annually.

S. a. 'Vitellina' (Golden willow) If this is treated in the same way as *S. a.* 'Chermesina' the reward will be brilliant yellow winter stems. Cut back each spring. Increase from hardwood cuttings taken during winter. 1.2–1.5 m (4–5 ft) if pruned back annually.

S. daphnoides (Violet willow)
If cut back hard as recommended for the other willows this will yield the most lovely violet winter stems. Propagate from hardwood cuttings during winter. 1.2–1.5 m (4–5 ft) if pruned back annually.

Taxodium distichum (Swamp cypress)
Only for the large bog garden. A very fine deciduous conifer of pyramidal habit. Summer foliage pale green turning russet as autumn approaches. When well established in really wet conditions it produces strange knobbly breathing roots or 'knees'.

The bark of the trunk is fibrous and red-brown; the branches are orange-brown. It can be propagated from summer cuttings or seed sown during spring or early summer. 20 m (66 ft).

Vaccinium angustifolium (Lowbush blueberry)
A shrub of neat habit requiring very wet acid soil. The pale green lance-shaped leaves turn fiery red and orange in autumn. The flowers are small, bell shaped, white, or red tinted, and produced in abundance during late spring. Fruits blue-black, sweet and edible. Increased by cuttings taken during spring or autumn. 1.5 m (5 ft).

V. arboreum (Farkleberry)
A large deciduous shrub with leathery, glossy, oval leaves that turn bright orange-red in autumn. Flowers small, white and bell shaped in spring. Fruits black and inedible. Increased by cuttings taken during spring or autumn. 1.5–3 m (5–10 ft).

V. corymbosum (Swamp blueberry)
A dense-growing shrub with oval or lance-shaped leaves of bright green turning scarlet and bronze in autumn. Flowers pale pink or white and produced freely during late spring. Fruits large, black and edible. Increased by cuttings taken during spring or autumn. 90 cm–1.5 m (3–5 ft).

APPENDICES

WATER GARDEN PLANTS
Hardy Water Lilies
Tropical Water Lilies
Pond Lilies
Sacred Lotus
Deep-water Aquatics
Hardy Marginal Plants
Tender Marginal Plants
Hardy Submerged Plants
Tender Submerged Plants
Hardy Floating Plants
Tender Floating Plants
Bog Garden Plants
Bog Garden Ferns
Shrubby Bog Plants

EASY PROPAGATION
GUIDE

USEFUL INFORMATION

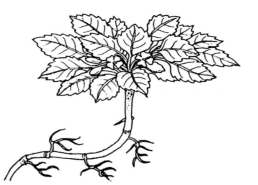

1. WATER-GARDEN PLANTS

Hardy Water Lilies (*Nymphaea*)

No indication of spread is given here as this tends to vary according to the depth of water in which the plant is growing. The surface spread of a properly maintained plant can be judged as being between one and one and a half times the depth at which the plant is growing. Therefore an individual plant suited to growing in 60 cm (2 ft) of water and living in that depth will have a spread of between 60–90 cm (2–3 ft).

Name	Flower/Foliage	Season	Depth
'Albatross'	white	summer	30–60 cm (1–2 ft)
'Amabilis'	salmon pink	summer	45–60 cm (1½–2 ft)
'American Star'	pink	summer	45–90 cm (1½–3 ft)
'Andreana'	red, streaked cream	summer	60–90 cm (2–3 ft)
'Arc-en-ciel'	blush pink; foliage variegated rose, purple, white and bronze	summer	45–60 cm (1½–2 ft)
'Arethusa'	rose pink	summer	45–60 cm (1½–2 ft)
'Atropurpurea'	crimson	summer	30–45 cm (1–1½ ft)
'Attraction'	garnet red	summer	60 cm–1.2 m (2–4 ft)
'Aurora'	yellow through orange to red	summer	30–45 cm (1–1½ ft)
N. *candida*	white	summer	30–45 cm (1–1½ ft)
N. *caroliniana*	pink	summer	30–45 cm (1–1½ ft)
N. *c.* 'Nivea'	white	summer	30–45 cm (1–1½ ft)
N. *c.* 'Perfecta'	salmon pink	summer	30–45 cm (1–1½ ft)
N. *c.* 'Rosea'	rose pink	summer	30–45 cm (1–1½ ft)
'Charles de Meurville'	plum to deep wine	summer	60 cm–1.2 m (2–4 ft)
'Col. A. J. Welch'	soft yellow	summer	60 cm–1.2 m (2–4 ft)
'Collosea'	flesh pink	summer	60 cm–1.8 m (2–6 ft)
'Comanche'	orange to bronze	summer	30–45 cm (1–1½ ft)
'Conqueror'	crimson, flecked white	summer	45–60 cm (1½–2 ft)
'Ellisiana'	wine red	summer	30–60 cm (1–2 ft)
'Escarboucle'	crimson	summer	60 cm–1.8 m (2–6 ft)
'Formosa'	bright pink	summer	45–75 cm (1½–2½ ft)
'Froebeli'	blood red	summer	45–60 cm (1½–2 ft)
'Gladstoniana'	white	summer	60 cm–2.4 m (2–8 ft)
'Glorie de Temple sur Lot'	double rose pink	summer	45–90 cm (1½–3 ft)
'Gloriosa'	currant red	summer	45–90 cm (1½–3 ft)
'Gonnere'	double white	summer	45–75 cm (1½–2½ ft)
'Graziella'	orange red	summer	30–60 cm (1–2 ft)
'Hermine'	white	summer	45–75 cm (1½–2½ ft)
'Indiana'	orange red	summer	45–75 cm (1½–2½ ft)
'James Brydon'	crimson	summer	45–90 cm (1½–3 ft)
N. × *laydekeri* 'Alba'	white	summer	30–60 cm (1–2 ft)
N. × *l.* 'Fulgens'	crimson	summer	30–60 cm (1–2 ft)
N. × *l.* 'Lilacea'	soft pink	summer	30–60 cm (1–2 ft)
N. × *l.* 'Purpurata''	vinous red	summer	30–60 cm (1–2 ft)
N. × *l.* 'Rosea'	deep rose	summer	30–60 cm (1–2 ft)
'Louise'	deep red	summer	60–90 cm (2–3 ft)
'Madame Wilfron Gonnere'	double, white to deep rose	summer	45–75 cm (1½–2½ ft)

Name	Flower/Foliage	Season	Depth
N. × *marliacea* 'Albida'	white	summer	45–90 cm (1½–3 ft)
N. × *m*. 'Carnea'	pink	summer	45 cm–1.5 m (1½–5 ft)
N. × *m*. 'Chromatella'	yellow; foliage green, heavily mottled maroon	summer	45–75 cm (1½–2½ ft)
N. × *m*. 'Flammea'	fiery red, flecked white	summer	45–75 cm
N. × *m*. 'Ignea'	deep crimson	summer	45–75 cm (1½–2½ ft)
N. × *m*. 'Rosea'	pink	summer	45 cm–1.2 m (1½–4 ft)
'Masaniello'	rose pink	summer	45–90 cm (1½–3 ft)
'Meteor'	crimson	summer	45–75 cm (1½–2½ ft)
'Moorei'	soft yellow	summer	45–75 cm (1½–2½ ft)
'Mrs. Richmond'	pale rose pink to crimson	summer	45–75 cm (1½–2½ ft)
'Norma Gedye'	semi-double rose pink	summer	30–45 cm (1–1½ ft)
'Odalisque'	rose pink	summer	45–75 cm (1½–2½ ft)
N. *odorata*	white	summer	45–75 cm (1½–2½ ft)
N. *o*. var. *minor*	white	summer	30 cm (1 ft)
N. *o*. var. *rosea*	soft pink	summer	45–60 cm (1½–2 ft)
N. *o*. 'Eugene de Land'	deep apricot pink	summer	45–75 cm (1½–2½ ft)
N. *o*. 'Firecrest'	deep pink	summer	45–90 cm (1½–3 ft)
N. *o*. 'Helen Fowler'	deep rose pink	summer	45–90 cm (1½–3 ft)
N. *o*. 'Sulphurea'	canary yellow; foliage green, mottled	summer	30 cm (1 ft)
N. *o*. 'Sulphurea Grandiflora'	canary yellow; foliage green, mottled	summer	45–60 cm (1½–2 ft)
N. *o*. 'Turicensis'	soft rose	summer	45–75 cm (1½–2½ ft)
N. *o*. 'William B. Shaw'	creamy pink and red	summer	45–60 cm (1½–2 ft)
'Pearl of the Pool'	double, bright pink	summer	45–75 cm (1½–2½ ft)
'Picciola'	deep crimson	summer	45 cm–1.5 m (1½–3½ ft)
'Pink Opal'	coral pink	summer	45–75 cm (1½–2½ ft)
'Pink Sensation'	pink	summer	45–75 cm (1½–2½ ft)
N. × *pygmaea* 'Alba'	white	summer	up to 30 cm (up to 1 ft)
N. × *p*. 'Helvola'	yellow; foliage heavily mottled purple and brown	summer	up to 30 cm (up to 1 ft)
N. × *p*. 'Rubra'	blood red	summer	up to 30 cm (up to 1 ft)
'René Gérard'	rose pink splashed crimson	summer	45–75 cm (1½–2½ ft)
'Rose Arey'	rose pink	summer	45–75 cm (1½–2½ ft)
'Sioux'	yellow, passing through orange to crimson; foliage green, mottled purple	summer	30–45 cm (1–1½ ft)
'Somptuosa'	double pink	summer	45–60 cm (1½–2 ft)
'Sultan'	cherry red streaked white	summer	45–75 cm (1½–2½ ft)
'Sunrise'	canary yellow	summer	45–90 cm (1½–3 ft)

Name	Flower/Foliage	Season	Depth
N. tuberosa var. *rosea*	pink	summer	60 cm−1.2 m (2−4 ft)
N. t. 'Richardsonii'	white	summer	75 cm−1 m (2½−3½ ft)
'Virginia'	white	summer	60 cm−1.2 m (2−4 ft)
'Virginalis'	white	summer	45−75 cm (1½−2½ ft)
'William Falconer'	blood red	summer	45−75 cm (1½−2½ ft)

Tropical Water Lilies *(Nymphaea)* Day blooming

Name	Flower/Foliage	Season	Depth
Aviator Pring	yellow	summer	45−75 cm (1½−2½ ft)
'Blue Beauty'	deep blue	summer	45−90 cm (1½−3 ft)
'Daubeniana'	blue	summer	15 cm (6 in)
'General Pershing'	deep pink	summer	45−75 cm (1½−2½ ft)
'Panama Pacific'	reddish purple	summer	45−75 cm (1½−2½ ft)
'St. Louis'	canary yellow	summer	45−75 cm (1½−2½ ft)

Tropical Water Lilies *(Nymphaea)* Night blooming

Name	Flower/Foliage	Season	Depth
'Emily Grant Hutchings'	pinkish red	summer	45−75 cm (1½−2½ ft)
'Maroon Beauty'	maroon	summer	45−75 cm (1½−2½ ft)
'Missouri'	white	summer	75 cm−1 m (2½−3½ ft)
'Red Flare'	red	summer	45−75 cm (1½−2½ ft)

Pond Lilies *(Nuphar)*

Name	Flower/Foliage	Season	Depth
N. advena	yellow tinged purple	summer	45 cm−1.5 m (1½−5 ft)
N. japonica	yellow	summer	45−75 cm (1½−2½ ft)
N. lutea	yellow	summer	30 cm−2.4 m (1−8 ft)
N. minimum	yellow	summer	30−45 cm (1−1½ ft)
N. polysepala	golden yellow	summer	30 cm−1.5 m (1−5 ft)
N. sagittifolia	yellow	summer	30 cm−1.5 m (1−5 ft)

186

Sacred Lotus *(Nelumbo)*

Name	Flower/Foliage	Season	Height
N. nucifera	vivid rose to flesh	summer	up to 1.8 m (up to 6 ft)
N. pentapetala	sulphur yellow	summer	90 cm (3 ft)
'Kermesina'	double red	summer	1.2 m (4 ft)
'Lily Pons'	salmon pink	summer	1.2 m (4 ft)
'Mrs. Perry D. Slocum'	double rose pink	summer	1.2 m (4 ft)
'Momo Botan'	double carmine	summer	45–75 cm (1½–2½ ft)
'Pygmaea Alba'	white	summer	30 cm (1 ft)

Deep-water Plants

Name	Flower/Foliage	Season	Depth
Aponogeton distachyos	white and black	late spring–autumn	30–90 cm (1–3 ft)
Nymphoides peltata	yellow	summer–early autumn	30–75 cm (1–2½ ft)
Orontium aquaticum	white and yellow	early summer	45 cm (1½ ft)

Hardy Marginal Plants

Most marginal plants will grow in conditions of mud and up to 15 cm (6 in) of water. The spread of most plants depends on the size of container in which they are grown.

Name	Flower/Foliage	Season	Height
Acorus calamus	green foliage	summer	90 cm (3 ft)
A. c. 'Variegatus'	green, cream and rose foliage	summer	60–90 cm (2–3 ft)
A. gramineus	dark green foliage	summer	15 cm (6 in)
A. g. 'Variegatus'	cream and dark green foliage	summer	15 cm (6 in)
Alisma plantago-aquatica	pink and white	summer	60–90 cm (2–3 ft)
A. parviflora	white or pinkish	summer	30–75 cm (1–2½ ft)
A. ranunculoides	rose or blush	late summer	15 cm (6 in)
Butomus umbellatus	pink	late summer	60–90 cm (2–3 ft)
Calla palustris	white, orange-red fruits	spring and autumn	15–30 cm (6 in–1 ft)
Caltha leptosepala	white	late spring	15–45 cm (6 in–1½ ft)
C. palustris	golden yellow	spring	30–60 cm (1–2 ft)
C. p. alba	white	spring	30–45 cm (1–1½ ft)
C. p. 'Flore Pleno'	double golden yellow	spring	15–30 cm (6 in–1 ft)
C. polypetala	golden yellow	spring	60–90 cm (2–3 ft)
Carex pendula	brownish	summer	90 cm–1.2 m (3–4 ft)
C. riparia 'Aurea'	golden foliage	spring and summer	30–75 cm (1–2½ ft)
C. r. 'Variegata'	green and white foliage	spring and summer	30–75 cm (1–2½ ft)
Cotula coronopifolia	yellow	summer	15 cm (6 in)
Cyperus longus	brown	summer	90 cm–1.2 m (3–4 ft)
C. vegetus	reddish brown	summer	30–60 cm (1–2 ft)
Damasonium alisma	white	summer	15–20 cm (6–8 in)
Decodon verticillatus	rose pink; red foliage in autumn	summer	90 cm–1.5 m (3–5 ft)
Eriophorum angustifolium	white	early summer	30–45 cm (1–1½ ft)
E. latifolium	white	early summer	30–45 cm (1–1½ ft)
Glyceria aquatica 'Variegata'	green and cream foliage	summer	60 cm–1.2 m (2–4 ft)

Name	Flower/Foliage	Season	Height
Houttuynia cordata	cream; foliage purplish	summer	15–30 cm (6 in–1 ft)
H. c. 'Plena'	double cream; foliage purplish	summer	15–30 cm (6 in-1 ft)
H. c. 'Variegata'	purplish and yellow foliage	summer	15–30 cm (6 in–1 ft)
Hypericum elodes	yellow	summer	8–15 cm (3–6 in)
Iris laevigata	blue	early summer	60–90 cm (2–3ft)
I. l. 'Alba'	white	early summer	60–90 cm (2–3 ft)
I. l. 'Atropurpurea'	purple-blue	early summer	60–90 cm (2–3 ft)
I. l. 'Colchesteri'	violet-purple and white	early summer	60–90 cm (2–3 ft)
I. l. 'Mottled Beauty'	white, mottled blue	early summer	60–90 cm (2–3 ft)
I. l. 'Muragumo'	blue, double	early summer	60 cm (2 ft)
I. l. 'Regal'	magenta	early summer	60–75 cm (2–2½ ft)
I. l. 'Rose Queen'	soft pink	early summer	60–75 cm (2–2½ ft)
I. l. 'Semperflorens'	blue	early summer	60–90 cm (2–3 ft)
I. l. 'Snowdrift'	white	early summer	60–90 cm (2–3 ft)
I. l. 'Variegata'	blue; foliage gold and green	summer	60–75 cm (2–2½ ft)
I. l. 'Violet Parasol'	violet-blue	early summer	60–90 cm (2–3 ft)
I. pseudacorus	yellow	early summer	75 cm–1.2 m (2½–4 ft)
I. p. var. *bastardii*	creamy yellow	early summer	75–90 cm (2½–3 ft)
I. p. 'Beuron'	yellow	early summer	75–90 cm (2½–3 ft)
I. p. 'E. Turnipseed'	creamy white	early summer	75–90 cm (2½–3 ft)
I. p. 'Flore-plena'	double yellow	early summer	75–90 cm (2½–3 ft)
I. p. 'Golden Queen'	golden yellow	early summer	75–90 cm (2½–3 ft)
I. p. 'Sulphur Queen'	sulphurous yellow	early summer	75–90 cm (2½–3 ft)
I. p. 'Variegata'	yellow; foliage cream and green	early summer	60–75 cm (2–2½ ft)
I. versicolor	violet-blue, purple and yellow	early summer	60–75 cm (2–2½ ft)
I. v. 'Alba'	white	early summer	60–75 cm (2–2½ ft)
I. v. 'Claret Cup'	deep claret purple	early summer	60–75 cm (2–2½ ft)
I. v. 'Kermesina'	deep plum	early summer	60–75 cm (2–2½ ft)
I. v. 'Rosea'	rose purple	early summer	60–75 cm (2–2½ ft)
I. v. 'Stella Main'	blue	early summer	60–75 cm (2–2½ ft)
Juncus effusus 'Spiralis'	foliage green, twisted	summer	30–45 cm (1–1½ ft)
J. e. 'Vittatus'	foliage gold and green	summer	30–45 cm (1–1½ ft)
Ludwigia palustris	foliage green	summer	30 cm (1 ft)
Mentha aquatica	lilac pink	summer	30–45 cm (1–1½ ft)
Menyanthes trifoliata	white	spring	20–30 cm (8 in–1 ft)
Mimulus luteus	yellow	summer	20–30 cm (8 in–1 ft)
M. ringens	lavender to blue	summer	45 cm (1½ ft)
Myosotis scorpioides	blue	summer	20 cm (8 in)
M. s. var. *alba*	white	summer	20 cm (8 in)
M. s. 'Mermaid'	blue	summer	20 cm (8 in)
M. s. 'Semperflorens'	blue	summer	20 cm (8 in)
Narthecium ossifragum	yellow	summer	20–30 cm (8 in–1 ft)
Peltandra alba	whitish green	summer	45 cm (1½ ft)
P. virginica	greenish	summer	45–60 cm (1½–2 ft)
Phragmites australis	silvery white	summer	1.2–1.5 m (4–5 ft)
P. a. 'Variegatus'	foliage cream and green	summer	90 cm–1.2 m (3–4 ft)
Polygonum amphibium	rosy red	late summer	floating foliage
Pontederia cordata	blue	late summer	60–90 cm (2–3 ft)
P. lanceolata	blue	late summer	90 cm–1.2 m (3–4 ft)
Preslia cervina	blue	late summer	30 cm (1 ft)
Ranunculus flammula	golden yellow	early summer	25–30 cm (10 in–1 ft)
R. lingua	yellow	early summer	60–90 cm (2–3 ft)
R. l. 'Grandiflora'	yellow	early summer	60–90 cm (2–3 ft)
Rumex hydrolapathum	foliage crimson	autumn	up to 3m (up to 10 ft)
R. h. var. *maximus*	foliage crimson	autumn	up to 2.1 m (up to 7 ft)

188

Name	Flower/Foliage	Season	Height
Sagittaria japonica	white	summer	45–60 cm (1½–2 ft)
S. j. 'Flore Pleno'	double white	summer	45–60 cm (1½–2 ft)
S. latifolia	white	summer	90 cm–1.2 m (3–4 ft)
S. l. 'Flore Pleno'	double, white	summer	90 cm–1.2 m (3–4 ft)
S. l. var. *pubescens*	white	summer	90 cm–1.2 m (3–4 ft)
S. sagittifolia	white	summer	45–60 cm (1½–2 ft)
Saururus cernuus	creamy white	summer	30 cm (1 ft)
S. loureri	creamy white	summer	30 cm (1 ft)
Scirpus lacustris	dark green foliage	summer	60–90 cm (2–3 ft)
S. tabernaemontani	steely grey foliage	summer	90 cm–1.5 m (3–5 ft)
S. t. 'Albescens'	sulphurous white foliage	summer	90 cm–1.2 m (3–4 ft)
S. t. 'Zebrinus'	green and white foliage	summer	90 cm (3 ft)
Sparganium erectum	greenish	summer	45–90 cm (1½–3 ft)
S. emersum	greenish	summer	45–90 cm (1½–3 ft)
S. minimum	greenish	summer	floating
Triglochin palustris	greenish white	summer	30 cm (1 ft)
Typha angustifolia	brown	late summer	90 cm–1.8 m (3–6 ft)
T. latifolia	brown	late summer	90 cm–1.8 m (3–6 ft)
T. l. 'Variegata'	brown; foliage cream and green	summer	90 cm–1.2 m (3–4 ft)
T. laxmanii	brown	late summer	90 cm–1.2 m (3–4 ft)
T. minima	brown	late summer	45 cm (1½ ft)
Veronica beccabunga	blue	summer	15–20 cm (6–8 in)
Zizania aquatica	green	summer	1.8–2.4 m (6–8 ft)
Z. latifolia	green	summer	1.2–1.5 m (4–5 ft)

Tender Marginal Plants

Name	Flower/Foliage	Season	Height
Acorus gramineus	foliage green	summer	25 cm (10 in)
A. g. 'Variegatus'	foliage green and cream	summer	25 cm (10 in)
Colocasia esculenta	foliage green	summer	90 cm–1 m (3–3½ ft)
C. e. 'Fontanesii'	foliage green	summer	90 cm–1 m (3–3½ ft)
C. e. 'Illustris'	foliage dark green and purple	summer	90 cm–1 m (3–3½ ft)
Cyperus 'Haspan'	foliage green	all year	60–90 cm (2–3 ft)
Thalia dealbata	violet	summer	1.5 m (5 ft)
T. geniculata	violet	summer	1.8 m (6 ft)
Zantedeschia aethiopica	white	spring and summer	60–90 cm (2–3 ft)
Z. a. 'Crowbrough'	white	spring and summer	60–75 cm (2–2½ ft)

Hardy Submerged Plants

These vary in size according to the depth of water in which they are growing. None will tolerate much more than 90 cm (3 ft) of water.

Name	Flower/Foliage	Season
Apium inundatum	green; flowers white	spring, summer and autumn
Callitriche hermaphroditica	green	all year
C. platycarpa	green	spring and summer
C. stagnalis	green	summer
Ceratophyllum demersum	dark green	spring, summer and autumn
C. submersum	dark green	spring, summer and autumn
Chara aspera	light green	spring and summer
Eleocharis acicularis	green	all year
Elodea canadensis	dark green	all year
Fontinalis antipyretica	dark green	all year
F. gracilis	dark green	all year
Hottonia inflata	green; flowers white to pale lilac	spring, summer and autumn
H. palustris	green; flowers white to pale lilac	spring, summer and autumn
Isoetes lacustris	olive green	all year
Lagarosiphon major	dark green	all year
Lobelia dortmanna	dark green; flowers lavender	all year
Myriophyllum proserpinacoides	blue–green	spring, summer and autumn
M. spicatum	bronze green	spring, summer and autumn
M. verticillatum	bright green	spring, summer and autumn
Oenanthe fluviatilis	green	spring, summer and autumn
Potamogeton crispus	bronze green; flowers red and creamy white	spring, summer and autumn
P. pectinatus	bronze green	spring, summer and autumn
P. nodosus	green, flushed bronze	spring, summer and autumn
Ranunculus aquatilis	green; flowers white and gold	spring, summer and autumn
Tillaea recurva	green; flowers white	all year

Tender Submerged Plants

Name	Flower/Foliage	Season
Anubias lanceolata	green	all year
Bacopa caroliniana	mid- pale green	all year
Cabomba caroliniana	bright green	all year
Cryptocoryne ciliata	deep green	all year
C. spiralis	purplish green	all year
Echinodorus intermedius	green	all year
E. radicans	green	all year
Egeria densa	green	all year
Heteranthera graminea	green; flowers yellow	all year
H. zosteraefolia	green, flowers blue	all year
Hygrophila polysperma	pale green	all year
Ludwigia mulertii	bronze green and crimson	all year
Marsilea quadrifolia	green	all year
Myriophyllum hippuroides	green	all year
M. scabratum	red bronze	all year
Riccia fluitans	green	all year
Sagittaria lorata	green; flowers white	all year
S. subulata	green; flowers white	all year
Vallisneria gigantea	green	all year
V. spiralis	green	all year
V. s. 'Torta'	dark green	all year

Hardy Floating Plants

These are of an indeterminate size as they often grow in spreading colonies.

Name	Flower/Foliage	Season
Azolla caroliniana	foliage green or crimson	summer
Hydrocharis morsus-ranae	white	summer
Lemna trisulca	foliage dark green	spring, summer and autumn
Stratiotes aloides	creamy white	summer
Trapa natans	white	summer
Utricularia minor	primrose yellow	summer
U. vulgaris	yellow	summer
Wolffia arrhiza	foliage green	summer

Tender Floating Plants

Name	Flower/Foliage	Season
Ceratopteris pteridoides	foliage green	all year
C. thalictroides	foliage green	all year
Eichornia crassipes	blue and lilac	spring and summer
Pistia stratiotes	foliage green	all year
Salvinia auriculata	foliage green	all year
S. natans	foliage green	all year
Utricularia exoleta	yellow	summer

Bog Garden Plants

It is difficult to determine accurately the spread of a bog garden plant. The heights given are the maximum that the plant attains at any particular stage in its life.

Name	Flower/Foliage	Season	Height
Aconitum napellus	navy blue	summer	1.2−1.5 m (4−5 ft)
A. n. 'Bicolor'	blue and white	summer	90 cm−1.2 m (3−4 ft)
A. n. 'Bressingham Spire'	violet-blue	summer	90 cm (3 ft)
A. n. 'Carneum'	shell pink	summer	90 cm (3 ft)
A. n. 'Grandiflorum Album'	white	summer	90 cm (3 ft)
A. n. 'Spark's Variety'	violet-blue	summer	90 cm (3 ft)
A. vulparia	soft yellow	summer	90 cm−1.2 m (3−4 ft)
A. wilsonii	bright blue	autumn	1.2−1.8 m (4−6 ft)
Ajuga pyramidalis	gentian blue	summer	15−30 cm (6 in−1 ft)
A. p. 'Metallica'	blue; foliage bronze	summer	15−30 cm (6 in−1 ft)
A. reptans 'Burgundy Glow'	blue; foliage rosy	summer	15 cm (6 ins)
A. r. 'Jungle Beauty'	blue	summer	15−30 cm (6 in−1 ft)
A. r. 'Purpurea'	blue; foliage purple bronze	summer	15 cm (6 ins)
A. r. 'Rainbow'	blue; foliage multi-coloured	summer	15 cm (6 in)
Anemone rivularis	white	early summer	30−60 cm (1−2 ft)
A. virginiana	greenish white or greenish purple	early summer	45−90 cm (1½−3 ft)
Anemopsis californica	white	summer	30−45 cm (1−1½ ft)
Anthericum liliago	white	summer	60 cm (2 ft)
Aruncus dioicus	creamy white	late summer	90 cm−1.5 m (3−5 ft)
A. d. 'Kneiffii'	creamy white	late summer	90 cm (3 ft)
Asclepias incarnata	rose pink	summer	60−90 cm (2−3 ft)

Name	Flower/Foliage	Season	Height
A.i. var. *alba*	white	summer	60−90 cm (2−3 ft)
Aster puniceus	lilac to pale violet-purple	late summer early autumn	90 cm−1.5 m (3−5 ft)
Astilbe × arendsii 'Fanal'	deep crimson	mid-late summer	30−45 cm (1−1½ ft)
A. × a. 'Irrlicht'	white	mid-late summer	60−75 cm (2−2½ ft)
A. × a. 'Ostrich Plume'	rich pink	mid-late summer	75−90 cm (2½−3 ft)
A. × a. 'Peach Blossom'	salmon pink	mid-late summer	60−90 cm (2−3 ft)
A. × a. 'White Gloria'	white	mid-late summer	60−75 cm (2−2½ ft)
A. chinensis 'Pumila'	pinkish mauve	late summer	30−45 cm (1−1½ ft)
A. crispa 'Lilliput'	salmon pink	late summer	15 cm (6 in)
A. c. 'Perkeo'	deep pink	late summer	15 cm (6 in)
Buphthalmum salicifolium	yellow	summer	45−60 cm (1½−2½ ft)
B. speciosum	yellow	summer	90 cm−1.2 m (3−4 ft)
Cardamine pratensis	rosy lilac	spring	30−45 cm (1−1½ ft)
C. p. flore plena	double, rosy lilac	spring	30 cm (1 ft)
Eupatorium ageratoides	white	summer	60 cm−1.2 m (2−4 ft)
E. cannabinum	reddish purple	summer	60 cm−1.2 m (2−4 ft)
E. purpureum	purple	late summer, early autumn	1.2 m (4 ft)
Euphorbia palustris	yellow-green	summer	45−90 cm (1½−3 ft)
Filipendula hexapetala	creamy white	summer	60−90 cm (2−3 ft)
F. h. flore-pleno	double, creamy white	summer	60 cm (2 ft)
F. palmata	pale pink	mid-late summer	90 cm (3 ft)
F. purpurea	deep pink	mid-late summer	60 cm−1.2 m (2−4 ft)
F. rubra 'Magnifica'	deep peach pink	mid-late summer	90 cm−1.8 m (3−6 ft)
F. ulmaria	creamy white	mid-summer	90 cm−1.2 m (3−4 ft)
F. u. 'Aurea'	gold foliage	summer	60−90 cm (2−3 ft)
F. u. 'Flore Pleno'	double creamy white	mid-summer	90 cm (3 ft)
Gratiola officinalis	white, striped purple	summer	30 cm (1 ft)
Gunnera magellanica	foliage green	summer	7.5 cm (3 in)
G. manicata	foliage green	summer	1.8−2.4 m (6−8 ft)
Hemerocallis fulva	orange to brown	summer	90 cm−1.2 m (3−4 ft)
H. 'Black Prince'	deep velvety mauve	summer	60−90 cm (2−3 ft)
H. 'Bonanza'	light orange and maroon brown	summer	60−90 cm (2−3 ft)
H. 'Burning Daylight'	deep orange	summer	60−90 cm (2−3 ft)
H. 'Buzz Bomb'	velvety red	summer	60−90 cm (2−3 ft)
H. 'Chartreuse Magic'	canary yellow and green	summer	60−90 cm (2−3 ft)
H. 'Esther Walker'	golden yellow	summer	60−90 cm (2−3 ft)
H. 'Golden Orchid'	rich gold	summer	60−90 cm (2−3 ft)
H. 'Hornby Castle'	brick red and yellow	summer	60−90 cm (2−3 ft)
H. 'Hyperion'	lemon yellow	summer	90 cm−1.5 cm (3−5 ft)
H. 'Margaret Perry'	orange	summer	60−90 cm (2−3 ft)
H. 'Marion Vaughan'	canary yellow	summer	60−90 cm (2−3 ft)
H. 'Mikado'	orange, brown throat	summer	60−90 cm (2−3 ft)
H. 'Pink Charm'	pink	summer	60−75 cm (2−2½ ft)
H. 'Pink Damask'	rose pink	summer	60−90 cm (2−3 ft)
H. 'Salmon Sheen'	salmon pink	summer	60−90 cm (2−3 ft)
H. 'Spectacular'	gold and red	summer	60−90 cm (2−3 ft)
H. 'Stafford'	red	summer	60−90 cm (2−3 ft)
H. 'Tejas'	deep reddish orange	summer	60−90 cm (2−3 ft)
H. 'Whichford'	lemon yellow	summer	60−90 cm (2−3 ft)
Hosta crispula	lavender; foliage green and white	summer	60−75 cm (2−2½ ft)

Aruncus sylvester is also known as goat's beard on account of its feathery cream flowers. First class for the bog garden.

Lysichiton americanum or American skunk cabbage provides startling early colour to the waterside. It has large leaves and needs thoughtfully placing.

Astilbe 'Fanal' is a favourite among these bog garden plants, providing bold colour during high summer.

Vaccinium corymbosum is one of the most versatile shrubby swamp lovers. A plant for acid soil, it has wonderful autumn foliage colour.

xxxi

Primula pulverulenta is a very colourful plant for pool or streamside. Hardy, resilient and easily raised from seed.

Name	Flower/Foliage	Season	Height
H. fortunei	lilac to violet; foliage grey-green	summer	75–90 cm (2½–3 ft)
H. f. 'Albo-picta'	foliage green and yellow	summer	75–90 cm (2½–3 ft)
H. f. 'Aurea'	foliage bright yellow	summer	60–75 cm (2–2½ ft)
H. f. 'Aureo-marginata'	foliage dark green and gold	summer	75–90 cm (2½–3 ft)
H. lancifolia	deep purple; foliage green	summer	60 cm (2 ft)
H. l. 'Kabitan'	bright gold and green foliage	summer	30–60 cm (1–2 ft)
H. plantaginea	white; foliage green	summer	60–75 cm (2–2½ ft)
H. p. 'Grandiflora'	white; foliage green	summer	60–75 cm (2–2½ ft)
H. p. 'Royal Standard'	white; foliage green	summer	60–75 cm (2–2½ ft)
H. sieboldiana	lilac; foliage glaucous	summer	60–75 cm (2–2½ ft)
H. s. 'Elegans'	white to pale lilac; foliage glaucous	summer	60–75 cm (2–2½ ft)
H. s. 'Mira'	white to pale lilac; foliage glaucous	summer	75–90 cm (1½–3 ft)
H. tardiflora	purple; foliage glossy green	summer	60 cm (2 ft)
H. undulata	lilac; foliage green and white	summer	60 cm (2 ft)
H. u. 'Albo-marginata'	foliage green and white	summer	60 cm (2 ft)
H. u. 'Erromena'	lavender, foliage green	summer	60 cm (2 ft)
H. u. 'Univittata'	foliage green and white	summer	60 cm (2 ft)
H. ventricosa	deep violet; foliage green	summer	90 cm (3 ft)
H. v. 'Aureomaculata'	foliage green and yellow	summer	90 cm (3 ft)
H. v. 'Variegata'	foliage green and creamy yellow	summer	90 cm (3 ft)
Iris aurea	golden yellow	early summer	1.2 m (4 ft)
I. bulleyana	blue	early-mid-summer	60–75 cm (2–2½ ft)
I. chrysographes	rich velvety purple	early summer	60 cm (2 ft)
I. kaempferi	deep purple	mid-summer	60–75 cm (2–2½ ft)
I. k. 'Blue Heaven'	rich purple-blue and yellow	mid-summer	60–75 cm (2–2½ ft)
I. k. 'Landscape at Dawn'	pale rose lavender	mid-summer	60–75 cm (2–2½ ft)
I. k. 'Mandarin'	deep violet	mid-summer	60–75 cm (2–2½ ft)
I. k. 'Tokyo'	mixed colours	mid-summer	60–75 cm (2–2½ ft)
I. k. 'Variegata'	violet-blue; foliage cream and green	mid-summer	60 cm (2 ft)
I. ochroleuca	yellow and white	mid-summer	1.5 m (5 ft)
I. sibirica	blue	mid-summer	90 cm (3 ft)
I. s. 'Emperor'	deep violet-purple	mid-summer	90 cm (3 ft)
I. s. 'Ottawa'	deep violet	mid-summer	90 cm (3 ft)
I. s. 'Perry's Blue'	sky blue	mid-summer	90 cm (3 ft)
I. s. 'Perry's Pygmy'	deep violet	mid-summer	45 cm (1½ ft)
Ligularia clivorum	orange	late summer	90 cm–1.2 m (3–4 ft)
L. c. 'Golden Queen'	golden yellow	late summer	90 cm–1.2 m (3–4 ft)
L. c. 'Orange Princess'	orange	late summer	90 cm–1.2 m (3–4 ft)
L. stenocephala 'The Rocket'	yellow	late summer	1.5–1.8 m (5–6 ft)
L. veitchianus	yellow	late summer, early autumn	90 cm–2 m (3–6½ ft)
Lobelia cardinalis	red	late summer	60–90 cm (2–3 ft)
L. fulgens	red; foliage maroon	late summer	60–90 cm (2–3 ft)
L. 'Huntsman'	scarlet	late summer	60–90 cm (2–3 ft)
L. 'Queen Victoria'	red	late summer	60–90 cm (2–3 ft)
L. syphilitica	blue	late summer	60–90 cm (2–3 ft)
L. × *vedrariensis*	violet	late summer	75–90 cm (2½–3 ft)
Lysichiton americanum	yellow	spring	60–90 cm (2–3 ft)
L. camtschatcense	white	spring	60–90 cm (2–3 ft)
Lysimachia nummularia	yellow	summer	5 cm (2 in)
L. n. 'Aurea'	yellow; foliage golden	summer	5 cm (2 in)
L. punctata	yellow	summer	60–90 cm (2–3 ft)
Lythrum salicaria	rose purple	mid-late summer	1.2 m (4 ft)
L. s. 'Brilliant'	pink	mid-late summer	90 cm–1.2 m (3–4 ft)
L. s. 'Lady Sackville'	rose pink	mid-late summer	90 cm–1.2 m (3–4 ft)

Name	Flower/Foliage	Season	Height
L. s. 'Robert'	soft pink	mid-late summer	90 cm−1.2 m (3−4 ft)
L. virgatum	purple	mid-late summer	45 cm (1½ ft)
L. v. 'Dropmore Purple'	deep purple	mid-late summer	45 cm (1½ ft)
Mimulus cardinalis	scarlet-orange	late summer	45−60 cm (1½−2 ft)
M. 'Highland Pink'	pink	summer	15 cm (6 in)
M. 'Highland Red'	red	summer	15 cm (6 in)
M. 'Hose-in-Hose'	double yellow	summer	20−30 cm (8 in−1 ft)
M. lewisii	rose lilac	summer	30−45 cm (1−1½ ft)
M. 'Monarch Strain'	mixed colours	summer	20−30 cm (8 in−1 ft)
M. 'Whitecroft Scarlet'	scarlet	summer	10 cm (4 in)
Parnassia palustris	white	early summer	15−30 cm (6 in−1 ft)
Peltiphyllum peltatum	pink; foliage bronze green	spring	45−90 cm (1½−3 ft)
Petasites japonicus	greenish white	early spring	1.5 m (5 ft)
Phormium tenax	foliage bronze green	spring, summer and autumn	90 cm−1.5 m (3−5 ft)
P. t. 'Atropurpurea'	foliage reddish purple	spring, summer and autumn	90 cm−1.2 m (3−4 ft)
P. t. 'Variegata'	foliage green, yellow and white	spring, summer and autumn	75−90 cm (2½−3 ft)
P. 'Cream Delight'	foliage creamy yellow and green	spring, summer and autumn	75−90 cm (2½−3 ft)
P. 'Dark Delight'	foliage deep maroon	spring, summer and autumn	75−90 cm (2½−3 ft)
P. 'Emerald Green'	foliage green	spring, summer and autumn	75−90 cm (2½−3 ft)
P. 'Maori Maiden'	foliage red, pink and brown	spring, summer and autumn	45−60 cm (1½−2 ft)
Primula alpicola	yellow to white	summer	15−60 cm (6 in−2 ft)
P. a. alba	white	summer	15−60 cm (6 in−2 ft)
P. a. luna	sulphurous yellow	summer	15−60 cm (6 in−2 ft)
P. a. violacea	purple to violet	summer	15−60 cm (6 in−2 ft)
P. anisodora	brownish purple	summer	30−60 cm (1−2 ft)
P. aurantiaca	reddish orange	early summer	60−90 cm (2−3 ft)
P. beesiana	rosy carmine	early summer	60−75 cm (2−2½ ft)
P. bulleyana	orange	early summer	60−90 cm (2−3 ft)
P. burmanica	reddish purple	early summer	60 cm (2 ft)
P. capitata	deep violet	summer	15−30 cm (6 in−1 ft)
P. c. mooreana	deep violet	summer	15−30 cm (6 in−1 ft)
P. c. sphaerocephala	deep violet	mid-late summer	15−30 cm (6 in−1 ft)
P. chungensis	pale orange	early summer	60−75 cm (2−2½ ft)
P. cortusoides	purplish rose	spring and early summer	15−30 cm (6 in−1 ft)
P. denticulata	lilac, pink or purple	spring	30−60 cm (1−2 ft)
P. d. var. alba	white	spring	30−60 cm (1−2 ft)
P. d. var. cachmireana	purple	spring	30−60 cm (1−2 ft)
P. d. 'Rosea'	rich crimson	spring	30−60 cm (1−2 ft)
P. florindae	sulphur yellow	mid-summer, early autumn	60−90 cm (2−3 ft)
P. f. 'Art Shades'	primrose to orange	mid-summer, early autumn	60−90 cm (2−3 ft)
P. 'Harlow Car Hybrids'	mixed colours	summer	60−75 cm (2−2½ ft)
P. helodoxa	vivid yellow	summer	60−90 cm (2−3 ft)
P. heucherifolia	mauve-pink to purple	spring and early summer	15−30 cm (6 in−1 ft)
P. 'Inverewe'	bright orange	early summer	45−75 cm (1½−2½ ft)
P. japonica	deep red	late spring, early summer	45−75 cm (1½−2½ ft)
P. j. 'Miller's Crimson'	crimson	late spring, early summer	45−75 cm (1½−2½ ft)

Name	Flower/Foliage	Season	Height
P. j. 'Postford White'	white	late spring, early summer	45−75 cm (1½−2½ ft)
P. muscarioides	deep purplish blue	summer	30−45 cm (1−1½ ft)
P. poissonii	deep purplish crimson	early summer	30−45 cm (1−1½ ft)
P. polyneura	pale rose to purple	spring	15−30 cm (6 in−1 ft)
P. pulverulenta	deep red	late spring, early summer	60−90 cm (2−3 ft)
P. p. 'Bartley Strain'	pink	late spring, early summer	60−90 cm (2−3 ft)
P. rosea	pink	spring	10−15 cm (4−6 in)
P. r. 'Delight'	rose pink	spring	10−15 cm (4−6 in)
P. r. 'Grandiflora'	rose pink	spring	10−15 cm (4−6 in)
P. saxatilis	rosy violet to pinkish mauve	spring, early summer	10−30 cm (4 in−1 ft)
P. secundiflora	reddish purple	summer	30−45 cm (1−1½ ft)
P. sieboldii	white, pink or purple	early summer	15−20 cm (6−8 in)
P. sikkimensis	soft yellow	summer	45−75 cm (1½−2½ ft)
P. sinoplantaginea	deep purple	late spring	15−20 cm (6−8 in)
P. sinopurpurea	violet-purple	late spring	30−45 cm (1−1½ ft)
P. viali	red and bluish purple	late spring, early summer	30−45 cm (1−1½ ft)
P. waltoni	deep wine purple	late spring, early summer	30−45 cm (1−1½ ft)
P. yargongensis	mauve, pink, purple	late spring	10−30 cm (4 in−1 ft)
Rheum palmatum	creamy white, foliage green	summer	1.5−1.8 m (5−6 ft)
R. p. var. tanguticum	pink, rose; foliage purplish green	summer	1.5−1.8 m (5−6 ft)
R. p. 'Bowles Crimson'	crimson; foliage purplish red	summer	1.5−1.8 m (5−6 ft)
Rodgersia tabularis	creamy white; foliage pale green	summer	90 cm−1.2 m (3−4 ft)
Schizostylis coccinea	red	autumn	30−60 cm (1−2 ft)
S. c. 'Grandiflora'	red	autumn	30−60 cm (1−2 ft)
S. c. 'Mrs Hegarty'	rose pink	autumn	30−60 cm (1−2 ft)
Symplocarpus foetidus	purple green	spring	75−90 cm (2½−3 ft)
Trollius asiaticus	deep yellow	spring	30−45 cm (1−1½ ft)
T. chinensis	yellow	spring	30−45 cm (1−1½ ft)
T. × cultorum 'Earliest of All'	canary yellow	spring	30−45 cm (1−1½ ft)
T. × c. 'Fireglobe'	reddish orange	spring	30−45 cm (1−1½ ft)
T. × c. 'Golden Queen'	yellow	spring and early summer	30−45 cm (1−1½ ft)
T. × c. 'Orange Globe'	orange	spring and early summer	30−45 cm (1−1½ ft)
T. europaeus	lemon yellow	spring and early summer	30−60 cm (1−2 ft)
T. yunnanensis	yellow	late spring	60 cm (2 ft)

Bog Garden Ferns

Name	Foliage	Season	Height
Dryopteris palustris	pale green	spring, summer	30 cm (1 ft)
Matteucia struthiopteris	bright green	spring, summer	90 cm (3 ft)
Onoclea sensibilis	rose pink to green	spring, summer	45−60 cm (1½−2 ft)
Osmunda regalis	green	spring, summer	1.2−1.8 m (4−6 ft)
O. r. 'Cristata'	green	spring, summer	90 cm−1.2 m (3−4 ft)
O. r. 'Purpurescens'	purplish green	spring, summer	1.2−1.8 m (4−6 ft)
O. r. 'Undulata'	green	spring, summer	90 cm−1.2 m (3−4 ft)
Woodwardia virginica	olive green	spring, summer	60 cm (2 ft)

Shrubby Bog Plants

Name	Flower/Foliage/Stem	Season	Height
Cornus alba	stems red	winter	1.2 m (4 ft)
C. a. 'Sibirica'	stems red	winter	90 cm–1.2 m (3–4 ft)
C. a. 'Spaethii'	foliage gold and green	summer	90 cm–1.2 m (3–4 ft)
C. stolonifera 'Flaviramea'	stems yellow	winter	90 cm–1.2 m (3–4 ft)
Salix alba 'Chermesina'	stems orange-scarlet	winter	1.2–1.5 m (4–5 ft)
S. a. 'Vitellina'	stems yellow	winter	1.2–1.5 m (4–5 ft)
S. daphnoides	stems violet	winter	1.2–1.5 m (4–5 ft)
Taxodium distichum	foliage green turning russet	spring, summer and autumn	20 m (66 ft)
Vaccinium angustifolium	flowers white tinted red; foliage turns red; fruits blue-black	spring, summer and autumn	1.5 m (5 ft)
V. arboreum	flowers white; foliage turns orange-red; fruits black	spring, summer and autumn	1.5 –3 m (5–10 ft)
V. corymbosum	flowers pale pink to white; foliage turns scarlet; fruits black	spring, summer and autumn	90 cm–1.5 m (3–5 ft)

2. EASY PROPAGATION GUIDE

Deep-water Plants

Name	Method	Season	Remarks
Nymphaea, hardy	eyes	summer	under glass
N. × *pygmaea* 'Alba'	seed	spring, summer	under glass
Nymphaea, tropical	tubers, plantlets	spring, summer	under glass
Nuphar	division, eyes	spring, summer	
Nelumbo	division	spring	under glass
Aponogeton	division, seed	spring, summer	fresh seed under glass
Nymphoides	division, runners	spring, summer	
Orontium	seed	summer	fresh seed

Hardy Marginal Plants

Name	Method	Season	Remarks
Acorus	division	spring, summer	
Alisma	seed, division	summer	
Butomus	bulbils, division	spring, summer	
Calla	division, seed	spring, summer	
Caltha species	division, seed	spring, summer	fresh seed
Caltha cultivars	division	spring, summer	fresh seed
Carex species	division, seed	spring, summer	
Carex cultivars	division	spring, summer	
Cotula	seed	spring	
Cyperus	division, seed	spring, summer	
Damasonium	division, seed	spring, summer	
Decodon	division, stem cuttings	spring, summer	cuttings during summer
Eriophorum	division	spring	

Name	Method	Season	Remarks
Glyceria	division	spring	
Houttuynia	division	spring	
Hypericum	seed, division, stem cuttings	spring, summer	cuttings during summer
Iris species	division, seed	spring, summer	division after flowering
Iris cultivars	division	summer	after flowering
Juncus cultivars	division	spring, summer	
Ludwigia	seed, division, stem cuttings	spring, summer	cuttings during summer
Mentha	stem cuttings, division	spring, summer	cuttings during summer
Menyanthes	division	spring	
Mimulus species	seed, division, stem cuttings	spring, summer	cuttings during summer
Myosotis species	seed, division	spring, summer	
Myosotis cultivars	division	spring	
Narthecium	seed, division	spring, summer	
Peltandra	division	spring	
Phragmites	division	spring	
Polygonum	division	spring	
Pontederia	seed, division	spring, summer	fresh seed
Preslia	stem cuttings	summer	
Ranunculus	division	spring	
Rumex	division, seed	spring	
Sagittaria	division	spring	
Saururus	division	spring	
Scirpus	division	spring	
Sparganium	seed, division	spring, summer	
Triglochin	seed, division	spring, summer	
Typha	division	spring	
Veronica	stem cuttings	summer	
Zizania (annual)	seed	spring	
Zizania (perennial)	seed, division	spring	

Tender Marginal Plants

Name	Method	Season	Remarks
Acorus	division	spring, summer	under glass
Colocasia	division	winter, spring	under glass
Cyperus	division	spring	under glass
Thalia	seed, division	spring, summer	under glass, fresh seed
Zantedeschia	division	winter, spring	under glass

Tender Floating Plants

Name	Method	Season
Ceratopteris	plantlets	summer
Eichornia	division	summer
Pistia	division	summer
Salvinia	division	summer
Utricularia	division	summer

Hardy Submerged Plants

Name	Method	Season
Apium	division	spring, summer
Callitriche	stem cuttings	spring, summer
Ceratophyllum	stem cuttings, division	spring, summer
Chara	division	spring, summer
Eleocharis	division	spring, summer
Elodea	stem cuttings	spring, summer
Fontinalis	division	spring, summer
Hottonia	stem cuttings	summer
Isoetes	division	spring, summer
Lagarosiphon	stem cuttings	spring, summer
Lobelia	division	spring, summer
Myriophyllum	stem cuttings	spring, summer
Oenanthe	division, seed	spring, summer
Potamogeton	stem cuttings	spring, summer
Ranunculus	stem cuttings	spring, summer
Tillaea	stem cuttings	spring, summer

Tender Submerged Plants

Name	Method	Season
Anubias	division	spring, summer
Bacopa	stem cuttings	spring, summer
Cabomba	stem cuttings	spring, summer
Cryptocoryne	division	spring, summer
Echinodorus	division	spring, summer
Egeria	stem cuttings	spring, summer
Heteranthera	division	spring, summer
Hygrophila	stem cuttings	spring, summer
Ludwigia	stem cuttings	spring, summer
Marsilea	division	spring, summer
Myriophyllum	stem cuttings	spring, summer
Riccia	division	spring, summer, autumn
Sagittaria	division	spring, summer
Vallisneria	division	spring, summer

Hardy Floating Plants

Name	Method	Season
Azolla	division	summer
Hydrocharis	division	summer
Lemna	division	spring, summer
Stratiotes	division	summer
Trapa	seed	spring
Utricularia	division	summer
Wolffia	division	summer

Bog Garden Plants

Name	Method	Season	Remarks
Aconitum species	seed, division	winter, spring	seed, spring only
Aconitum cultivars	division	winter, spring	
Ajuga	division	spring	
Anemone	seed	spring	
Anemopsis	division	winter, spring	
Anthericum	division, seed	spring	seed, ideally when it ripens, summer
Aruncus	division	winter, spring	
Asclepias	division	spring	
Aster	division	spring	
Astilbe	division	spring	
Buphthalmun	seed, division	winter, spring	seed in spring only
Cardamine species	seed, division	winter, spring	seed in spring only
Cardamine forms	division	winter	
Eupatorium	division	spring	
Euphorbia	division	spring	
Filipendula	division	winter, spring	
Gratiola	division	spring	
Gunnera	division, seed	spring	fresh seed in late summer
Hemerocallis	division	winter, spring	
Hosta	division	spring	species can also be increased from seed
Iris species	seed, division	spring, summer	division immediately after flowering
Iris cultivars	division	summer	after flowering
Ligularia	division	winter, spring	
Lobelia	division, seed, stem cuttings	spring	stem cuttings in summer
Lysichiton	seed	summer	fresh seed
Lysimachia (creeping)	stem cuttings	spring, summer	
Lysimachia (others)	division	winter, spring	
Lythrum	division	winter, spring	
Mimulus	division, seed, stem cuttings	spring	stem cuttings in summer
Parnassia	seed	spring	pot grow seedlings
Peltiphyllum	division	spring	
Petasites	division	winter	
Phormium species	division, seed	spring	
Phormium cultivars	division	spring	
Primula species	seed, division	spring	fresh seed also in summer
Primula cultivars	division	spring	one or two can also be grown true from seed
Primula, candelabra/drumstick	root cuttings	winter	this is an additional propagation method for these
Rheum species	seed, division	spring	
Rheum cultivars	division	winter, spring	
Rodgersia	seed, division	spring	
Schizostylis	division	spring	
Symplocarpus	division	winter, early spring	
Trollius species	seed, division	winter, spring	Seed in spring only
Trollius cultivars	division	winter, spring	

Bog Garden Ferns

Name	Method	Season	Remarks
Dryopteris	division	spring	
Matteuccia	division	spring	
Onoclea	division	spring	
Osmunda species	spores, division	spring	fresh spores only, late summer
Osmunda cultivars	division	spring	
Woodwardia	division	spring	

Shrubby Bog Plants

Name	Method	Season	Remarks
Cornus	hardwood cuttings	winter	
Salix	hardwood cuttings	winter	
Taxodium	soft cuttings	summer	sow seed when available in spring
Vaccinium	stem cuttings	summer	cuttings with a heel

3. USEFUL INFORMATION

Calculating Capacities

Rectangular Pools (or Aquaria)

Multiply length by width by depth (all in metres) to obtain volume in cubic metres. Multiply this by 28.41 to give the capacity in litres.

Multiply length by width by depth (all in feet) to obtain volume in cubic feet. Multiply this by 6.25 to give the capacity in gallons.

Circular Pools

Multiply depth in metres by the square of the diameter in metres by 20.74 to give approximate capacity in litres.

Multiply depth in feet by the square of the diameter in feet by 4.9 to give approximate gallonage.

Other Useful Information

One imperial gallon of water occupies 0.16 cubic feet, and weighs 10lb.

One US gallon is equivalent to 0.83268 imperial gallons, and weights 8.3lb.

One cubic foot of water is equivalent to 6.24 imperial gallons or 28.3 litres, and weighs 62.32lb.

One imperial gallon equals 160 fluid ounces or 4.546 litres.

One litre equals 1.76 imperial pints or 0.22 imperial gallons or 35.196 fluid ounces.

One litre equals 0.264 US gallons.

Easy Reference Tables for Rectangular Pools

Capacity of rectangular pools, 30 cm average depth, in litres.

Breadth (m)	Length (m)						
	0.6	1.2	1.8	2.4	3.0	3.6	4.8
0.6	113	227	340	454	568	681	909
0.9	172	340	509	681	846	1251	1363
1.2	227	454	681	909	1137	1363	1818
1.5	281	568	846	1137	1410	1706	2272
1.8	340	681	1023	1363	1706	2047	2727

Capacity of rectangular pools, one foot average depth, in imperial gallons.

Breadth (ft)	Length (ft)						
	2	4	6	8	10	12	16
2	25	50	75	100	125	150	200
3	38	75	112	150	186	275	300
4	50	100	150	200	250	300	400
5	62	125	186	250	310	375	500
6	75	150	225	300	375	450	600

Easy Reference Tables for Circular Pools

Capacity of circular garden pools in litres

Diameter (m)	Average depth of water in centimetres				
	30	45	60	76	91
1.2	354	531	709	887	1064
1.8	800	1201	1601	2002	2402
2.4	1424	2138	2848	3562	4272
3.0	2224	3339	4449	5564	6674
3.6	3207	4813	6415	8021	9623

Capacity of circular garden pools in imperial gallons

Diameter (ft)	Average depth of water in inches				
	12	18	24	30	36
4	78	117	156	195	234
6	176	264	352	440	528
8	313	470	626	783	939
10	489	734	978	1,223	1,467
12	705	1,058	1,410	1,763	2,115

Volume — Rate of Flow

An important factor when installing a fountain or waterfall.

Gallons per minute	Gallons per hour	Litres per minute	Litres per hour
1	60	4.55	272.7
2	120	9.09	545.5
3	180	13.64	818.3
4	240	18.18	1,091
5	300	22.73	1,363
6	360	27.27	1,636
7	420	31.82	1,909
8	480	36.37	2,182
9	540	40.91	2,454
10	600	45.46	2,727
11	660	50.00	3,000
12	720	54.55	3,273
13	780	59.10	3,545
14	840	63.64	3,818
15	900	68.10	4,091
16	960	72.74	4,364
17	1,020	77.28	4,636
18	1,080	81.83	4,909
19	1,140	86.38	5,182
20	1,200	90.92	5,455

Index